VANCOUVER
HANDBOOK

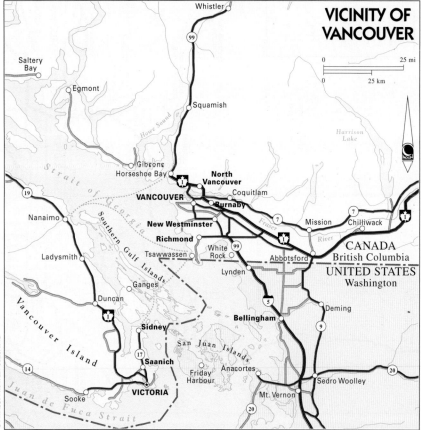

VICINITY OF VANCOUVER

0   25 mi
0   25 km

Whistler

99

Saltery Bay

Egmont

Squamish

Howe Sound

Harrison Lake

Gibsons
Horseshoe Bay

North Vancouver

VANCOUVER

Coquitlam

Burnaby

7

Mission

Chilliwack

19

Strait of Georgia

Nanaimo

Southern Gulf Islands

New Westminster

Fraser River

Richmond

Ladysmith

Tsawwassen

White Rock

99

Abbotsford

CANADA
British Columbia

Ganges

Lynden

UNITED STATES
Washington

Duncan

1

5

Deming

Sidney

Vancouver Island

17

Saanich

San Juan Islands

Friday Harbour

Anacortes

Bellingham

9

14

VICTORIA

Sooke

Juan de Fuca Strait

Mt. Vernon

20

Sedro Woolley

20

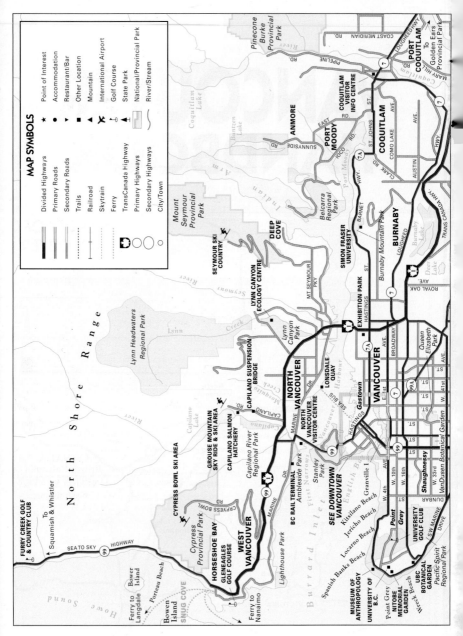

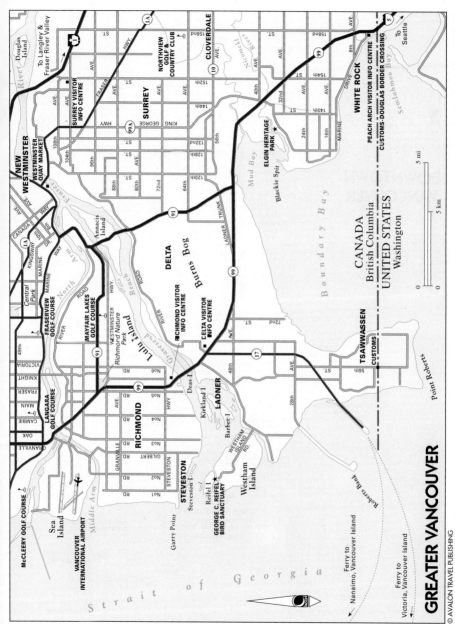

GREATER VANCOUVER

© AVALON TRAVEL PUBLISHING

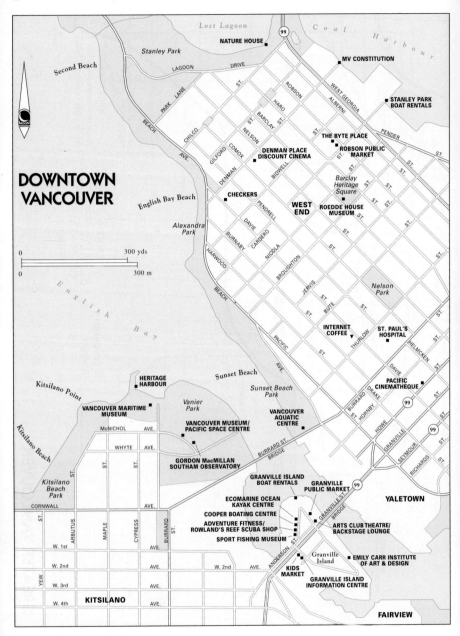

DOWNTOWN VANCOUVER

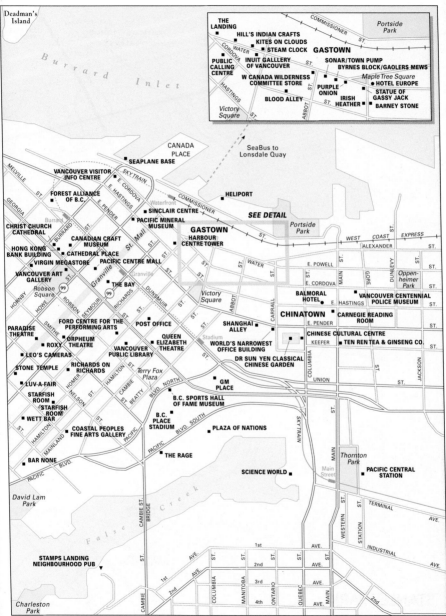

Deadman's Island

Burrard Inlet

GASTOWN (DETAIL)

THE LANDING
HILL'S INDIAN CRAFTS
KITES ON CLOUDS
STEAM CLOCK
PUBLIC CALLING CENTRE
INUIT GALLLERY OF VANCOUVER
W CANADA WILDERNESS COMMITTEE STORE
BLOOD ALLEY
SONAR/TOWN PUMP
BYRNES BLOCK/GAOLERS MEWS
Maple Tree Square
HOTEL EUROPE
PURPLE ONION
IRISH HEATHER
STATUE OF GASSY JACK
BARNEY STONE
Victory Square
Portside Park
COMMISSIONER ST.
WATER ST.
CORDOVA ST.
HASTINGS ST.
ABBOTT ST.

CANADA PLACE
SeaBus to Lonsdale Quay
SEAPLANE BASE
VANCOUVER VISITOR INFO CENTRE
FOREST ALLIANCE OF B.C.
HELIPORT
SEE DETAIL
SINCLAIR CENTRE
PACIFIC MINERAL MUSEUM
GASTOWN
HARBOUR CENTRE TOWER
Portside Park
WEST COAST EXPRESS
ALEXANDER ST.

CHRIST CHURCH CATHEDRAL
CANADIAN CRAFT MUSEUM
HONG KONG BANK BUILDING
CATHEDRAL PLACE
VIRGIN MEGASTORE
PACIFIC CENTRE MALL
VANCOUVER ART GALLERY
Robson Square
THE BAY

E. POWELL
E. CORDOVA
E. HASTINGS
Oppenheimer Park

BALMORAL HOTEL
VANCOUVER CENTENNIAL POLICE MUSEUM
CHINATOWN
CARNEGIE READING ROOM
E. PENDER
CHINESE CULTURAL CENTRE
TEN REN TEA & GINSENG CO.
KEEFER
Victory Square

PARADISE THEATRE
FORD CENTRE FOR THE PERFORMING ARTS
POST OFFICE
ORPHEUM THEATRE
ROXY
QUEEN ELIZABETH THEATRE
LEO'S CAMERAS
VANCOUVER PUBLIC LIBRARY
STONE TEMPLE
RICHARDS ON RICHARDS
Terry Fox Plaza
SHANGHAI ALLEY
WORLD'S NARROWEST OFFICE BUILDING
DR SUN YEN CLASSICAL CHINESE GARDEN
LUV-A-FAIR
STARFISH ROOM
STARFISH ROOM
WETT BAR
GM PLACE
B.C. SPORTS HALL OF FAME MUSEUM
COASTAL PEOPLES FINE ARTS GALLERY
B.C. PLACE STADIUM
PLAZA OF NATIONS
BAR NONE
THE RAGE
SCIENCE WORLD
Thornton Park
PACIFIC CENTRAL STATION

David Lam Park
STAMPS LANDING NEIGHBOURHOOD PUB
Charleston Park
False Creek

TERMINAL AVE.
INDUSTRIAL AVE.

© AVALON TRAVEL PUBLISHING

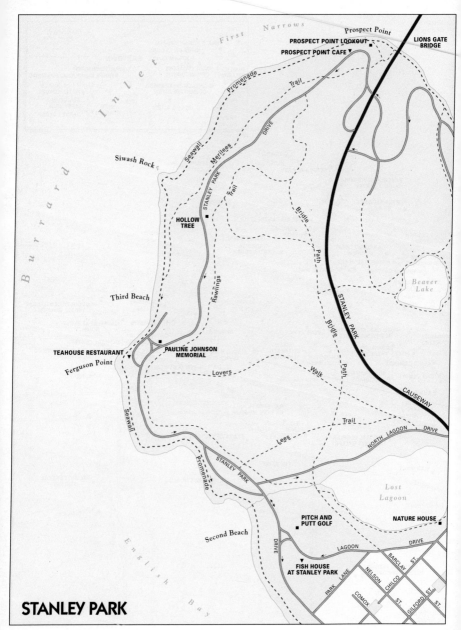

STANLEY PARK

First Narrows

Prospect Point

PROSPECT POINT LOOKOUT
PROSPECT POINT CAFE ▼

LIONS GATE BRIDGE

Promenade

Trail

B u r r a r d   I n l e t

Seawall

STANLEY PARK DRIVE

Merilees

Trail

Siwash Rock

HOLLOW TREE ■

Bridle

Beaver Lake

Rawlings

Path

STANLEY PARK

Third Beach

TEAHOUSE RESTAURANT ▼

PAULINE JOHNSON MEMORIAL ■

Ferguson Point

Lovers

Walk

Bridle

Path

CAUSEWAY

Seawall

Lees

Trail

NORTH LAGOON   DRIVE

Promenade

STANLEY PARK

Lost Lagoon

DRIVE

PITCH AND PUTT GOLF ■

NATURE HOUSE ■

Second Beach

DRIVE

LAGOON   DRIVE

BARCLAY ST.

E n g l i s h   B a y

FISH HOUSE AT STANLEY PARK ▼

PARK LANE

NELSON ST.

CHILCO ST.

GILFORD ST.

ST.

COMOX

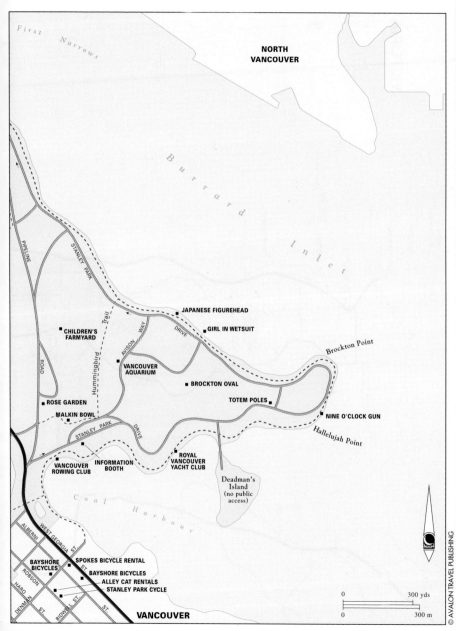

First Narrows

NORTH VANCOUVER

Burrard Inlet

PIPELINE

STANLEY PARK

ROAD

Hummingbird Trail

AVISON WAY

DRIVE

JAPANESE FIGUREHEAD

GIRL IN WETSUIT

CHILDREN'S FARMYARD

VANCOUVER AQUARIUM

Brockton Point

BROCKTON OVAL

ROSE GARDEN

TOTEM POLES

MALKIN BOWL

NINE O'CLOCK GUN

STANLEY PARK DRIVE

Hallelujah Point

VANCOUVER ROWING CLUB

INFORMATION BOOTH

ROYAL VANCOUVER YACHT CLUB

Deadman's Island (no public access)

Coal Harbour

ALBERNI ST.

WEST GEORGIA ST.

ROBSON ST.

HARO ST.

DENMAN ST.

BIDWELL ST.

BAYSHORE BICYCLES

SPOKES BICYCLE RENTAL

BAYSHORE BICYCLES

ALLEY CAT RENTALS

STANLEY PARK CYCLE

VANCOUVER

0   300 yds
0   300 m

© AVALON TRAVEL PUBLISHING

viii

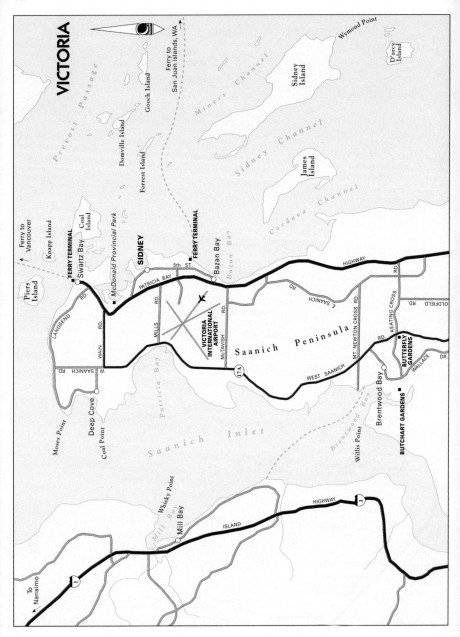

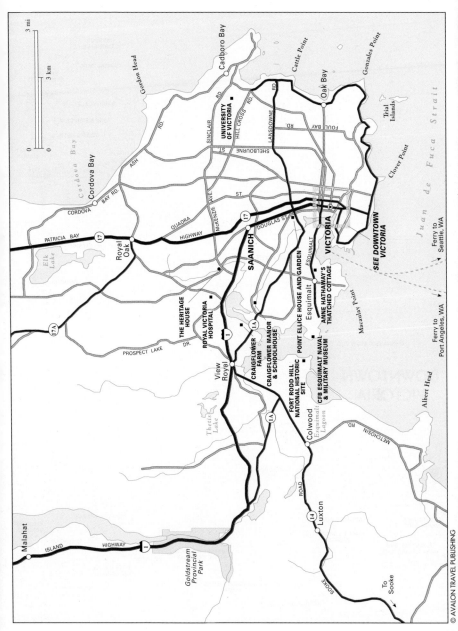

© AVALON TRAVEL PUBLISHING

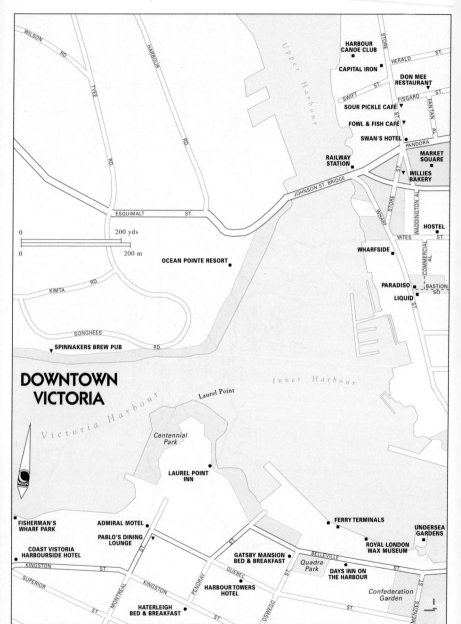

DOWNTOWN VICTORIA

HARBOUR CANOE CLUB
CAPITAL IRON
DON MEE RESTAURANT
SOUR PICKLE CAFÉ
FOWL & FISH CAFÉ
SWAN'S HOTEL
MARKET SQUARE
RAILWAY STATION
WILLIES BAKERY
HOSTEL
WHARFSIDE
PARADISO
LIQUID
OCEAN POINTE RESORT
SPINNAKERS BREW PUB
LAUREL POINT INN
FISHERMAN'S WHARF PARK
ADMIRAL MOTEL
PABLO'S DINING LOUNGE
COAST VICTORIA HARBOURSIDE HOTEL
GATSBY MANSION BED & BREAKFAST
HARBOUR TOWERS HOTEL
HATERLEIGH BED & BREAKFAST
FERRY TERMINALS
UNDERSEA GARDENS
ROYAL LONDON WAX MUSEUM
DAYS INN ON THE HARBOUR

Upper Harbour
Inner Harbour
Victoria Harbour
Laurel Point
Centennial Park
Quadra Park
Confederation Garden

WILSON RD.
HARBOUR RD.
TYEE RD.
SWIFT ST.
STORE ST.
HERALD ST.
FISGARD ST.
FANTAN AL.
PANDORA ST.
JOHNSON ST. BRIDGE
ESQUIMALT ST.
WHARF ST.
WADDINGTON AL.
YATES ST.
COMMERCIAL AL.
BASTION SQ.
KIMTA RD.
SONGHEES RD.
KINGSTON ST.
SUPERIOR ST.
MONTREAL ST.
PENDRAY ST.
QUEBEC ST.
OSWEGO ST.
BELLEVILLE ST.
MENZIES ST.

0   200 yds
0   200 m

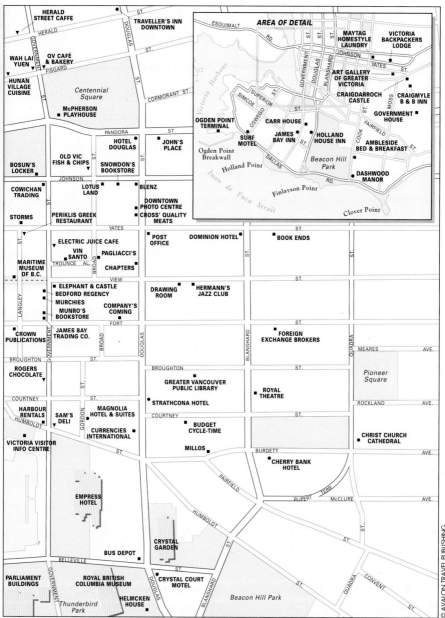

HERALD STREET CAFFE
TRAVELLER'S INN DOWNTOWN
HERALD ST.
GOVERNMENT
DOUGLAS ST.

WAH LAI YUEN
QV CAFÉ & BAKERY
FISGARD
HUNAN VILLAGE CUISINE
Centennial Square
McPHERSON PLAYHOUSE
CORMORANT ST.

PANDORA ST.
HOTEL DOUGLAS
JOHN'S PLACE
OLD VIC FISH & CHIPS
SNOWDON'S BOOKSTORE
JOHNSON
BOSUN'S LOCKER
BLENZ
COWICHAN TRADING
LOTUS LAND
DOWNTOWN PHOTO CENTRE
STORMS
PERIKLIS GREEK RESTAURANT
CROSS' QUALITY MEATS
YATES

ELECTRIC JUICE CAFE
VIN SANTO
PAGLIACCI'S
POST OFFICE
DOMINION HOTEL
BOOK ENDS
MARITIME MUSEUM OF B.C.
TROUNCE AL.
BROAD
CHAPTERS
VIEW ST.
LANGLEY
ELEPHANT & CASTLE
BEDFORD REGENCY
MURCHIES
MUNRO'S BOOKSTORE
COMPANY'S COMING
DRAWING ROOM
HERMANN'S JAZZ CLUB
FORT

CROWN PUBLICATIONS
JAMES BAY TRADING CO.
GOVERNMENT
BROAD
DOUGLAS
BLANSHARD
FOREIGN EXCHANGE BROKERS
QUADRA
MEARES AVE.
BROUGHTON
ROGERS CHOCOLATE
BROUGHTON ST.
Pioneer Square
COURTNEY
GREATER VANCOUVER PUBLIC LIBRARY
STRATHCONA HOTEL
ROYAL THEATRE
ROCKLAND AVE.
HARBOUR RENTALS
HUMBOLDT
SAM'S DELI
GORDON
MAGNOLIA HOTEL & SUITES
COURTNEY ST.
BUDGET CYCLE-TIME
CHRIST CHURCH CATHEDRAL
VICTORIA VISITOR INFO CENTRE
CURRENCIES INTERNATIONAL
MILLOS
BURDETT AVE.
CHERRY BANK HOTEL
FAIRFIELD
RUPERT
FERN
McCLURE AVE.
EMPRESS HOTEL
HUMBOLDT
BELLEVILLE
BUS DEPOT
CRYSTAL GARDEN
QUADRA
CONVENT
PARLIAMENT BUILDINGS
GOVERNMENT
ROYAL BRITISH COLUMBIA MUSEUM
CRYSTAL COURT MOTEL
DOUGLAS
BLANSHARD
Beacon Hill Park
HELMCKEN HOUSE
Thunderbird Park

AREA OF DETAIL
ESQUIMALT RD.
MAYTAG HOMESTYLE LAUNDRY
VICTORIA BACKPACKERS LODGE
JOHNSON
YATES ST.
GOVERNMENT
DOUGLAS
BLANSHARD
ART GALLERY OF GREATER VICTORIA
Victoria Harbour
SUPERIOR ST.
SIMCOE
OSWEGO
CRAIGDARROCH CASTLE
MOSS
CRAIGMYLE B & B INN
OGDEN POINT TERMINAL
CARR HOUSE
FAIRFIELD
GOVERNMENT HOUSE
SURF MOTEL
JAMES BAY INN
HOLLAND HOUSE INN
COOK
AMBLESIDE BED & BREAKFAST
Ogden Point Breakwall
DALLAS
Beacon Hill Park
Holland Point
DASHWOOD MANOR
Juan de Fuca Strait
Finlayson Point
Clover Point

© AVALON TRAVEL PUBLISHING

VANCOUVER HANDBOOK

INCLUDING VICTORIA
FIRST EDITION

ANDREW HEMPSTEAD

MOON
TRAVEL
HANDBOOKS

VANCOUVER HANDBOOK
FIRST EDITION

Published by
Avalon Travel Publishing
5855 Beaudry St.
Emeryville, CA 94608, USA

Printed by
Colorcraft, Ltd.

Please send all comments, corrections,
additions, amendments, and critiques to:

**VANCOUVER HANDBOOK
C/O MOON TRAVEL HANDBOOKS
AVALON TRAVEL PUBLISHING
5855 BEAUDRY ST.
EMERYVILLE, CA 94608, USA
e-mail: travel@moon.com
www.moon.com**

Printing History
1st edition—May 2000
5 4 3 2 1 0

ISBN: 1-56691-198-2
Library of Congress Cataloging-In-Publication-Data has been applied for.

Editor: Deana Corbitt Shields
Production & Design: Stephanie Bird
Cartography: Mark Stroud/Moon Street Cartography
Index: Gina Wilson Birtcil

Front cover photo: © Jan Strømme/Picturesque, 2000

All photos by Andrew Hempstead unless otherwise noted.
All illustrations by Bob Race unless otherwise noted.

Distributed in the United States and Canada by Publishers Group West

Printed in China

CONTENTS

VANCOUVER

INTRODUCTION . . . . 3~12

The Land 3
    Flora and Fauna; Climate
History 5
    The Earliest Inhabitants; European Exploration; Permanent Settlement;
    The Coming of the Railway; The Early 1900s; Recent Times

SPECIAL TOPICS

Totem Poles 6   The Hippy Capital of Canada 11

SIGHTS . . . . 13~39

Downtown 13
    Gastown; Chinatown; West End; Stanley Park; False Creek
Central Vancouver 25
    Vanier Park; University of British Columbia; Parks and Gardens
Farther South 29
    Richmond; South of the Fraser River
The North Shore 31
    North Vancouver; West Vancouver and Vicinity
East from Downtown 35
    Burnaby; Vicinity of Coquitlam; New Westminster; Langley; Fraser River
    Valley

SPECIAL TOPICS

Getting Oriented 14-15   Robson Street 21
Vancouver Views 16-17   Vancouver for Kids 36
"Gassy Jack" Deighton 18   Harrison Hot Springs 38

RECREATION . . . . 40~62

Fun in the Sun 40
    Walking and Hiking; Bicycling; Golf; Water Sports; Skiing; Spectator
    Sports; Tours
Arts and Entertainment 51
    Drinking and Dancing; Live Music and Comedy; Performing Arts;
    Cinemas
Shopping 55
Festivals and Events 57
    Spring; Summer; Fall; Winter

SPECIAL TOPICS

Whitewater Rafting 41   Shopping for
Vancouver Beaches 44   Native Arts and Crafts 56
Skiing at Whistler/Blackcomb 47   Public Holidays 57
The Remarkable Terry Fox 50   So, It's Raining Outside,
                                              but You Still Feel Active 60

ACCOMMODATIONS . . . . **63~77**

Hotels and Motels 63
Downtown; Robson Street; West End; North Vancouver and Vicinity;
South of Downtown; East of Downtown
Bed and Breakfasts 73
Backpacker Lodges 74
Hostelling International; Other Backpacker Lodges; More Options for
Budget Travelers
Campgrounds 76

SPECIAL TOPIC
....
Accommodations Ratings Chart *64*

FOOD . . . . **78~94**

Downtown Dining 79
Cafés and Cheap Eats; Restaurants; Gastown; Chinatown; Robson
Street; West End
Dining in Other Parts of the City 91
Granville Island and Vicinity; Kitsilano; West Broadway; North Vancouver

SPECIAL TOPICS
....
East Hastings Street . . . . *86*   *A Hidden Central Vancouver*
                                                Dining Gem. *92*

VICTORIA
....

INTRODUCTION . . . . **97~98**
History

SPECIAL TOPIC
....
Victoria in a Day from Vancouver *98*

SIGHTS . . . . **99~108**
Inner Harbour; Old Town; South of the Inner Harbour; Rockland and Oak
Bay; West of Downtown; Saanich Peninsula

SPECIAL TOPIC
....
Exploring the Rest of Vancouver Island *106-107*

RECREATION . . . . **109~113**
Fun in the Sun; Arts and Entertainment; Shopping; Festivals and Events

ACCOMMODATIONS . . . . **114~120**

Hotels and Motels 114
Downtown; Other Parts of the City
Bed and Breakfasts 117
Budget Accommodations 119
Backpacker Lodges; Other Options; Campgrounds

FOOD . . . . **121~124**

SPECIAL TOPIC
....
Two Out of Town Splurges *123*

BASICS

VANCOUVER BASICS . . . . 127~143
Getting There 127
  Air; Rail; Bus; Ferry
Getting Around 133
  Translink; Car; Taxi, Boat, and Bike
Services 136
  Visas and Officialdom; Money; Health; Communications and
  Measurements; Photography
Information 140
  Information Centers; Books and Bookstores; Newspapers and
  Periodicals

SPECIAL TOPICS

Departure Taxes *128*	*Currency Exchange* *137*
Cutting Flight Costs *129*	*Heading Farther Afield?* *141*
Inside Passage Cruises *132*	

VICTORIA BASICS . . . . 144~147
Getting There 144
  Air; Bus; Ferry
Getting Around 146
  Bus and Taxi; Car Rental; Bikes and Such
Services and Information 147

BOOKLIST . . . . 148~150

INDEXES . . . . 151~158
Accommodations 151-152
Restaurants 153-154
General Index 155-158

MAPS

COLOR SUPPLEMENT

Vicinity of Vancouver i
Greater Vancouver . . . . ii-iii
Downtown Vancouver . . . . iv-v
Stanley Park . . . . vi-vii
Victoria . . . . viii-ix
Downtown Victoria . . . . x-xi

ACCOMMODATIONS

Downtown Vancouver Accommodations 66-67

FOOD

Downtown Vancouver Dining 82-83

VANCOUVER BASICS

Downtown Vancouver Bookstores 142

ACKNOWLEDGMENTS

Thanks to all my friends in Vancouver, old and new, for helping guide me in the right direction and offering insider tips for the city they are so proud to call home; you know who you all are.

DROP US A LINE

Although we have strived to produce the most up-to-date guidebook humanly possible, things change—restaurants and accommodations open and close, attractions come and go, and prices go up. If you come across a great out-of-the-way place, a new restaurant or lodging, or if you think a particular sight warrants a mention, please write to us. Letters from tour operators and people in the tourism and hospitality industries are also appreciated.

Write to:

Vancouver Handbook
c/o Moon Travel Handbooks
Avalon Travel Publishing
5855 Beaudry Street
Emeryville, CA 94608

e-mail: travel@moon.com

ACCOMMODATIONS RATINGS CHART

To make choosing an accommodation that comes within your budget easy, all hotels and motels, bed and breakfasts, backpacker lodges, and campgrounds have been afforded a one-word "rating" in this book. The rating is based on high season (summer) double occupancy rates. In the off-season, prices will often drop to a less expensive category, as will many city hotels on weekends. The rating is only a price indication and has no bearing on the facilities offered at each establishment.

Except for campgrounds, an eight percent provincial hotel and motel tax, a two percent tourism tax, and, like the rest of Canada, the seven percent goods and services tax must be added; the latter is refundable to visitors from outside the country.

Budget: up to $60
Inexpensive: $60-90
Moderate: $90-120
Expensive: $120-150
Premium: $150-180
Luxury: $180 and up

VANCOUVER

Let your mind fill with images of dramatic, snowcapped mountains rising high above a city skyline. Century-old inner-city buildings and steel-and-glass skyscrapers facing the sheltered shores of a large wide inlet. Manicured suburbs perching along the edge of the sea, fringed by golden sandy beaches. Lush tree-filled parks and brilliant flower gardens overflowing with color. An outdoor-loving population keen to take advantage of magnificent surroundings. Flocks of Canada geese overhead, noisily honking to one another as they fly toward the setting sun. These are the magnificent images of Vancouver, largest city in British Columbia, Canada's westernmost province.

If you view this gleaming mountain- and sea-dominated city for the first time on a beautiful sunny day, you're bound to fall for it in a big way. But even gray skies can't dampen the city's vibrant, outdoorsy atmosphere. By day, the active visitor can enjoy boating right from downtown, or perhaps venture out to one of the nearby provincial parks for hiking and skiing. More urban-oriented visitors can savor the aromas of just-brewed coffee and freshly baked bread wafting from cosmopolitan sidewalk cafés, join in the bustle at seaside markets, or simply relax on one of the many city beaches. By night, Vancouver's myriad fine restaurants, nightclubs, and performing-arts venues beckon visitors to continue enjoying themselves on into the wee hours.

Rain or shine, night or day, it is an alluring and unforgettable city.

INTRODUCTION

THE LAND

Greater Vancouver is contained by the geological boundary of the Coast Mountains to the north and the Strait of Georgia to the west, and the political boundary of an international border to the south. These borders hold a great variety of landforms, although most of the city is laid out across a massive coastal delta at the mouth of the Fraser River. For millions of years, silt, sand, and gravel have been washing down from the river's 200,000-square kilometer watershed, slowly filling a fjord that originally extended inland over 150 kilometers. This gradual process was fast-tracked at the end of the last Ice Age, around 11,000 years ago, when glacial silt left behind by the retreating sheet of ice built up high enough to extend the coastline to its present position. The process continues to this day—fly into the city on a clear day and you'll see a massive fan of brown water extending far into the Strait of Georgia from the mouth of the Fraser River. Vancouver's beaches are a result of the same process. Over thousands of years, sediment washed out of the Fraser River has been forced northward by ocean currents, then pushed into the shoreline by tidal action, creating a string of sandy beaches extending from Point Grey all the way around English Bay to Stanley Park.

Downtown itself rises from a peninsula jutting northward into Burrard Inlet and is linked to Central Vancouver by a low-lying isthmus of land, much of which has been artificially reclaimed from the waters of False Creek. The peninsula is volcanic in origin, but it rises less than 50 meters above sea level at its highest point; one distinctive outcrop of volcanic origin is Siwash Rock, which stands in open water off the end of Stanley Park.

South of Central Vancouver, the North Arm of the Fraser River runs along the northern extent of the delta, then splits near the coast to form low-lying Sea Island, upon which Vancouver International Airport lies. To the south, Richmond lies on another island formed by the split of the Fraser River. South of the South Arm, suburban Delta and Surrey extend along the delta to shallow Boundary Bay and the international border.

Rising precipitously to the north of Burrard Inlet is the North Shore Range, the southern arm of the Coast Mountains. The highest peak of the North Shore Range is 1,725-meter Cathedral Mountain, but many of the Golden Ears

Group peaks are around 1,700 meters and capped in snow almost year-round. The range is broken by four valleys, including one that holds Indian Arm, a tidal waterway draining into Burrard Inlet. Over millions of years, excessive rainfall has eroded many other watercourses through these mountains, including the Capilano River, which has carved a 70-meter-deep gorge into its forested flanks.

FLORA AND FAUNA

When the first Europeans sailed into Burrard Inlet in the late 1700s, most of what is now Vancouver was covered in a temperate rainforest of Douglas fir, western red cedar, hemlock, and Sitka spruce. The only remaining tract of this forest can be found in Stanley Park, including a magnificent stand of western red cedar near Third Beach.

Stanley Park is also the best place to view the city's fauna. Coyotes, raccoons, skunks, and a variety of squirrels call the park home. Beavers live in many waterways within Greater Vancouver, but the most accessible spot to view these industrious critters is Burnaby Lake. On the North Shore, the forested provincial parks such as Golden Ears, Cypress, Indian Arm, and Mount Seymour hold populations of larger mammals, including deer, mountain goats, and black and grizzly bears.

Marinelife in the waters around Vancouver is abundant, a major drawcard for scuba divers and anglers alike. Whales, seals, and sea lions are all present, and they occasionally venture

bald eagle

into Burrard Inlet. All five species of North Pacific salmon spawn in local river systems—chum, chinook, coho, pink, and sockeye—and along with halibut, perch, and lingcod make for excellent fishing. On a smaller scale, tidal rock pools hold a great variety of marinelife: wander down to Stanley Park's shoreline at low tide and you'll see sea urchins, crabs, sea anemones, and sea cucumbers.

Over 350 bird species have been reported within Greater Vancouver. The Fraser River delta is an important migratory stop for hundreds of thousands of birds. It's on the Pacific Flyway, along which birds winter in South America and migrate north each spring to Siberia, then make the return trip south each fall. The highest concentration of migrating birds can be viewed at the George C. Reifel Bird Sanctuary, where up to 50,000 snow geese stop over in November. Nearby, 4,000-hectare Burns Bog, one of the world's largest peat bogs, is home to 140 species of birds. The delta's wetlands are also an important wintering ground for many species, including trumpeter swans, the world's largest waterfowl. Birdlife is also prolific in Stanley Park, where Lost Lagoon holds a large population of ducks, Canada geese, herons, and white swans. Brackendale, 70 km north of downtown along Hwy. 99, is home to the world's largest winter concentration of bald eagles. Between mid-December and the end of January over 3,000 of

grizzly bear

Canada goose

a lot. Most precipitation, though, falls in winter, and summers are relatively dry. Precipitation is strongly influenced by the lay of the land, which means there is a large variation in rainfall across the city. In the south of the city rainfall averages just 900 millimeters annually, while North Vancouver, in the shadow of the North Shore Range, averages 2,400 millimeters.

Summer is by far the most popular time to visit Vancouver. July daytime temperatures average a pleasant 23° C (73° F), while the hottest day on record reached 33.3° C (92° F). In summer, city paths come alive with joggers, cyclists, and in-line skaters; the beaches and outdoor pools with swimmers and sunbathers; and the nearby mountain parks with hikers, anglers, and campers.

Temperatures through spring and fall are, naturally, cooler than in summer, but in many ways these are prime travel periods. June and September are especially pleasant, as crowds are minimal. The average daytime temperature during both April and October is 14° C (57° F).

Vancouver's main winter attraction is as a gateway to major ski resorts, including Whistler/Blackcomb, which is open from early November, and three local ski areas within sight of the city. Winter temperatures remain relatively mild (on a few occasions each year snow does fall in downtown Vancouver, but it melts quickly), with January's average high being 5° C (41° F).

Most city attractions are open year-round, although summer hours are longer. Hotels and motels charge more in summer than the rest of the year, reducing rates most in winter. Outside of summer, many accommodations offer package deals, which, for example, may include meals and discounted admissions to theater performances.

these magnificent creatures descend on this stretch of the Squamish River to feed on spawned-out salmon.

CLIMATE

Vancouver boasts the mildest climate of all Canadian cities except for nearby Victoria. But the mild climate comes with one drawback—it rains

HISTORY

THE EARLIEST INHABITANTS

The first Europeans to set eyes on the land encompassing today's city of Vancouver were gold-seeking Spanish traders who sailed through the Strait of Georgia in 1790. Although the forested wilderness they encountered seemed impenetrable, it had been inhabited by humans since becoming ice-free some 10,000 years earlier. The

ancestors of these earliest inhabitants had migrated from northeast Asia across a land bridge spanning the Bering Strait. During this time, the northern latitudes of North America were covered by an ice cap, forcing these people to travel south down the west coast before fanning out across the ice-free southern latitudes. As the ice cap receded northward, the people drifted north also, perhaps only a few kilometers in an

TOTEM POLES

Traveling through the Pacific Northwest you can't help but notice all the totem poles that decorate the landscape, and many can be found in Vancouver. All totem poles are made of red (or occasionally yellow) cedar painted black, red, blue, yellow, and white with colored pigment derived from minerals, plants, and salmon roe. They are erected as validation of a public record or documentation of an important event. Six types of poles are believed to have evolved in the following order: house post (an integral part of the house structure), mortuary (erected as a chief's or shaman's grave post, often with the bones or ashes in a box at the top), memorial (commemorating special events), frontal (a memorial or heraldic pole), welcome, and shame poles. None is an object of worship; each tells a story or history of a person's clan or family. The figures on the pole represent family lineage, animals, or a mythical character.

Since a government ban on potlatch ceremonies—of which the raising of totem poles is an integral part—was lifted in 1951, the art form has been revived. Over the years, many totem poles have been relocated from their original sites. Both historic and more modern poles can be viewed in Vancouver. **Stanley Park** has a small collection of authentic totem poles. They were collected from along the coast in the early 1900s and are mostly the work of the Kwagiulth, who lived on the mainland opposite the northern tip of Vancouver Island. The poles stand near Brockton Point.

The world's best collection of totem poles is housed inside the **Museum of Anthropology,** on the UBC campus at Point Grey. The Haida, of the Queen Charlotte Islands, were renowned for their totem poles. Many "totem villages," long since abandoned, remain on the remote southern tip of the archipelago, but for those not lucky enough to travel that far north, there's a re-creation of a village behind the museum. Three Gitskan-style poles can be viewed at the Plaza of Nations, while a 30-meter-high Kwagiulth-style pole towers over the entrance to the Maritime Museum, and a replica of a pole from the Haida village of Skedans greets visitors at the Douglas Border Crossing. If you'd like your own totem pole, head to **Hills Indian Crafts,** 165 Water St., tel. (604) 685-4249, or search out the **Coastal Peoples Fine Arts Gallery** at 1072 Mainland St., Yaletown, tel. (604) 685-9298, and expect to pay up to $15,000 for a four-meter-high pole.

Totem poles can be found throughout Vancouver, including here in Stanley Park.

entire generation. They settled in areas with an abundance of natural resources, such as around the mouth of the salmon-rich Fraser River. Known as the **Coast Salish,** these earliest inhabitants lived a very different lifestyle from the stereotypical "Indian"—they had no bison to depend on, they didn't ride horses, nor did they live in tepees, but instead they developed a unique and intriguing culture that revolved around the ocean and its bountiful resources.

The oldest archaeological sites in the Lower Mainland are ancient middens of clam and mussel shells, which accumulated as garbage dumps for native villages. The largest known of these is the Marpole Midden, in southern Vancouver, which at three hectares in area and up to five meters deep represents a thousand years of seasonal living beginning around 2,500 years ago. The end of the "Marpole Phase" coincided with prehistoric technological advances, which made living in larger, more permanent communities more practical. Distinct bands then began forming within the Coast Salish nation. The largest was the **Musqueam**, 3,000 of whom lived in a village beside the Fraser River. The **Squamish** lived on the north side of Burrard Inlet and along Howe Sound. Both formed highly specialized societies and a distinctive and highly decorative arts style featuring animals, mythical creatures, and oddly shaped human forms believed to be supernatural ancestors. Like other west coast tribes, both emphasized the material wealth of each chief and his tribe, displayed to others during special events called potlatches. The potlatch ceremonies were held to mark important moments in tribal society, such as marriages, puberty celebrations, deaths, or totem-pole raisings. The wealth of a tribe became obvious when the chief gave away enormous quantities of gifts to his guests—the nobler the guest, the better the gift. The potlatch exchange was accompanied by much feasting, speech-making, dancing, and entertainment, all of which could last many days. Stories performed by hosts garbed in elaborate costumes and masks educated, entertained, and affirmed each clan's historical continuity.

PROVINCIAL ARCHIVES OF BRITISH COLUMBIA

George Vancouver

EUROPEAN EXPLORATION

The first Europeans to venture along North America's west coast north of the 49th parallel were in search of a northwest passage to the Orient. This fabled route across the top of the continent was first attempted from the east by Martin Frobisher in 1576, but it wasn't until the 1770s that the route was attempted from the west. Three Spanish ex-

peditions and a fourth led by Captain James Cook, with George Vancouver as navigator, sailed past the entrance to the Strait of Georgia, but none of these ships entered the waters upon which the city now lies. In 1792, Vancouver returned to the area as Captain Vancouver, leading an expedition sent to chart the waters of the strait. In the process, Vancouver entered Burrard Inlet and claimed the land for Great Britain.

Fur and Gold

The next wave of Europeans to arrive on the west coast came overland in search of fur-bearing mammals. The first to reach the coast was Simon Fraser, who was sent west by the North West Company to establish a coastal trading post. In 1806 he reached the Pacific Ocean via the river that was later named for him, and in 1808 he built a fur fort east of today's Vancouver. In 1827, the Hudson's Bay Company established its own trading post, Fort Langley, on the Fraser River 48 km east of present-day downtown Vancouver. Neither of these two outposts spawned a permanent settlement, although Fort Langley was relocated farther upstream in 1839.

When gold was discovered on the upper reaches of the Fraser River in the late 1850s, the British government, worried that the influx of Americans was a threat to its sovereignty, declared the whole western expanse of Canada a British colony, as it had for Vancouver Island in 1849. The most important task for James Douglas, the colony's first governor, was to establish a permanent settlement. Unimpressed by the location of Fort Langley, Douglas selected a site farther downstream and named it New Westminster.

PERMANENT SETTLEMENT

By 1860 a rough track had been carved through the wilderness between New Westminster and

Burrard Inlet, where seams of coal had been reported. The government tried selling off the surrounding land, but with the coal deemed uneconomical to extract, little interest was generated.

Although seams of coal did exist around Burrard Inlet, lumber formed the basis of Vancouver's first industry. In 1863 a small sawmill was established at Moodyville, across Burrard Inlet to the north; then two years later another, owned by Captain Edward Stamp, began operation on the south side of the inlet. They were linked to each other by a steam-powered ferry and to New Westminster by a stagecoach trail. Both sawmill companies provided accommodation and board for single workers, and while most lumber was for export, married employees were given wood to build themselves simple dwellings.

Slowly, two rough-and-tumble townships were carved out of the wilderness.

Gastown and Granville

Alcohol was banned from the company towns, so a number of saloons sprang up on their outskirts, including one west of Stamp's Mill operated by infamous "Gassy Jack" Deighton. The smattering of buildings that quickly went up around Gassy Jack's enterprise became known to early residents as Gastown. This small saloon, nothing more than a couple of planks lying across empty wooden barrels, protected from the elements by a canvas tent, was the embryo of what is today Vancouver.

In 1870, as Gassy Jack was selling liquor to thirsty sawmill workers, the government began selling off the land surrounding Gastown under the official name of Granville. Land was sold for $1 an acre, on the condition that the owner occupy his holding for a minimum of two years. The government also began establishing naval reserves at strategic locations throughout the region, and more trails were cut through the wilderness, including one that linked a reserve beside False Creek to New Westminster (along the route taken by the modern-day Kingsway). Settlers also began moving farther afield, establishing the first farms on the Fraser River delta.

THE COMING OF THE RAILWAY

In 1871, with the promise of a transcontinental railway, British Columbia officially became part of Canada. But it was to be another 15 years until the first train rolled into Vancouver. Originally, Port Moody, at the head of Burrard Inlet, was to be the line's western terminus, but influential landowners convinced the Canadian Pacific Railway that Granville would be a more suitable option, and so the original decision was reversed, but this wasn't announced until 1885, by which time the CPR had bought up large chunks of land around the planned terminus. At this time Granville consisted of a short block of waterfront buildings and boasted a population of around

The arival of the first train on May 23, 1887, heralded Vancouver's emergence as the major metropolis of western Canada.

PROVINCIAL ARCHIVES OF BRITISH COLUMBIA

400, but within six months of the public announcement real estate prices had skyrocketed, and hundreds of buildings lined the waterfront. The surrounding land was still densely forested, so in anticipation of the coming of the railway, the CPR employed William Hamilton to map streets out of the wilderness. As he had done previously in Regina and Calgary, he laid out a downtown core in a grid pattern, naming streets after CPR officials (and one after himself).

The following year, on 6 April 1886, Granville, population 1,000, was officially incorporated as the City of Vancouver, in honor of the first Englishman to sail through the heads. Two months later, fire roared through the timber city. Just about everything burned to the ground, and 28 people perished in the blaze. With true pioneering spirit the rebuilding process began immediately.

Terminal City

By the end of the 1880s, the railway had arrived, and Vancouver had become "Terminal City," Canada's transportation gateway to the Orient. In the process, its population increased 10-fold, to 10,000, eclipsing that of New Westminster.

As well as port facilities at the end of the rail line, more sawmills were built to fill the never-ending demand for lumber, most of which was used in housing. Other industries also sprouted, including a floating cannery on Coal Harbour. Granville and Hastings Streets developed as commercial strips, with the former leading from the original Gastown through a large tract of CPR-owned land to False Creek. By 1890 other aspects of the city

of today had taken shape—400 acres west of the downtown had been set aside as Stanley Park, wealthy residents began building large houses in the West End, European workers built houses in Yaletown, and Chinese workers that had been brought in to help build the railway were concentrated at the east end of Hastings Street.

Continuing Growth

Vancouver continued to boom through the last decade of the 1800s, due to the city's strategic location more than anything else. Lead, silver, and copper mines were operating throughout the province's interior, and Vancouver, with a rail line and developing port facilities, was the focal point for export. This, in turn, spurred the development of manufacturing industries. The city's wealthier residents began demanding the finer things in life: a streetcar system came into operation in 1890, a golf course opened behind Jericho Beach in 1892, and a new 2,000-seat opera house hosted its first production in 1897.

By the turn of the 20th century, Vancouver's population reached 24,000, having doubled yet again within the space of a decade, this time surpassing the population of Victoria, the provincial capital.

THE EARLY 1900s

With Vancouver developing as an important manufacturing and financial center, in the early years of the century the young city experienced a population and real estate boom: in the first decade the population *quadrupled*. The West End and the CPR mainstay of Shaunessey Heights became enclaves of the wealthy, Yaletown continued to be home to the working class, and the middle-class suburbs of Central Vancouver, such as Kitsilano, Kerrisdale, and Fairview, sprang up. Wholesale and commercial buildings continued to be centered in Gastown, while Granville Street developed into a commercial corridor and financial institutions set up business along W. Hastings Street.

World War I and Continued Expansion
After the Great Fire of 1886, stone and brick buildings replaced the burnt out timber ones, and while many of Gastown's buildings are from this era, it wasn't until 1913 that the first skyscraper, the World Building, was completed. At the time, this 17-story-high structure (known today as the Old Sun Tower) was the tallest building in the British Empire. The economic depression of 1913 slowed the local economy, and then the onset of WW I saw thousands of working-age men head off to Europe, but Vancouver was less affected by those two world-changing events than elsewhere. The war created a demand for new ships, and by 1918 shipbuilding had become Vancouver's largest industry. Additionally, the opening of the Panama Canal in 1915 created the perfect outlet for transporting the province's abundant nonrenewable resources and grain crops from the prairies to North America's east coast and Europe, resulting in further development of the port facilities and railyards. By 1920 False Creek and the far reaches of Burrard Inlet sprawled with industry, and while the West End continued to develop as a residential area, population growth was mostly south of the Fraser River in Richmond, Surrey, and Delta.

During the 1920s Vancouver's population grew from 175,000 to 230,000, and by 1936, when the city celebrated its 50th birthday, the figure had grown above 250,000.

Development on the North Shore
Today, Vancouver's most sought after residential addresses are on the North Shore, but just 70 years ago, with no land-based link to Vancouver, it was an untamed wilderness, like the city itself had been a further 50 years prior. That all changed

in 1932 when the Guinness family of Ireland invested $20 an acre in buying 4,000 acres of land at West Vancouver. To boost the resale value of their investment, the family financed the Lions Gate Bridge, which at the time of construction was the world's longest steel cable bridge.

The opening of the Lions Gate Bridge exponentially spurred development north of the inlet, but at the same time the city itself boomed as it took advantage of a thriving provincial economy, which was mostly due to high mineral and lumber prices.

1954 British Empire Games
In 1954 the rest of the world got to see Vancouver and its fabulous natural setting in all its glory as host city for the British Empire Games. The games were the first major sporting event shown on television, an event in itself that put the city under the international spotlight, but it was the "Miracle Mile" that made the games most memorable. The race was a much-awaited clash between Australia's John Landy and England's Roger Bannister, the only two men in the world to have run a mile in under four minutes. In the end it was Bannister who crossed the line first, but both ran the distance in under four minutes, a classic finish that graced the first cover of *Sports Illustrated*.

RECENT TIMES

City limits continued to expand through the 1960s, keeping house prices steady, but then real estate speculation reached a peak in the early 1970s, when downtown house prices more than doubled in the first five years. Unable to afford housing near the city center, many families began to move to the outer suburbs, and into apartment buildings, which were slowly replacing the grand old houses of the West End and Central Vancouver. The boom also forced many of the remaining downtown industries to relocate to outlying areas—and so the sawmills and industry around Burrard Inlet and False Creek closed, leaving an industrial wasteland. Originally, the plan was to raze the old warehouses along Gastown's Water Street and build a waterfront expressway, diverting traffic away from the downtown core. Amid an outpouring of public opposition, the plan was thrown out, and Gastown was reborn as a tourist attraction, complete with

THE HIPPY CAPITAL OF CANADA

During the 1960s, in stark contrast to the modernization of downtown, Kitsilano's 4th Ave. became a mecca for the counter-culture movement, a Haight-Ashbury of the north.

The aura of this era lives on in a few local Kitsilano restaurants, but its biggest impact was the formation of **Greenpeace**, an organization of activists now headquartered in Amsterdam but active worldwide in the fight to make governments and big business environmentally responsible for the planet. It all started in 1967 when a small group of Vancouver locals began expressing their dismay among themselves at U.S. government testing of nuclear weapons in the waters off the Alaskan coastline. Convinced that they could do something about it, the group chartered a small ship and amid much publicity sailed north for the test site. The year was 1971, the ship was named *Greenpeace,* and the rest, as they say, is history.

restaurants and boutiques scattered through some of the city's oldest buildings.

The preeminent architect of this time was a local boy, University of British Columbia graduate Arthur Erickson, whose distinct style can be seen today in notable buildings such as the Vancouver Museum, the Museum of Anthropology, and Simon Fraser University.

Immigration

Federal immigration laws were relaxed in the 1960s, but it wasn't until the '70s that the largest influx of Chinese, Greek, and Italian immigrants settled in the city, reflected in a change to the local restaurant scene and to commercial areas such as Main Street. The city's new multicultural look went a lot further than the surface; economic ties with Asia have strengthened as exports to Asia surpassed those to the United States by the mid-'70s. By 1980, most of Vancouver's prime downtown real estate was foreign owned.

The Changing Face of False Creek

With the relocation of downtown industry complete by 1980, False Creek had become an industrial wasteland. A farmers' market in rejuvenated Gastown met with little success, so the concept was tried on False Creek's government-owned Granville Island. The market opened in conjunction with an island-based arts school, small businesses such as boat building, and a variety of artistic endeavors, boutiques, and restaurants. At the same time, much of the rest of the land around False Creek was rezoned, allowing only residential developments that included large tracts of greenspace. The earliest of these rose on the south side of Burrard Inlet, between Granville Island and the Cambie Street Bridge. The most recent phases are taking place on the downtown side, with the beautification of False Creek slated to continue well into the future.

Expo86

In 1986, at just 100 years old, Vancouver was showcased to the world during Expo86, boldly declaring itself the "City of the Century" to the world exposition's 20 million visitors. The main Expo site was spread around the head of False Creek, and although most of the infrastructure has since been removed, the BC Pavilion (now Plaza of Nations) and Expo Preview Centre (now Science World) remain. But Expo's biggest legacy was the Canada Pavilion, now a city icon known as Canada Place. In keeping with the Expo theme, "Man in Motion," the SkyTrain, a driverless computer-operated light transit system, opened in the mid-'80s.

The 1990s

The worldwide economic downturn of the late 1980s and early '90s was felt less in Vancouver than in other major cities, mainly due to continued strong foreign investment from Asia. After the 1984 agreement by Great Britain to hand Hong Kong back to China, the nationals of that small Asian country invested in Vancouver with added zeal. By the time the actual takeover took place in 1997, it was estimated that Hong Kong interests owned 90% of the land in the downtown core. Immigration continued to be strongest from Asian countries throughout the '90s, and by the end of the decade the people of almost 100 countries called Vancouver home.

A New Millennium

From what began as a cluster of ramshackle buildings centered around a saloon just 120 years

British traditions are still strong in Vancouver. Wander down to Coal Harbour at any time to the Vancouver Rowing Club, where the city's rowing teams push off.

ago, Vancouver has blossomed into one of the world's greatest cities. Vancouver's population is currently quoted as 600,000, but, in reality, the city sprawls well beyond any arbitrary boundary, and over 2.6 million residents call Greater Vancouver home. And while the city holds onto the largest port on North America's west coast, boasting 20 specialized terminals that handle more tonnage than any other port in Canada, it is now a lot less reliant on its traditional economic heart for its growth. Tourism contributes over $5 billion annually to the local economy, with finance, real estate, insurance, and manufacturing also forming large slices of the local economic pie. Newer industries also contribute; Vancouver is North America's third-largest movie-making center, employing up to 25,000 on as many as 30 simultaneous productions.

the Seawall Promenade

SIGHTS
DOWNTOWN

Canada Place

The stunning architectural curiosity with the billowing 27-meter-high Teflon-coated "sails" on Burrard Inlet—the one that looks as if it might weigh anchor and cruise off into the sunset at any moment—is Canada Place, Vancouver's convention center and cruise-ship dock. Built as the Canada Pavilion for Expo86, the impressive building at the foot of Burrard Street also houses the luxurious Pan Pacific Hotel (the glass marvel with domed top), restaurants, shops, and an IMAX theater. Start your self-guided tour at the information booth near the main entrance, then allow at least an hour to wander through the complex. Don't miss walking the outside promenade—three city blocks long—for splendid views of the harbor, the North Shore, the Coast Mountains, and docked Alaska-bound cruise ships.

Vancouver Art Gallery

Francis Rattenbury, architect of Victoria's Empress Hotel and many other masterpieces, designed Vancouver's imposing neoclassical-revival courthouse, which now houses Vancouver Art Gallery, 750 Hornby St., tel. (604) 662-4700. The exterior retains its original 1911 design while the interior was renovated in 1983 by Arthur Erickson, a prominent Vancouver architect.

The gallery houses a large collection of works by Canada's preeminent female artist, **Emily Carr,** who was born on Vancouver Island in 1871 and traveled the world honing her painting and drawing skills before settling in Vancouver in 1906. Her style reflects the time she spent with the natives of the Pacific Northwest coast, but she was also influenced by techniques acquired during periods she lived in London and Paris. Carr combined these influences to create unique works, and the gallery is well worth visiting for these alone. The Carr collection is on the third floor, along with the works of many other local artists. The gallery also holds pieces by other contemporary artists, from both North America and Europe, as well as an impressive collection of historical art.

GETTING ORIENTED

Vancouver isn't a particularly easy city to find your way around, although an excellent transit system helps immensely. The color maps provided at the front of this book—highlighting all sights, accommodations, and restaurants listed within these pages—should suffice. For more detail, consider the 88-page map book produced by Pathfinder Maps, a locally based company. It costs just $4 and is available at bookstores and convenience stores throughout the city.

The **City of Vancouver** incorporates downtown and Central Vancouver. Surrounding this central core, many population centers have been incorporated as individual cities but in reality are part of the city sprawl and are referred to as **Greater Vancouver.** You'll also hear reference made to the **Lower Mainland;** this encompasses the entire Fraser River Valley, including downtown Vancouver.

Highways and Byways
Vancouver is one of the few North American cities without a freeway system. The closest it comes is Hwy. 1, the TransCanada Hwy., which enters the city from the east, crosses the Fraser River at Burnaby, then crosses Burrard Inlet at the Second Narrows Bridge and skirts through the back of the North Shore to Horseshoe Bay. Getting to downtown from Hwy. 1 is easiest by taking Exit 28B and heading west along the Grandview Hwy., then merging left onto Broadway (Hwy. 7) and turning north on Main, Cambie, or Granville Street. From the south, Hwy. 99 (Hwy. 5 south of the border) passes through 45 km of residential and industrial sprawl (and countless traffic lights) before crossing onto the downtown peninsula via the Granville Street Bridge. From the north, take Exit 13 from Hwy. 1 south along Taylor Way, turn left onto Marine Drive, then take the first right after crossing the Capilano River; the next thing you know you are high above Burrard Inlet on the Lions Gate Bridge. This three-lane bridge becomes one of the city's worst bottlenecks during peak hours; try to avoid traveling southbound 7-9 a.m. and northbound 4:30-6:30 p.m.

Streets and Avenues
As a city that has grown in spurts, with no real planning, Vancouver's street numbering system is surprisingly easy to understand. Throughout Greater Vancouver avenues run east to west and streets north to south. For numbering purposes the downtown east-west division is Carrall St. (from where "east" and "west" designations are given), and in Central Vancouver it's Ontario St.; from north to south the numbering system begins at Waterfront Rd., along Burrard Inlet, continuing south through Central Vancouver. Streets on the downtown peninsula actually run parallel to its spine, meaning they run in a northwest to southeast and southwest to northeast direction and are named for a variety of individuals.

In the south, avenues are numbered progressively from the border, all the way to the Fraser River, while on the North Shore avenues are numbered progressively from Burrard Inlet.

NEIGHBORHOODS, SUBURBS, AND CITIES

Downtown
Downtown Vancouver lies on a spit of land bordered to the north and east by Burrard Inlet, to the west by English Bay, and to the south by False Creek, which almost cuts the city center off from the rest of the city. **Granville Street** was Vancouver's first commercial corridor, and if today you stand at its junction with W. Georgia St., you're as close to the "center" of the city as it's possible to be. Within a five-block radius of this intersection are Canada Place, Vancouver Art Gallery, the main information center, all major banking institutions, shopping centers, and the city's best hotels. To the west, and still within easy walking distance, is the oldest part of the city, **Gastown.** To the south, between Dunsmuir and Robson Streets, is the **theater district** and Library Square. **Yaletown,** the current yuppie hot spot for living, shopping, and dancing the night away, is farther south, between Homer and Mainland Streets.

Reach the **West End** and enormous **Stanley Park** by walking along **Robson St.,** a two-km-long strip of boutiques and restaurants.

East of downtown is North America's third largest **Chinatown** and **Pacific Central Station,** terminus for all long-distance trains and buses.

Central Vancouver

South and west from downtown, between False Creek and the Fraser River, is Central Vancouver. Here lie the trendy beachside suburb of **Kitsilano** (known as "Kits" to the locals), home to Vancouver Museum, and **Point Grey,** home of the University of British Columbia. Central Vancouver also holds some of Vancouver's most expensive suburbs, including **Shaughnessy Heights.**

South

South of Central Vancouver, the low-lying Fraser River delta extends all the way south to the border. Between the north and south arms of the river is **Richmond,** home of **Vancouver International Airport.** South of the south arm is the mostly industrial area of **Delta,** as well as **Tsawwassen,** departure point for ferries to Vancouver Island. Immediately east is **Surrey,** another of those never-ending suburbs, this one with a population of over 300,000.

North

Across Burrard Inlet to the north of downtown, the **North Shore** is a narrow developed strip backed up to the mountains and connected to the rest of the city by the Lions Gate Bridge. Immediately north of downtown is **North Vancouver;** to its west are the suburbs of **West Vancouver,** an upscale neighborhood, and **Horseshoe Bay,** departure point for Sunshine Coast and Vancouver Island ferries. From Horseshoe Bay, Hwy. 99 continues north to **Whistler.**

East

With Vancouver growing at an incredible rate, and as development to the south and north are restricted—by the international border and the North Shore Range—there's no where to go but east. The residential sprawl continues east from Central Vancouver along the TransCanada Hwy., with the highway bisecting **Burnaby, New Westminster,** and **Coquitlam** before crossing the Fraser River and continuing along its southern bank through **Langley, Abbotsford,** and **Chilliwack.**

Guided tours are available. Kids will enjoy the children's gallery, while adults will appreciate the special-events program, including a lecture series, films, and concerts. The gift shop sells a wide selection of art books, jewelry, and gifts, and the gallery café is always crowded.

Summer hours are Mon.-Sat. 10 a.m.-6 p.m. (until 9 p.m. on Thursday), Sunday noon-5:30 p.m. Between October and May, the gallery is closed Monday and Tuesday. Admission is adult $9.75, senior $7.75, children under 12 free.

Near the Art Gallery

Diagonally opposite the art gallery and behind Cathedral Place is the **Canadian Craft Museum,** 639 Hornby St., tel. (604) 687-8266, which catalogs the history of arts and crafts throughout the ages. Mediums displayed include glass, wood, clay, metal, and fabric materials. The emphasis is on Canadian work, but a couple of other displays and touring exhibitions bring an international feel to the museum. As you'd expect, the gift shop offers an excellent choice of unique craft items; prices are reasonable. Admission to the museum is $4, and it's open Mon.-Sat. 10 a.m.-5 p.m. (Thursday until 9 p.m.), Sunday noon-5 p.m.

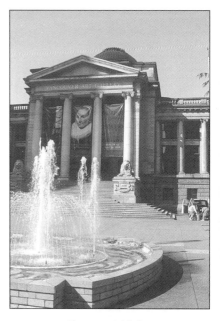

Vancouver Art Gallery

VANCOUVER VIEWS

DOWNTOWN

The Lookout!
For immediate orientation from downtown, catch the high-speed, stomach-sinking glass elevator up the outside of 40-story Harbour Centre Tower, 555 W. Hastings St., tel. (604) 689-0421. The ride takes less than a minute and ends at The Lookout!, an enclosed room 167 meters above street level, from where views extend as far away as Mt. Baker, 140 km to the south. Walk around the circular room for 360-degree views and interpretive panels describing interesting facts about the panorama below and beyond. In summer, the elevator runs daily 8:30 a.m.-10:30 p.m., the rest of the year daily 9:30 a.m.-9 p.m. The trip to the top costs adult $8, senior or child $7; keep the receipt and you can return at any time during the same day (the top of the

looking southwest across the city (the distinctive domed building is B.C. Place Stadium) from The Lookout! atop the Harbour Centre Tower

tower is a great place to watch the sun setting over the Strait of Georgia).

Down on the Waterfront
From Vancouver Visitor Info Centre, continue down Burrard St. to **Canada Place** and wander around the west side promenade for neck-straining views of the city close up, as well as North Vancouver and the rugged mountains beyond. For a look at the skyline and sparkling Canada Place from sea level, take the SeaBus from the adjacent Waterfront Station across Burrard Inlet to **Lonsdale Quay** ($2.25). Taking to the air offers the opportunity to get a bird's-eye view of the city. **Harbour Air,** tel. (604) 688-1277, offers a 20-minute flightseeing trip from a seaplane base on the west side of Canada Place for $72 pp, and **Vancouver Helicopters** flights, tel. (604) 270-1484, take off from the heliport on the east side of Canada Place (enter through Waterfront Station) for a 30-minute trip over the heart of downtown, Stanley Park, and the North Shore for $195 pp.

Stanley Park
Drive, walk, or cycle Stanley Park's 10-km-long **Seawall Promenade** to appreciate the skyline to the east, the busy shipping lanes of First Narrows to the north, and the sandy beaches of English Bay to the west. Sunsets from **English Bay Beach,** in the West End, are delightful. Relax on the beach or soak up the sunset from the lounge in the Sylvia Hotel or the outdoor terrace of the Teahouse Restaurant.

NORTH SHORE

The best views from the north side of Burrard Inlet are gained by taking the **Grouse Mountain Skyride,** Nancy Greene Way, tel. (604) 984-0661, up the slopes of Grouse Mountain. The panorama extends back across the inlet to downtown and beyond to Mt. Baker, in Washington State, and west to Vancouver Island. In summer, the gondola departs the base station every 10 minutes 10 a.m.-10 p.m.; adult $16.95, senior $14.95, child $5.95. From the summit, **Grouse Mountain Helicopters,** tel. (604) 525-1484, offers a 10-minute, $50 pp joy-flight providing views from even higher elevations.

On the way back down, turn onto Hwy. 1 and continue west to Cypress Bowl Rd., which climbs to **Cypress Provincial Park** and more spectacular city vistas (there's a particularly good view from the parking lot at the second switchback). Continue west to Horseshoe Bay, then return to the city along Marine Dr., which parallels Burrard Inlet, providing many glimpses of the city skyline. At **Lighthouse Park,** along this route, English Bay, Stanley Park, and Kitsilano Beach are laid out in all their glory from Point Atkinson.

CENTRAL VANCOUVER

South of downtown, the **Kitsilano** foreshore provides that well-known view of the city skyline backed by the Coast Mountains. The south side of the city is relatively flat. The high point is 152-meter-high **Little Mountain,** in Queen Elizabeth Park, where the city skyline and abruptly rising mountains contrast starkly with the residential sprawl of Central Vancouver all around.

Cathedral Place, built in 1991, is worth visiting for the grand art deco-style lobby. Next door is the **Hongkong Bank** building, which features a massive 27-meter-long aluminum pendulum in the lobby. Next door again, on the corner of W. Georgia and Burrard Streets, is **Christ Church Cathedral.** Built in 1895, it is Vancouver's oldest church. Across W. Georgia St. from these three buildings is the **Hotel Vancouver,** which dates to 1939. The original hotel was built in 1887, but it burnt to the ground in 1932. The hotel today reflects the heritage of the Canadian Pacific Hotels and Resorts chain, with its distinctive château-style design topped by a copper roof.

Mining and Forestry Displays
The **Pacific Mineral Museum** has a small exhibit at 840 W. Hastings St., tel. (604) 681-4321. A large three-dimensional map of the province shows mineral deposits and current mining operations, while other displays point out the importance of the industry to the province. Open Mon.-Fri. 8:30 a.m.-4:30 p.m. Also downtown, the **Forest Alliance of B.C. Information Centre,** 1055 Dunsmuir St., tel. (604) 685-7507, is a good place to learn about the forestry industry through interactive displays, computer programs, information boards describing the various woods and wood products, free seed kits, and a quiet area stacked with relevant literature. It's open Mon.-Fri. 8 a.m.-5 p.m.

GASTOWN

Just three blocks east of Canada Place, Gastown is a marvelous place to spend a few hours. It was the birthplace of Vancouver, officially named Granville in 1870 but always known as Gastown, for saloon owner "Gassy Jack" Deighton.

The Great Fire of 1886 destroyed almost all of Gastown's wooden buildings, but the district was rebuilt in stone and brick. By 1900, the heart of the city had moved away from the waterfront, and as Gastown declined in importance it became run-down. By the 1960s, this historic district held nothing more than decrepit Victorian-era buildings and empty warehouses. The government originally planned to redevelop the entire district, including construction of an expressway through the heart of Gastown. The public outcry was loud and clear; Vancouverites were becoming more aware of their heritage. The plans were scuttled and Gastown was saved. A massive rejuvenation program commenced, and today historic Gastown is one of the city's most popular tourist attractions. Tree-lined cobblestone streets and old gas lamps front brightly painted restored buildings housing galleries, restaurants, and an abundance of gift and souvenir shops.

A Gastown Walking Tour
Most of the action centers along **Water Street,** which branches east off Cordova St. and slopes gently toward the site of Gassy Jack's original saloon (now the Alhambra Hotel).

As you first enter Water St., you're greeted by the **The Landing,** a heritage building that has had its exterior restored to its former glory and its interior transformed to an upmarket shopping arcade. It also holds a number of eateries and the Steamworks Brewing Co., a pub/restaurant boasting harbor views.

On the corner of Water and Cambie Streets is a **steam clock,** one of only two in the world

"GASSY JACK" DEIGHTON

Born in England in 1830, John Deighton took to the high seas at a young age in search of adventure and fortune. Partnering with an American businessman, he set up a crude saloon at New Westminster, quenching the thirst of Cariboo-bound prospectors and getting the nickname "Gassy," which in British slang described an obnoxious drunk. Forced out of New Westminster by his business partner, he set off to make his fortune elsewhere. On 4 July 1867, with just his native wife and a barrel of whiskey, Gassy Jack beached his small boat on the shore of Burrard Inlet below the sawmill owned by Captain Edward Stamp. Because Stamp had banned alcohol from his company town, Gassy Jack found an eager market for his liquor. The next morning, enlisting the help of locals, he erected a ramshackle saloon. With a rousing speech to the workers, he declared free drinks for the rest of the day and was on his way to making a small fortune.

The Globe Saloon, as Deighton's enterprise became known, soon became a social center, and more buildings sprang up around his business. Three years after serving his first tot of whiskey, Gassy Jack became the first official landowner when he purchased Lot 1 of the newly laid out settlement of Granville. With tax collectors on his tail, he was forced to move his operation into a more permanent building, and so he opened a hotel on his lot, providing both liquor and accommodations.

Life as a saloon owner took its toll on the entrepreneur: wild drunken brawls brought unwanted attention from local police officers, he was continually hounded by tax collectors, and his wife died at a young age. Gassy himself died in a summer heat wave aged just 45; his funeral cost an unheard-of $136.

(the other is a replica of this, the original one). Built by a local clock maker in the mid-1970s, it is powered by a steam system originally put in place to heat buildings along a 10-km-long underground pipeline that snakes through downtown. Watch for the burst of steam every 15 minutes, which sets off steam whistles to the tune of Westminster chimes.

Continue east along Water St. to the 1899 **Dominion Hotel,** then half a block south down Abbott St. to **Blood Alley,** the hangout of many infamous turn-of-the-century rogues. Most buildings still standing along Water St. were built immediately after the Great Fire of 1886, but the **Byrnes Block,** at 2 Water St., is generally regarded as the oldest; it stands on the site of Deighton House, Gassy Jack's second and more permanent saloon. Behind this building is **Gaolers Mews,** the site of Vancouver's first jail.

Water Street ends just around the corner at cobbled **Maple Tree Square,** the intersection of Water, Carrall, Powell, and Alexander Streets. Here you'll find a bronze **statue of Gassy Jack** watching over the square and the site of his original saloon from the top of a whiskey barrel. The **Alhambra Hotel,** which occupies the actual saloon site, was built in 1886 from bricks used as ballast in ships that sailed into Burrard Inlet. Across from the statue is the **Hotel Europe,** a narrow triangular building. After its 1892 opening, the hotel quickly became recognized as the city's finest hostelry.

Vancouver Centennial Police Museum

This museum, beyond the east end of Gastown at 240 E. Cordova St., tel. (604) 665-3346, catalogs the history of Vancouver's police and the notorious criminals they chased. Formerly the city morgue, the museum houses historic police equipment, some intriguing seized items, and re-creations of the city's most famous crime scenes. Summer hours are Mon.-Sat. 10 a.m.-3 p.m., the rest of the year Mon.-Fri. 9 a.m.-3 p.m. Admission is adults $5, seniors and children $3. To get there, avoid walking E. Hastings St. for safety's sake and instead take bus no. 3, 4, 7, or 8 north from Granville Mall.

CHINATOWN

Chinese were brought into the city in the 1880s to help with rail line construction. Most settled around an area known as Shanghai Alley, at the west end of today's Chinatown. The Chinese cleared the surrounding land and began growing produce that was sold at markets along what is now Pender Street. This is the heart of Chinatown today, which lies several blocks southeast of Gastown, along E. Pender St. between Carrall and Gore Streets. Its commercial center is the block bordered by Main, E. Pender, Gore, and Keefer Streets. With a population exceeding 30,000, it is the second-largest Chinese community in North America and one of the largest outside Asia.

Stroll through the neighborhood to admire the architecture—right down to the pagoda-roofed telephone booths—or to seek out one of the multitude of restaurants. You'll find the markets and genuine Cantonese-style cuisine east of Main St. and tamer Chinese-Canadian dishes along Main St. and to the west. While Chinatown is an exciting place any time of year, it's especially lively during a Chinese festival or holiday, when thronging masses follow the ferocious dancing dragon, avoid exploding firecrackers, sample tasty tidbits from outside stalls, and pound their feet to the beat of the drums.

The district's intriguing stores sell a mind-boggling array of Chinese goods—wind chimes, soy sauce, teapots, dried mushrooms, delicate paper fans, and much, much more. Along Main St. a number of shops sell ginseng, sold by the Chinese ounce (38 grams). Cultivated ginseng costs from $10 an ounce, while wild ginseng goes for up to $400 an ounce. In addition to selling the herb, the staff at **Ten Ren Tea and Ginseng Co.,** 550 Main St., tel. (604) 684-1566, explains ginseng preparation methods to buyers and offers tea tastings as well.

To get to Chinatown from downtown catch bus no. 19 or 22 east along Pender Street. Try to avoid E. Hastings St. at all times; it's Vancouver's skid row, inhabited by unsavory characters day and night.

Chinese Cultural Centre

This cultural center at 50 E. Pender St., tel. (604) 687-0729, holds a museum and library cataloging the history of the Chinese in Vancouver; admission is $3 and it's open Tues.-Sun. 11

*Chinese
Cultural Centre*

a.m.-3 p.m. The center also sponsors exhibitions and displays ranging from bonsai to watercolor paintings; admission varies according to what's going on.

Dr. Sun Yat-Sen Classical Chinese Garden

Gardening enthusiasts won't want to miss this peaceful and harmoniously designed garden at 578 Carrall St. (behind the Cultural Centre), tel. (604) 662-3207. Designed by artisans from Suzhou, China—a city famous for its green-thumbed residents—the garden features limestone rockeries, a waterfall and tranquil pools, and beautiful trees and plants hidden away behind tall walls. The garden is styled around Taoist traditions of balance and harmony, achieved through the use of buildings, rocks, plants, and water. The buildings and other manmade elements, including woodcarvings and sculptures, were shipped from China. This was the first authentic classical Chinese garden built outside China, and it remains to this day the largest. It's open daily from 10 a.m.; admission is adults $6.50, seniors and students $5. Tours are conducted four to six times daily. During summer, "Enchanted Evenings" held on the first Friday of each month give visitors a chance to tour the gardens and taste teas from around the world. Adjacent to the gardens is **Dr. Sun Yat-Sen Park,** where admission is free.

World's Narrowest Office Building

Opposite the entrance to Dr. Sun Yat-Sen Classical Chinese Garden, at 8 W. Pender St., is the Sam Kee Building, best known as the narrowest office building in the world. When city developers widened surrounding streets in 1912, the Chinese consortium that owned the lot decided to proceed with its planned building, just making it narrower than at first planned. The result is a building 1.8 meters wide, noted in the *Guinness Book of Records* as the "narrowest building in the world."

WEST END

Pretty, park-fringed **English Bay Beach** is part of the section of Vancouver that locals call the West End (not to be confused with the West Side, in Central Vancouver, or West Vancouver, on the north side of the harbor). The golden sands, tree-shaded grassy roadsides, and sidewalks are popular places to find walkers, joggers, cyclists, and sun worshippers. It has been a popular area for the wealthy to live since the late 1800s, when CPR began building large homes for its high-ranking officials. In 1901, a streetcar line opened down Robson St., linking downtown to English Bay Beach and in the process increasing the popularity of the West End as a summer getaway. As real estate prices across the city rose early last century, the original mansions were replaced by apartment buildings, and today the West End is one of Canada's most densely populated neighborhoods. Today, the streets are lined with ritzy condos, high-rise apartment blocks, and the occasional Edwardian-era home. Denman St. harbors trendy cafés and restaurants; on Sunday, large numbers of Vancouverites congregate here for brunch and an afternoon stroll along the bay. The more energetic head north to walk the Seawall Promenade around magnificent Stanley Park.

Roedde House Museum

Built in 1893, this restored house at 1415 Barclay St. (take Broughton St. off Robson St.), tel. (604) 684-7040, is a classic example of Vancouver's Edwardian architecture. The two-story residence was designed by Francis Rattenbury, architect of Victoria's Empress Hotel. It's furnished in period style and open to the public. Tours of the house are conducted Monday, Wednesday, and Friday at 2 p.m. (call to reserve a spot).

The house is on **Barclay Heritage Square,** a precinct of nine houses from the same era, each looking much as it would have when first built, right down to the style of surrounding gardens.

STANLEY PARK

Beautiful Stanley Park, a lush 405-hectare tree-and garden-carpeted peninsula jutting out into Burrard Inlet, is a sight for sore eyes in any weather—an enormous peaceful oasis sandwiched between city center's skyscrapers and the North Shore at the other end of Lions Gate Bridge. It was named after Lord Stanley, Canada's governor-general from 1888 to 1893, who had the foresight to preserve the peninsula as a park for "the

ROBSON STREET

After WW II, European immigration to Vancouver reached its peak, with Robson St. between Burrard and Bute Streets becoming an enclave of German businesses and transforming itself into **Robsonstrasse.** Today, the colorful and exciting theme of these two blocks has extended almost all the way down Robson St. to the West End's Denman St. and grown to become one of Vancouver's most fashionable shopping and dining precincts. If you like to shop in designer boutiques, sample European delicacies, and sip lattes at sidewalk cafés, then this is the place to do it.

A Walking Tour to the West End
The downtown end of this upmarket commercial corridor is glass-topped **Robson Square** (at Hornby St.). At the same intersection is the **Law Courts,** a magnificent glass structure designed by architect Arthur Erickson that sits opposite the original courthouse, now the Vancouver Art Gallery. Cross to the art gallery side of the road and search out **Duthie Books,** 919 Robson St., an outlet of western Canada's most successful bookstore chain. Success on a different scale is flaunted at the nearby **Virgin Megastore,** at Burrard St., a massive music store owned by English entrepreneur Richard Branson. Heading east, the next few blocks hold the largest concentration of boutiques, cafés and restaurants. If anywhere in the city could be called "coffee row," then this would be it. Local companies **Blenz,**

Bagel Street Café, and the **Bread Garden** are well represented, and Seattle-based **Starbucks** has three outlets, including two kitty-corner to each other at Thurlow Street. There's not a latte in sight, though, at **Murchie's Tea and Coffee,** 970 Robson St., which sells packaged teas and coffees from around the world. Of the many bars and restaurants along this strip, the best place for a beer or a full meal is **Joe Fortes Seafood and Chophouse,** 777 Thurlow St., which offers some of the city's best seafood and a rooftop patio overlooking Robson Street. Sweettooths are not forgotten; head to **Daniel le Chocolate Belge,** 1105 Robson St., for chocolate treats and **Cows,** 1301 Robson St., for delicious ice cream.

From the intersection with Jervis St., Robson St. begins its gradual descent to the West End. The hustle and bustle is behind you, and the corridor is lined with hotels and motels that offer some of the best value to be found in Vancouver, a variety of restaurants, and apartment buildings from the 1960s and '70s. At 1610 Robson St., **Robson Public Market** occupies an impressive atrium-topped building filled with meat, seafood, dairy products, fruits and veggies, nuts, flowers, craft vendors, fresh juice and salad bars, and an international food fair.

Two blocks farther west you find yourself at Denman St · turn left and you'll reach English Bay Beach after passing through another restaurant-clogged section of the city; turn right and you'll find bike rental outlets catering to Stanley Park-bound cyclists.

use and enjoyment of all peoples of all colors, creeds, and customs for all time."

Walk or cycle the 10-km **Seawall Promenade** or drive the perimeter via **Stanley Park Drive** to take in beautiful water and city views. Travel along both is one-way in a counterclockwise direction. For vehicle traffic, the main entrance to Stanley Park is the beginning of Stanley Park Dr., which veers right from the end of Georgia St.; on foot, follow Denman St. to its north end and you'll find a pathway leading around Coal Harbour into the park. Either way, you'll pass a small information booth where park maps are available. Just before the booth, take Pipeline Rd. to access **Malkin Bowl,** home to outdoor theater productions; a **rose garden;** and forest-encircled **Beaver Lake.** Pipeline Rd. rejoins

Stanley Park Dr. near the Lions Gate Bridge, but by not returning to the park entrance you'll miss most of the following sights.

Vancouver Aquarium
In the forest behind the information booth is Canada's largest aquarium, the third largest in North America. Guarding the entrance is a five-meter-long killer whale sculpture by preeminent native artist Bill Reid. Over 8,000 aquatic animals and 600 species are on display, representing all corners of the planet, from the oceans of the Arctic to the rainforests of the Amazon. A number of exhibits highlight regional marinelife. The newly opened Pacific Canada Pavilion is of particular interest, as it contains a wide variety of sealife from local waters, including the giant

fish of the deep, halibut, and playful little sea otters who frolic in the kelp. The most popular (and controversial) part of the aquarium is the pool where orca (killer) and beluga whales strut their stuff in a "natural" environment. In the Amazon Rainforest Gallery, there's a computer-generated hourly tropical rainstorm and creatures such as crocodiles and piranhas as well as fascinating misfits such as a four-eyed fish. A part of the complex is also devoted to the rehabilitation of injured marine mammals, and there's a packed interpretive program of talks and tours. The aquarium is open in summer daily 9:30 a.m.-7 p.m., the rest of the year daily 10 a.m.-5:30 p.m. Admission is adult $9.50, senior $8.25, child $6.25. For information call (604) 659-3474.

Until the mid-1990s, Stanley Park was home to a zoo; what remains is the **Children's Farmyard,** where you can see all types of domesticated animals. It's linked to the aquarium by a short walking path and is open daily 10 a.m. till dusk.

Seawall Sights

The following sights are listed from the information booth, which overlooks Coal Harbour, in a counterclockwise direction. From this point, Stanley Park Dr. and the Seawall Promenade pass the Royal Vancouver Yacht club and **Deadman's Island.** Now a naval reserve, the island has a dark history, having seen many battles between native tribes, been the burial place of the last of the Coast Salish people, and been used as a quarantine station during an early smallpox epidemic.

The first worthwhile stop at **Brockton Point** (which refers to the entire eastern tip of the park) is a collection of authentic totem poles from the Kwagiulth people, who lived along the coast north of present-day Vancouver. Before rounding the actual point itself, you'll pass the **Nine o'Clock Gun,** which is fired each evening at, you guessed it, 9 p.m. Its original purpose was to allow ship captains to set their chronometers to the exact time. Much of the Brockton Point peninsula is dedicated to sporting fields, and on any sunny afternoon young Vancouverites can be seen playing traditional British pursuits such as rugby and cricket. Around the point, the road and the seawall continue to hug the shoreline, passing the famous *Girl in Wet Suit* bronze sculpture and a figurehead commemorating Vancouver's links to

Look out for the Girl in Wet Suit *sculpture as you travel around the Seawall Promenade.*

Japan. Then the two paths divide: the seawall passes directly under the Lions Gate Bridge while the road loops back to a higher elevation to Prospect Point Lookout, a memorial to the SS *Beaver* (which was the first HBC steamship to travel along this stretch of the coast), and a café (a stairway leads up from the seawall to the café).

The Lions Gate Bridge marks the halfway point of the seawall and a change in scenery. From this point to Second Beach the views are westward toward the Strait of Georgia and across English Bay to Central Vancouver. The next stretch of pleasant pathway, about two kilometers long, is sandwiched between the water and steep cliffs, with **Siwash Rock** the only distinctive landmark. This volcanic outcrop sits just offshore, rising over 15 meters from the lapping waters of English Bay. If you're traveling along Stanley Park Dr., park at the **Hollow Tree** and walk back up the hill to a lookout high above the rock.

Continuing south, the seawall and Stanley Park Dr. converge at the south end of **Third Beach,** a popular swimming and sunbathing spot (and a great place to watch the setting sun). The beach's southern end is guarded by **Ferguson Point,** where a fountain marks the final resting spot of renowned native poet Pauline Johnson. One km farther back toward the city is **Second Beach,** where you'll find an outdoor swimming pool, a pitch-and-putt golf course, a putting green, tennis courts, and lawn bowling greens. On summer evenings an area behind the beach is set aside for local dance clubs to practice their skills. From Second Beach it's only a short distance to busy Denman St. and English Bay Beach, or you can cut across the park back to Coal Harbour.

Lost Lagoon

At the time of European settlement, Coal Harbour extended almost all the way across the peninsula to Second Beach. With the receding of the tides, the water would drain out from the head of the inlet, creating a massive tidal flat and inspiring native-born Pauline Johnson to pen the poem "Lost Lagoon," a name that holds to this day. A bridge across the harbor was replaced with a causeway

Native poet Pauline Johnson's "Lost Lagoon" is the namesake of the massive tidal flat.

in 1922, blocking the flow of the tide and creating a "real" lagoon. Over the years it has become home to large populations of waterfowl, including great blue herons, trumpeter swans, grebes, and a variety of ducks. It is also a rest stop for migrating Canada geese each spring and fall. In the center of the lake, a fountain erected to celebrate the park's 50th anniversary is illuminated each night. A 1.5-km walking trail encircles the lagoon, passing the **Nature House** at the southeast corner, tel. (604) 257-8544, which holds natural history displays and general park information.

Getting Around the Park

Even at a casual pace, it's possible to walk the seawall in under three hours, but it's easy to spend a whole day detouring to the main attractions, taking in the panoramas from the many lookouts, or just relaxing on the benches and beaches along the way. Even if you find the

Lycra-clad cyclists racing around the seawall on their thousand-dollar bikes intimidating, exploring the park by bike is easy and fun. At the corner of Robson and Denman Streets a number shops rent decent bikes for under $20 for a full day. They include **Alley Cat Rentals,** 1779 Robson St., tel. (604) 684-5117; **Bayshore Bicycles,** at 745 Denman St., tel. (604) 688-2453, and at 1601 W. Georgia St., tel. (604) 689-5071; **Spokes Bicycle Rental,** 1798 W. Georgia St., tel. (604) 688-5141; and **Stanley Park Cycle,** 1741 Robson St., tel. (604) 608-1908.

Horse-drawn trams leave regularly from the information booth, tel. (604) 681-5115, on a one-hour tour in a 20-person carriage; adult $14.95, senior $13.95, child $9.95.

Between June and mid-September the city bus system operates a free shuttle around the park and to all major park attractions.

FALSE CREEK

B.C. Place Stadium and Vicinity

Another Vancouver landmark, this 60,000-seat stadium at 777 Pacific Blvd., tel. (604) 669-2300, is the world's largest air-supported domed stadium. It is the home of the B.C. Lions, one of the Canadian Football League teams, and is the venue for major trade shows, concerts, and other big events. At Gate A is the **B.C. Sports Hall of Fame and Museum,** tel. (604) 687-5520. Displays in the Hall of Champions catalog the careers of British Columbia's greatest sports achievers. Memorabilia, old photographs, and a few videos commemorate the greats, while the Participation Gallery allows you to run, jump, climb, row, and throw, testing yourself against professional athletes. The most moving displays are dedicated to cancer victim Terry Fox and wheelchair-bound Rick Hanson, whose courage in the face of adversity opened the eyes of all Canadians in the late 1970s and early '80s, respectively. The museum is open Tues.-Sun. 10

a.m.-5 p.m.; admission is adults $6, seniors and children $4. To get there, take the SkyTrain to Stadium Station, or take bus no. 15 or 17 south on Burrard Street.

Science World

The impressive, 17-story-high, geodesic-shaped silver dome (it's best known locally as "the golf ball") over the waters of False Creek on the southeast side of city center, 1455 Quebec St., tel. (604) 268-6363, was built as the Expo Preview Centre for Expo86. For a time it housed restaurants, shops, and the world's largest Omnimax theater. Today the Vancouver landmark is home to Science World, a museum providing exhibitions that "introduce the world of science to the young and the young at heart." The three main galleries explore the basics of physics, natural history, and music through hands-on displays, while a fourth gallery holds an ever-changing array of traveling exhibits. The Omnimax theater, with one of the world's largest such screens (28 meters in diameter), is still here, featuring science-oriented documentaries. Admission to Science World is adult $11.75, senior or child $7.75; to the theater $10.50 pp; or purchase a combination ticket to save a few bucks. The complex is open daily 10 a.m.-5 p.m.

The most enjoyable way to get to Science World is aboard a False Creek Ferry from Granville Island or the Vancouver Aquatic Centre. If you don't want to take the ferry, you can drive to the west end of Terminal Ave.—plenty of parking is available—or take the SkyTrain to Main Street Station then walk across the street.

Granville Island

Prior to the 1970s, Granville Island was the dowdy, all-but-abandoned center of Vancouver's maritime industries. When Vancouver was first settled by Europeans, it was nothing more than a sandbar, but tons of fill transformed it into an island. It soon became a center of industry (its official name is Industrial island), filled with factories and warehouses. Lacking space, city officials at one time proposed to reclaim all of False Creek, but in the end only a small section was filled—and Granville Island became joined to the mainland.

By the end of the 1970s Granville had become an industrial wasteland, so with a massive injection of funds from the federal government, the entire island got a facelift. The refurbished, jazzed-up island is *the* place to go on a bright sunny day—allow at least several hours or an entire afternoon for this hive of activity.

Start at **Granville Island Information Centre,** 1398 Cartwright St., tel. (604) 666-5784, website www.granvilleisland.com; open daily 9 a.m.-6 p.m., closed Monday in winter. The center offers a ton of local information, as well as displays and an audiovisual presentation detailing the island's colorful history.

After a preliminary stop at the information center, you can spend the better part of a day just walking around the island looking at the mari-

It's easy to see why Science World is known locally as "the Golf Ball."

na, the specialty businesses, the markets, the gift shops, the restaurants, and the theaters. Among the highlights are the **Emily Carr Institute of Art and Design,** 1399 Johnston St., tel. (604) 844-3800, where two galleries are worth perusing, and the colorful **Granville Island Public Market,** open daily 9 a.m.-6 p.m. Inside the market you'll find all kinds of things to eat—from fresh fruit and vegetables to prepared ready-to-go meals—as well as unique jewelry and crafts, potted plants, and cut flowers. If you're into fishing, the **Sport Fishing Museum,** 1502 Duranleau St., tel. (604) 683-1939, is worth a visit for the collection of historic rods and reels and the photographic history of fishing in the province. Museum admission is $3.50 and hours are Tues.-Sun. 10 a.m.-5:30 p.m. (For details of the best shopping the island has to offer, see Shopping in the Recreation chapter.) Grab a tasty bite at the market and take it out onto the wharf to enjoy all the False Creek harbor activity—in summer the water teems with sailboats, small ferries, and barges.

To get to the island by boat, jump aboard one of the small **False Creek Ferries.** The boats run regularly between the island, Vancouver Aquatic Centre at Sunset Beach ($1.75), and Vanier Park ($3). To get to the island by land, take a no. 50 (False Creek) bus from Howe St. to the stop under Granville Street Bridge at the entrance to the island, or take a Granville Island bus from downtown. Parking on the island is almost impossible, at best, especially on weekends when locals do their fresh-produce shopping. If you do find a spot, it'll have a three-hour maximum time limit.

CENTRAL VANCOUVER

Vancouver's three largest museums and a number of public gardens lie in Central Vancouver, a largely residential area of the city south of downtown and extending west to Point Grey and the University of British Columbia.

VANIER PARK

This stretch of parkland, which holds two not-to-be-missed museums, extends from Burrard Street Bridge to Kitsilano Beach. It's a popular spot for walkers, joggers, and cyclists and is home to the famous Bard on the Beach summertime theater. To reach the park catch bus no. 22 on Burrard St. and get off after Burrard Street Bridge at the Cornwall and Chestnut St. stop, or catch a ferry to Vanier Park from Granville Island or the Aquatic Centre at Sunset Beach. If you're driving, you'll find plenty of free parking.

Vancouver Museum
Regional history from Precambrian times to the present comes to life at Vancouver Museum, 1100 Chestnut St. in Vanier Park, tel. (604) 736-4431. The West Coast Archaeology and Culture galleries hold ravishing masks, highly patterned woven blankets, and fine baskets. The Discovery and Settlement Gallery details European exploration of British Columbia—both by land and by sea. After browsing through the forestry and mill-town displays and the metropolis of Vancouver exhibit, you'll end up in the gallery of changing exhibitions, where you never know what you'll find. The complex also holds a gift shop and a self-serve restaurant overlooking Vanier Park. It's open in summer daily 10 a.m.-5 p.m., the rest of the year Tues.-Sun. 10 a.m.-5 p.m. Admission is adult $8, child $5.50.

Pacific Space Centre
In the same building as the museum is the Pacific Space Centre, tel. (604) 738-7827, which features displays related to planet Earth, the surrounding universe, and space exploration. Many of these exhibits are hands-on and enjoyable for all ages. The Ground Station theater shows a 20-minute audiovisual presentation throughout the day on the universe. A highlight of the center is the Virtual Voyages Simulator, a flight simulator that makes a virtual reality journey through space. The "flight" lasts five minutes and is included in the price of general admission. The center is open in summer daily 10 a.m.-5 p.m., closed Monday the rest of the year. Admission is adult $12, senior $9.50, child $8. Combined tickets for the Pacific Space Centre

and Vancouver Museum are $15, $10, and $9 respectively.

The Space Centre also presents a popular laser rock music show in the HR MacMillan Star Theatre Wed.-Sun. at 9 p.m., with additional shows on Friday and Saturday nights at 10:30 p.m.; $8 per person.

Gordon MacMillan Southam Observatory

Adjacent to the museum complex is the Gordon MacMillan Southam Observatory, tel. (604) 738-2855, which is open for public stargazing Fri.-Sat. 7-11 p.m. when the skies are clear; admission is free.

Vancouver Maritime Museum

Just a five-minute stroll from Vancouver Museum is Vancouver Maritime Museum, 1905 Ogden Ave. (the end of Cypress Ave.) in Vanier Park, tel. (604) 257-8300. British Columbia's seafaring legacy is the focus here. Exhibits chronicle everything from the province's first sea explorers and their vessels to today's oceangoing adventurers, modern fishing boats, and fancy ships. Kids will love the Children's Maritime Discovery Centre and its model ships, computer terminals, underwater robot, and telescopes for viewing ships out in the harbor. The historic RCMP vessel *St. Roch* is dry-docked within the building, and admission includes a tour. Now a National Historic Site, the *St. Roch* was the first patrol vessel to successfully negotiate the infamous Northwest Passage. The museum is open in summer daily 10 a.m.-5 p.m., the rest of the year Tues.-Sat. 10 a.m.-5 p.m. and Sunday noon-5 p.m. Admission is adults $6, seniors and children $3. From downtown, take bus no. 22 south on Burrard St. or walk down Burrard St. to the Aquatic Centre and hop aboard a False Creek Ferry.

When you're through inside the museum, you can wander down to the water to view the small fleet of historic vessels docked in the protected harbor.

UNIVERSITY OF BRITISH COLUMBIA

The UBC campus sprawls across **Point Grey,** the westernmost point of Vancouver and the southern extremity of Burrard Inlet. It enjoys a spectacular coastal location, surrounded by parkland laced with hiking trails. Many of the trails provide access to the beach. As early as the 1880s, the government set aside a large tract of land on the point as a reserve, and although originally intended for military purposes, it became home to a branch of Montreal's famous McGill University in 1913. The outbreak of WW I stalled expansion plans, and it wasn't until 1925 that the University of British Columbia officially opened on what became University Endowment Lands. The campus of today encompasses over 400 hectares and serves up to 35,000 students at one time. Originally, the Endowment Lands were intended for future development, but in 1988 a 763-hectare section was set aside as **Pacific Spirit Regional Park,** a tract of second-growth forest protected for all

After you've toured the Maritime Museum, wander down to water's edge to view a small collection of historic vessels, including the Black Duck, which was used as a search and rescue boat in the 1950s.

time. The park extends from Burrard Inlet in the north to the North Arm of the Fraser River in the south, separating the campus from the Central Vancouver suburbs of Point Grey, Dunbar, and Mackenzie Heights.

If you're interested in learning more about the university, join one of the student-led tours that leave the Student Union Building (near the main university bus interchange) Mon.-Fri. at 10 a.m. and 2 p.m. Call (604) 822-8687 for information.

Museum of Anthropology

Containing the world's largest collection of arts and crafts of the Pacific Northwest native peoples, this excellent on-campus museum, 6393 Northwest Marine Dr., tel. (604) 822-5087, should not be missed. Designed by innovative Canadian architect Arthur Erickson, the ultramodern concrete-and-glass building perches on a high cliff overlooking the Pacific Ocean and mimics the post-and-beam structures favored by the Coast Salish.

The entrance is flanked by panels that create the shape of a Bent-box, which the Salish believed contained the meaning of life. Inside, a ramp lined with impressive sculptures by renowned modern-day carvers leads to the Great Hall, a cavernous 18-meter-high room dominated by towering totem poles collected from along the coast and interspersed with other ancient works. A museum highlight is the collection of works by Haida artist Bill Reid, which includes *The Raven* and the *First Men,* a sculpture carved from a four-ton chunk of cedar. Other displays include intricate carvings, baskets, and ceremonial masks, fabulous jewelry, and European ceramics. The museum holds over 200,000 artifacts, most of which are stored in uniquely accessible research collections. Instead of being stored in musty boxes out back and available only to crusty old anthropologists, the collections are stored in the main museum—in row upon row of glass-enclosed cabinets and in drawers that visitors are encouraged to open. Details of each piece are noted in handy catalogs.

Outside, a deliciously scented woodland path on the left side of the museum leads to a reconstructed Haida village and a number of contemporary totem poles with descriptive plaques.

In summer, the museum is open daily 10 a.m.-5 p.m., and till 9 p.m. on Tuesday nights. The rest of the year the museum is open Tues.-Sun. 11 a.m.-5 p.m. Admission is adult $6, senior and child $3.50, everyone free on Tuesday after 5 p.m. If you have your own vehicle, go armed with a fistful of quarters and park in the lot beside the museum.

Nitobe Memorial Garden

About 300 meters south of the Museum of Anthropology is the serene Nitobe Memorial Garden, tel. (604) 822-6038, a traditional Japanese garden of shrubs and miniatures spread over one hectare. The garden has two distinct sections: the Stroll Garden, laid out in a form that symbolizes the journey through life, and the Tea Garden, the place to contemplate life from a ceremonial teahouse. The garden is surrounded by high walls (which almost block out the noise of traffic from busy Marine Dr.), making it a peaceful retreat. In summer it's open daily 10 a.m.-6 p.m. and admission is adult $2.50, senior and child $1.50; the rest of the year it's open weekdays only 11 a.m.-3 p.m., but admission is free.

UBC Botanical Garden

Also on campus is the delightful UBC Botanical Garden, at 6804 Marine Dr. (at 16th Ave. 2.4 km south of the Museum of Anthropology), tel (604) 822-4208. Set among coastal forest, the 44-hectare garden dates to the turn of the 20th century and features eight separate sections, which hold around 10,000 species. The various gardens have themes of specific regions or environments. Highlights include Canada's largest collection of rhododendrons in the Asian Garden; a Native Garden alive with the plants, flowers, and shrubs found along the Pacific Northwest coast; a display of mountain plants from the world's continents in the Alpine Garden; and an interesting planting of fruit and vegetables in the Food Garden. The garden is open in summer 10 a.m.-6 p.m., the rest of the year 10 a.m.-2:30 p.m. Admission is adult $4.50, senior $2.25.

B.C. Golf Museum

On the east side of campus, a three-iron from the university golf course, is the B.C. Golf Museum, 2545 Blanca St., tel. (604) 222-4653, housed in a Tudor-style building that was originally a clubhouse. The museum holds a collection of British Columbia golfing memorabilia, extensive archives, and a library. It's open year-round Tues.-Sun. noon-4 p.m.; admission is by donation.

Getting to UBC
To get to the campus take bus no. 4 or 10 south along Granville Mall or no. 9 west along Broadway. All buses terminate at the "Bus Loop," in the middle of the campus near the junction of University Blvd. and Westbrook Mall. From this bus stop, the Museum of Anthropology is a 15-minute walk along Westbrook Mall. If you're driving, take 4th Ave. west out of Kitsilano. This street becomes Chancellor Blvd., which becomes Marine Dr., which loops around the outer edge of the campus and passes the Museum of Anthropology and both the gardens detailed above.

PARKS AND GARDENS

VanDusen Botanical Garden
This 22-hectare garden at 5251 Oak St., tel. (604) 878-9274, is the city's answer to Victoria's Butchart Garden, albeit on a smaller scale. Feast your eyes on more than 1,000 varieties of rhododendrons, as well as roses, all kinds of botanical rarities, an Elizabethan hedge maze, and a children's topiary garden featuring animal shapes. The complex includes a shop selling cards, perfumes, soaps, potpourri, and all kinds of gifts with a floral theme. At popular **Sprinklers Restaurant,** tel. (604) 261-0011, the light and airy decor, picture windows, and garden view bring the outside inside. Sprinklers is open daily 11:30 a.m.-3 p.m. for a reasonably priced lunch and 5:30-9 p.m. for a more expensive, dressier dinner; reservations recommended.

The garden is open in summer daily 10 a.m.-9 p.m., the rest of the year daily 10 a.m.-4 p.m. Admission is adult $5, senior $2.50. To get there by bus, take no. 17 south along Burrard Street. Oak Street runs parallel to Granville Street; access to the garden is on the corner of E. 33rd Avenue.

Queen Elizabeth Park
Less than two km from the VanDusen Botanical Garden, this 53-hectare park is a gardener's paradise of sweeping lawns, trees, flowering shrubs, formal flower gardens, and masses of rhododendrons—a vivid spectacle in May and June. The park sits atop 152-meter **Little Mountain,** the city's highest point, so magnificent views of Vancouver and the Coast Mountains are an added bonus. Admission to the park is free.

Within the park is the magnificent **Bloedel Floral Conservatory,** tel. (604) 257-8570, a glass-domed structure rising 40 meters and enclosing a temperature-controlled, humid tropical jungle. Inside you'll find a profusion of exotic flowering plants and a resident avian population including multihued parrots. The conservatory is open in summer Mon.-Fri. 9 a.m.-8 p.m. and Sat.-Sun. 10 a.m.-9 p.m., the rest of the year daily 10.a.m.-5 p.m. Admission is adults $3.50, seniors and children $2. The main entrance is by the junction of E. 33rd Ave. and Cambie St.; to get there from downtown take bus no. 15 south on Burrard Street.

Bloedel Observatory, Queen Elizabeth Park

JANE AND BRUCE KING

FARTHER SOUTH

When your plane touches down at Vancouver International Airport, it's actually landing on an island. A number of such islands are part of a massive alluvial fan formed over eons of time as silt and gravel have washed down the Fraser River and been deposited in the Strait of Georgia. The largest of these islands holds the city of Richmond, which is sandwiched between the North and South Arms of the river. Across the South Arm are Delta and Tsawwassen, from where ferries depart for Vancouver Island. Across Boundary Bay from Tsawwassen is White Rock, a large residential area that sits right on the border.

RICHMOND

Richmond lies on a large island at the mouth of the Fraser River. Most visitors to Vancouver cross the island on their way to or from the airport or Tsawwassen Ferry Terminal. Steveston (see below) is the main reason to visit Richmond, but on the way, consider escaping the suburban sprawl at **Richmond Nature Park** at the junction of Highways 91 and 99. This 85-hectare park has been left in its natural state; the only development comprises trails leading through to ponds and fens. The park is open daily during daylight hours.

Steveston

On the island's southwestern extremity, historic Steveston Fishing Village is a lively spot worth a visit. In the 1880s it had over 50 canneries and was the world's largest fishing port. The harbor still holds Canada's largest fleet of commercial fishing boats. For an introduction to the town's heritage, check out **Steveston Museum,** in the Royal Bank building at 3811 Moncton St., tel. (604) 271-6868. It's open Mon.-Sat. 9:30 a.m.-5 p.m. Then you can visit one of the many fishing-supply outlets or head for **Steveston Landing** on Bayview Road. The landing is lined with boutiques and restaurants, and bustles with activity in summer. Below the landing, fishing boats sell the day's catch. Shrimp are especially good

value (avoid the headless ones) at around $5 per pound. To watch all the action, grab a seat on the deck of **Shady Island Seafood,** 3800 Bayview Rd., tel. (604) 275-6587, where daily specials are around $7-9, a bowl of incredibly good clam chowder is $5, and burgers with fries start at $6. Farther along the harborfront you'll find the **Gulf of Georgia Cannery National Historic Site,** 12138 4th Ave., tel. (604) 664-9031, a salmon cannery that operated between 1894 and 1979. Much of the original cannery has been restored, and an audiovisual presentation is offered in the Boiler House Theatre. It's open in summer daily 10 a.m.-5 p.m. and in spring and fall Thurs.-Mon. 10 a.m.-5 p.m. Admission is adult $4, senior $3, child $2.

To get to Steveston, take bus no. 401, 406, or 407 south on Howe Street. If you're driving, take Hwy. 99 to the Steveston Hwy. exit, passing by a magnificent Buddhist temple before entering Steveston town center.

SOUTH OF THE FRASER RIVER

Delta

Pass under the south arm of the Fraser River via Hwy. 99 and the George Massey Tunnel and you'll emerge in the sprawling industrial and residential area of Delta. The first township in the Delta area was Ladner's Landing, which was developed as a port facility for local farmers. Take Hwy. 17 (Exit 28) south from Hwy. 99 and turn right on Ladner Trunk Rd. to access the site and **Delta Museum and Archives,** 4858 Delta St., tel. (403) 946-9322. This museum tells the story of the first inhabitants, the Salish, and the farming and fishing history of more recent times. It's open Tues.-Sat. 10 a.m.-2:30 p.m., Sunday 2-4 p.m.

The George Massey Tunnel passes under 70-hectare **Deas Island,** where marshes, dunes, and a high density of birdlife are protected within the boundaries of a regional park. Deas is linked to the mainland by a causeway; take the same exit from Hwy. 99 as detailed above, but cross under the highway and head north to McNeeleys Way, which crosses onto the island.

George C. Reifel Bird Sanctuary

This great attraction west of downtown Delta is missed by most visitors. The 350-hectare sanctuary protects the northern corner of low-lying Westham Island, a stopover for thousands of migratory birds in spring and fall. In the middle of a wide delta at the mouth of the Fraser River, the island is a world away from surrounding city life.

The best time for a visit is during the spectacular snow goose migration, which runs from early November to mid-December. Otherwise, you'll see abundant migratory birdlife anytime between October and April. The island also serves as a permanent home for many bird species, including bald eagles, peregrine falcons, herons, swans, and owls.

Within the sanctuary are many kilometers of trails, an observation tower, free birdseed, and a couple of picnic areas. It's open year-round daily 9 a.m.-4 p.m. Admission is adults $3.25, seniors

Birdlife is prolific around the wetlands of the Fraser River delta. One of the most common of the waders is the great blue heron, which calls Vancouver home year-round.

and children $1. To get there, follow 47th Ave. through Delta and follow the river's edge, crossing a short bridge to the sanctuary on Westham Island Road.

Point Roberts

In 1846, when it was agreed that the international boundary would run along the 49th parallel, an exception was made for Vancouver Island, which was retained as a Canadian possession, even though its southern extremity dipped well below this latitude. No such exception was made for Point Roberts, south of Tsawwassen and accessible by road only through Canada (take 56th St. south from Hwy. 17). Although most basic services are provided by British Columbia, the 12-square-km chunk of land is officially part of Washington State, and entry is controlled by a 24-hour border crossing. The point's main attractions are the beaches, which face the Strait of Georgia to the west and the warm, shallow waters of Boundary Bay to the east. At the end of the road is a park with picnic tables and a campground overlooking the water. Most visitors are Vancouver locals, who take advantage of not only the point's natural attractions but also cheap liquor at the two huge taverns (until provincial liquor laws in British Columbia were relaxed, these bars were *especially* popular on Sunday).

Surrey

Suburban Surrey sprawls from the Fraser River in the north to White Rock and the international boundary in the south and from Delta in the west to Langley in the east. Surrey's first settlers were the Stewarts, who built a homestead beside the Nicomekl River in 1894. The original homestead is now the centerpiece of **Elgin Heritage Park,** 13723 Crescent Rd., tel. (250) 543-3456. The farm's original workers' accommodations have been transformed into a weaving center, where textiles are created on antique looms and spinning wheels. Also on the property is a barn full of antique farm machinery. The park is open Tues.-Fri. 10 a.m.-4 p.m., Sat.-Sun. noon-4 p.m. To get there, take the King George Hwy. Exit off Hwy. 99, then the first right to Crescent Road.

The Nicomekl River drains into Boundary Bay just north of **Crescent Beach.** Most of the surrounding foreshore is protected as parkland, including a narrow finger of land that protrudes northward around the mouth of the river. A surrounding buildup of silt has created tidal flats that attract a wide variety of birdlife; almost 200 species have been recorded on the spit.

White Rock

Named for a 400-ton glacial erratic that sits by the shoreline, this residential area of the city lies right on the international border and surrounds the **Douglas Border Crossing.** It is the main border crossing for Vancouver-bound travelers heading north on Hwy. 5 from Seattle (Hwy. 99

north of the border). At the 24-hour checkpoint are duty-free shops and a 22-meter-high archway symbolizing the friendly relationship enjoyed between Canada and the U.S.

Take 8th Ave. west from the first interchange north of the border to reach seaside **Semiahoo Park** and the beginning of a five-km promenade that extends around Semiahoo Bay to West Beach. Along the way, you'll pass small **White Rock Museum,** in a restored railway station at 14970 Marine Dr., tel. (250) 541-2222. It's open daily 10 a.m.-4 p.m., and admission is by donation.

THE NORTH SHORE

To explore the many outdoor attractions north of Burrard Inlet, take the SeaBus from Waterfront Station to **Lonsdale Quay** (adults $2.25 each way). At the lively quay, a small information center (to the right as you come out of the SeaBus terminal) dispenses valuable information, and transit buses depart regularly for all the sights listed below. Locals come here to meet friends over coffee, or to stock up at a farmers' market full of fresh fruit and veggies, fish, meats, bread, flowers, and plants. Some take time out from shopping for a quick bite to eat, a cool drink, and a stunning harbor view from one of many in- or outdoor tables. The quay also features many gift shops and boutiques, restaurants, and the Lonsdale Quay Hotel.

NORTH VANCOUVER

Capilano Suspension Bridge

The first bridge across the Capilano River opened in 1899. That remarkable wood-and-hemp structure stretched 137 meters across the deep canyon. Today, several bridges later, the canyon is spanned by a wood-and-wire suspension bridge a fearsome 70 meters above the Capilano River. Allow 30 minutes to walk the bridge and the nature trails on the far side, view the totem-pole carvers in action in summer, and browse the requisite gift shop. Admission is a bit steep—adults $9.95, seniors $8.35—but it's one of Vancouver's most popular sights. (If you don't want to spend the money, you can get much the same thrill by crossing the free bridge in Lynn Canyon Park; see below). The Capilano

Suspension Bridge is open in summer daily 8 a.m.-dusk, the rest of the year daily 9 a.m.-5 p.m. For more information call (604) 985-7474. To get there by car, cross Lions Gate Bridge, turn east onto Marine Dr. then immediately north onto Capilano Rd., continuing to 3735 Capilano, on your left. By bus, take no. 246 north on Georgia St. or jump aboard the SeaBus and take bus no. 236 from Lonsdale Quay.

Capilano Salmon Hatchery and Regional Park

If you've always wanted to know more about the miraculous life cycle of salmon, or want some facts to back up your fish stories, visit this hatchery on the Capilano River, two km upstream from the suspension bridge (turn onto Capilano Park Rd. from Capilano Rd.), tel. (604) 666-1790. Along with educational displays and nature exhibits you can see what the fish see from an underwater point of view. From July through October, magnificent adult coho and chinook salmon fight their way upriver to the hatchery. It's open daily 8 a.m.-4 p.m., until 6 p.m. the rest of the year. Admission is free.

The hatchery is within **Capilano River Regional Park,** which extends north to **Cleveland Dam.** The dam was built in 1954 to form Capilano Lake—Vancouver's main drinking-water supply. Within the park are many kilometers of hiking trails, including one that leads all the way down to where the Capilano River drains into Burrard Inlet; seven km (two hours) each way.

Grouse Mountain

Continuing north, Capilano Rd. becomes Nancy Greene Way and ends at the base of the **Grouse**

Mountain Skyride, tel. (604) 984-0661. For an excellent view of downtown Vancouver, Stanley Park, the Pacific Ocean, and as far south as Mount Baker (Washington), take the almost-vertical eight-minute ride on the gondola to the upper slopes of 1,250-meter Grouse Mountain. Tickets are adults $16.95, seniors $14.95, children $5.95. The gondola runs year-round, departing every 15 minutes 10 a.m.-10 p.m. in summer.

Facilities at the top include the casual **Bar 98,** where you can drink in some high-elevation sunshine along with the view (open daily 11 a.m.-10 p.m.); the fancy **Grouse Nest Restaurant,** which provides free Skyride tickets with dinner reservations (open daily 5:30 p.m.-9:30 p.m.); and a picnic area. Theatre in the Sky is a bird's eye, wide-screen presentation of the outdoor wonders of the province. Entry is included in the Skyride ticket. In addition, the Peak Chair continues higher up the mountain, and paved paths and nature trails skirt mountain meadows. Of the many possible hikes, the one-km **Blue Grouse Interpretive Trail** is the easiest and most enjoyable, winding around a lake and through a rainforest. More ambitious hikers will have ready access to the rugged West Coast Range.

For a bit of extra excitement when you get to the top, get a bird's-eye view of Vancouver with a **Grouse Mountain Helicopter Tour,** tel. (604) 525-1484. The chopper tour costs $45 per person for five minutes, $70 for 10 minutes. Flights lift off daily, 11 a.m. to sunset. In summer you can also enjoy logging demonstrations, and you can often see hang-gliding enthusiasts taking to the air. In winter, skiers can choose from beginner to advanced runs on the slopes of Grouse Mountain, with the added magic of night skiing (see Skiing in the Recreation chapter).

To get to the gondola from downtown, take the SeaBus to Lonsdale Quay, then take bus no. 236 to the end of the road.

Lynn Canyon Park

On its way to Burrard Inlet, Lynn Creek flows through a deep canyon straddled by this 240-hectare park. Spanning the canyon is the "other" suspension bridge. The one here, built in 1912, is half as wide as its more famous counterpart over the Capilano River, but it's a few meters higher and, best of all, it's free. An ancient forest of Douglas fir surrounds the impressive canyon

and harbors a number of hiking trails. Also visit **Lynn Canyon Ecology Centre,** tel. (604) 981-3103, where displays, models, and free slide shows and films explore plant and animal ecology. The center is open daily 10 a.m.-5 p.m.; admission is free.

Lynn Canyon Park is seven km east of the Capilano River. To get there by car, take the Lynn Valley Rd. Exit off Hwy. 1, east of the Lions Gate Bridge. By public transport, take the SeaBus to Lonsdale Quay, then bus no. 228 or 229.

Farther upstream is **Lynn Headwaters Regional Park,** a remote tract of wilderness on the edge of the city. Contact the Ecology Centre for more information.

Mount Seymour Provincial Park and Vicinity

Hikers and skiers flock to this 3,508-hectare park 20 km northeast of downtown. The park lies off Mt. Seymour Parkway, which spurs east off the TransCanada Highway just north of Burrard Inlet. The long and winding access road to the park climbs steadily through an ancient forest of western hemlock, cedar, and Douglas fir to a small facility area at an elevation of 1,000 meters. From the parking lot, trails lead to the summit of 1,453-meter Mt. Seymour; allow one hour for the two km (one-way) trek.

If you continue along Mount Seymour Parkway instead of turning north toward the park, you end up in the scenic little village of **Deep Cove** on the west shore of Indian Arm (off the northeast end of Burrard Inlet)—an excellent spot for a picnic. Take your sack lunch to the waterfront park and watch the fishing and pleasure boats coming and going in the bay. More adventurous visitors can swim, kayak, or scuba dive.

WEST VANCOUVER AND VICINITY

Cypress Provincial Park

This 3,012-hectare park northwest of downtown encompasses a high alpine area in the North Shore Mountains. Even the road up to the park is worthwhile for the views; the roadside Highview Lookout provides a stunning panorama of the city. After passing a couple more lookouts, the road enters the park, ending at Cypress Bowl ski area. From the ski area parking lot, well-

Black bears are common throughout the North Shore Range.

marked hiking trails radiate out like spokes, through alpine meadows and to low peaks with views across Howe Sound. With a vivid imagination, maybe you'll spot Say-noth-kai, the two-headed sea serpent of native Salish legend, believed to inhabit the sound. On a clear day you can also make out the cone of Mt. Baker, one of a row of Pacific Coast volcanoes. It's to the southeast, in Washington State.

Another concentration of hiking trails surrounds the old Hollyburn Lodge, in the park's southeast corner. Among many short hikes possible here, a six-km (one-way) trail leads to the 1,325-meter summit of Hollyburn Mountain. The trail gains 450 meters in elevation; allow two and a half hours each way.

Aside from the ski resort, the park's only facilities are the picnic areas dotting the access road. Camping is permitted only in the backcountry. (For information on skiing within the park, see Skiing in the following chapter.) To get to the park, take the TransCanada Hwy. 12 km west of Lions Gate Bridge and turn north onto Cypress Bowl Road.

Lighthouse Park
On a headland jutting into Howe Sound, 70-hectare Lighthouse Park lies eight km west of the Lions Gate Bridge. Trails lead through the park to coastal cliffs and a lighthouse that guides shipping into narrow Burrard Inlet. Views from the lighthouse grounds are spectacular, extending west over the Strait of Georgia and east to Stan-ley Park and the Vancouver skyline. Get there along Marine Dr. or aboard bus no. 250 from Georgia Street.

Horseshoe Bay
The pretty little residential area of Horseshoe Bay offers plenty to see and do while you wait for the Vancouver Island or Sunshine Coast ferry. If you and your trusty vehicle are catching one of the ferries, buy your ticket at the car booth, move your automobile into the lineup, then explore the town. Several restaurants, a bakery, a supermarket, a pub, and a couple of good delis cater to the hungry and thirsty. A stroll along the beautiful waterfront marina is a good way to cool your heels and dawdle away some waiting time.

Bowen Island
From Vancouver, this is the most accessible of hundreds of islands dotting the Strait of Georgia. The island is only a short ferry trip from Horseshoe Bay, but it seems a world away from the city. The first European settlers were loggers, but Bowen Island has also been home to a fishing and whaling industry. Vancouverites began holidaying on the island as early as 1900, and soon a hotel, complete with tennis courts, lawn bowling, and grove of fruit trees, had opened. By the 1920s, the island was catering to tens of thousands of summer visitors annually and grand plans were put in place to open North America's most luxurious resort. The development never eventuated, and today the island is home

to a permanent population of 2,800, many of whom work in Vancouver, commuting daily across the water.

The ferry docks at the island's main settlement, **Snug Cove,** where you'll find all the services of a small town, including bed and breakfasts and cafés. There's good swimming at Mannion Bay, near Snug Cove, and **Bowen Island Sea Kayaking,** tel. (604) 947-9266, rents kayaks and offers tours, but the rest of island is also good to explore. A 1.5-km trail leads from Snug Cove to Killarney Lake, where birdlife is prolific and roads lead across to the island's west coast.

BC Ferries, tel. (604) 669-1211, operates service between Horseshoe Bay and the island daily 6 a.m.-9:45 p.m. approximately once an hour. The fare is adult $6, child $3. The ferries also take vehicles ($18.75), but these aren't necessary as most visitors set out on foot. Island information is available in the chamber of commerce office, at the corner of Government and Grafton Streets, during regular business hours.

EAST FROM DOWNTOWN

When you leave Vancouver and head due east, you travel through the most built-up and heavily populated area of British Columbia, skirting modern cities, residential suburbs, and zones of heavy industry. Greater Vancouver extends almost 100 km along the Fraser Valley, through mostly residential areas. The main route east is the TransCanada Hwy., which parallels the Fraser River to the south, passing through Burnaby, Langley, and Abbotsford. The original path taken by this highway crosses the Fraser River at New Westminster, the capital of British Columbia for short period in the 1860s.

BURNABY

Immediately east of downtown, Burnaby was incorporated as a city in 1992 (its population of 190,000 makes it British Columbia's third largest city), but in reality it's part of Vancouver's suburban sprawl. It extends east from Boundary Rd. to Coquitlam, while Burrard Inlet lies to the north and riverside New Westminster to the south. The TransCanada Hwy. bisects Burnaby, but access is easiest via the SkyTrain, which makes three stops within the city, including at **Metrotown,** which is British Columbia's largest shopping mall.

Burnaby's Heritage Village and Vicinity

This four-hectare open-air museum, tel. (604) 293-6501, lies in Deer Lake Park, on the south side of the TransCanada Hwy.; to get there take Exit 33 south, turn left onto Canada Way then right onto Deer Lake Ave., or take the SkyTrain to Metrotown Station and jump aboard bus no. 144. The village is a reconstruction of how a B.C. town would have looked in the first 20 years of the 1900s, complete with over 30 businesses, heritage-style gardens, a miniature railway, and costumed staff. But the highlight is a historic carousel with over 30 restored wooden horses. It's open through summer and in December 11 a.m.-4:30 p.m. Admission is adult $7, senior and child $5.

Deer Lake Park itself is a pleasant place to spend time on a sunny day. The lake is encircled by a five-km trail that passes **Burnaby Art Gallery,** 6344 Deer Lake Ave., tel. (604) 291-9441. The gallery, housed in Ceperley Mansion, features contemporary works by artists from throughout North America. Admission is $2. It's open Tues.-Fri. 9:30 a.m.-4:30 p.m., Sat.-Sun. 12:30-4:30 p.m.

Burnaby Mountain Park

This large park north of the TransCanada Hwy. surrounds the campus of **Simon Fraser University,** the province's second largest campus with a student population of 20,000. Centennial Way (off Burnaby Mountain Parkway) leads to the park's high point, where views extend down Burrard Inlet to North Vancouver and its stunning mountain backdrop. Also at the summit is a collection of totem poles, Japanese sculptures, a rose garden, and a restaurant. The university itself is worthy of inspection. Its unique design of "quadrants" linked by a massive fountain-filled courtyard is typical of architect Arthur Erickson, who was partly responsible for its design. Tours of the campus are offered year-round but must be booked in advance by calling (604) 291-3397. The **Museum of Archaeology and Ethnology,** in Academic Quadrangle 8602, tel. (604) 291-3325, holds a collection of native artifacts gathered from along the Pacific Northwest coast. Admission is by donation and it's open Mon.-Fri. 10 a.m.-4 p.m.

VICINITY OF COQUITLAM

Coquitlam is a sprawling residential area east of Burnaby. It lies at the head of Burrard Inlet, near Port Moody, which was once slated as the terminus of the transcontinental railway. There's nothing of real interest in Coquitlam itself, but Loco Rd. leads around Burrard Inlet to **Belcarra Regional Park,** which is lapped by the waters of Indian Arm.

Pinecone Burke Provincial Park

This newly declared park protects 38,000 hectares of the North Shore Range northeast of Coquitlam. It extends along the west shoreline of Pitt Lake (opposite Golden Ears Provincial Park) and as far west as the Boise Valley, scene of a short-lived gold rush in the late 1800s. Much of the park was logged over 100 years ago, but a few sections of old growth forest remain, including a 1,000-year-old stand of cedar in the Cedar Spirit Grove. To get to the park from Hwy. 7 take Coast Meridian Rd. north to Harper Rd., which leads to Munro and Bennett Lakes.

NEW WESTMINSTER

"New West," as it's best known, is a densely populated residential area 15 km southeast of downtown. Its strategic location, where the Fraser River divides, caused it to become a hub of river transportation and the provincial capital in the years 1866-68. Only a few historic buildings

VANCOUVER FOR KIDS

Vancouver offers plenty of attractions devoted especially to the needs of youngsters. A couple of pre-trip information sources are the **Kid Friendly Society of British Columbia,** tel. (604) 925-6063, which produces a free directory of kid-friendly facilities throughout the city, and Creative Options, tel. (604) 266-8986, which produces the brochure *Kids' Guide to Vancouver.*

Many of Vancouver's annual festivals include the needs of the younger set in their programs, but for a real treat, take the children down to Vanier Park through the last week of May for the **Vancouver International Children's Festival,** tel. (604) 708-5655, website www.youngarts. ca. Most of the fun is free, with music, dance, plays, and storytelling taking place under big-top tents.

Just for Fun

Kids will be kids, so even with an overabundance of outdoor-recreation opportunities, you may still want to spend time with the tribe at an old-fashioned fun park. The best of these is **Playland,** Exhibition Park, corner E. Hastings and Cassiar Streets, tel. (604) 253-2311, featuring plenty of old-fashioned amusements, including a merry-go-round, a wooden roller coaster, a games arcade, and a petting zoo. It's open in summer daily 11 a.m.-10 p.m., April-June and Sept.-Oct. weekends only and shorter hours. Admission is adults $24, children $21, which includes unlimited rides. To get there from downtown, take bus no. 14 or 16 north along Granville Mall. Farther east, **Kid City,** 19888 Langley Bypass, Langley, tel. (604) 532-8989, is a massive indoor facility filled with slides, climbing equipment, rope bridges, and bouncing rooms. It's open for those aged 4-13 only; $8 for a maximum of three hours.

The **Kids' Market,** 1496 Cartwright St., near the entrance to Granville Island, tel. (604) 689-8447, is the place to take the young ones on a sunny after-

noon. There's an outdoor waterpark, a playground, and birds to feed on the adjacent waterway.

A Little More Educational

Stanley Park holds many attractions for the little ones. Along Pipeline Rd. from the main entrance is the **Children's Farmyard,** a collection of domesticated animals including cows, sheep, chickens, and goats; open 10 a.m. until dusk. Adjacent is a **miniature railway,** tel. (604) 257-8351, with carriages pulled by replicas of historic locomotives. In the same part of the park is the **Vancouver Aquarium,** tel. (604) 659-3474, displaying a wide range of marinelife from around the world, with dolphins, orcas, and beluga whales the stars of the show.

Distinctively shaped **Science World,** southeast of downtown on False Creek, tel. (604) 268-6363, contains hands-on displays that help those of all ages understand the wonderful world of science. Get there by SkyTrain from downtown (but don't tell your children the train has no driver) or by ferry from Granville Island.

Kidsbooks, 3083 W. Broadway, tel. (604) 899-8675, offers a lot more than just books for kids. There are daily book talks and readings as well as puppet shows and puppets for sale.

an orca, star of the aquarium show

remain, and the old port area has been totally overtaken by modern developments. The north side of the river, along Columbia St., was redeveloped in the late 1980s, with a riverside promenade linking attractive stretches of green space to the Westminster Quay development and other modern shopping areas.

Sights
The center of the action is **Westminster Quay Market,** which holds markets of fresh produce, takeout food stalls, and specialty shops. Immediately to the south of the market is the *Samson V,* a retired paddlewheeler.

To the north of the market is the only **Russian submarine** in North America that is open to the public. Admission is adult $7, senior and child $5, and it's open daily 9:30 a.m.-6:30 p.m. For information call (604) 520-1073.

An easy walk from the riverfront is **Irving House,** 302 Royal Ave., tel. (604) 527-4640, once the home of riverboat captain William Irving and his family. Constructed in 1865, this Victorian-era mansion is one of western Canada's oldest standing residential buildings. The adjacent **New Westminster Museum** catalogs the history of the area. Both are open in summer Tues.-Sun. 11 a.m.-5 p.m., weekends 1-5 p.m. the rest of the year.

Getting to New West
The easiest way to reach New West from downtown is by SkyTrain. By vehicle, take the Kingsway out of the city. This stretch of road becomes 10th Ave., winding around the north side of New West's downtown commercial district before crossing the Fraser River as McBride Boulevard. Turn right at the last intersection (Columbia St.) on the north side of the river to reach the riverfront and the heart of the action. Alternatively, take the SkyTrain from any downtown station.

LANGLEY

Langley is a large residential area 50 km east of downtown that sprawls across both sides of the TransCanada Highway. It holds little of interest to the casual visitor, but on its northern outskirts Fort Langley is a re-creation of the Lower Mainland's first permanent European settlement.

Fort Langley National Historic Park
In 1827, the Hudson's Bay Company established a settlement 48 km upstream from the mouth of the Fraser River as part of a network of trading posts, provision depots, and administrative centers that stretched across western Canada. The original site was abandoned in 1839 in favor of another, farther upstream, where today the settlement has been re-created. It was the abundance of fur-bearing mammals that led to the region's settlement originally, but within a decade salmon had become its mainstay. Through its formative years, the fort played a major role in the development of British Columbia. Out its gates have vamoosed native fur and salmon traders, adventurous explorers who opened up the interior, company traders, and fortune seekers heading for the goldfields of the upper Fraser River. When British Columbia became a crown colony in 1858, the official proclamation was uttered here in the "big house."

Today the restored trading post springs to life as park interpreters in period costumes animate the fort's history. Admission is adult $4.50, child $2.50. It's open in summer daily 10 a.m.-4:30 p.m., closed Mon.-Tues. the rest of the year. To get there, follow Hwy. 1 for 50 km east from downtown and head north toward the Fraser River. It's well signposted from Hwy. 1, but the official address is 23433 Mavis St., Fort Langley, tel. (604) 888-4424.

FRASER RIVER VALLEY

This fertile valley east of the city encompasses rolling farmland dotted with historic villages, and beautiful mountains line the horizon in just about any direction. In summer you can pick and choose from an endless number of roadside stands selling fresh fruit at bargain prices—the raspberries in July are delectable. Two routes lead through the valley. The TransCanada Highway, on the south side of the Fraser River, speeds you out of southeast Vancouver through Abbotsford and scenic Chilliwack to Hope. Slower, more picturesque Hwy. 7 meanders along the north side of the Fraser River through Mission, named after a Roman Catholic mission school built in 1861. If you take the TransCanada Hwy., it's possible to cross the Fraser River at

HARRISON HOT SPRINGS

British Columbia is blessed with 60 documented hot springs. Many remain in their natural state while others attract visitors with luxurious resorts. The closest of these to Vancouver is **Harrison Hot Springs,** on the north side of the Fraser Valley 125 km east of downtown. Known as the "Spa of Canada," the springs lie on the sandy southern shores of southwestern B.C.'s largest body of water, **Harrison Lake,** and since the opening of the province's first resort in 1886, the springs have spurred much surrounding development. Coast Salish were the first to take advantage of the soothing water, then in the late 1850s gold miners stumbled across the springs, and by 1886 the St. Alice Hotel was enticing guests with a large bath house. Due to a historical agreement, only the Harrison Hot Springs Hotel has water rights, but the hotel operates **Harrison Public Pool,** right downtown on the corner of Harrison Hot Springs Rd. and Esplanade Ave., tel. (604) 796-2244. Scalding 74° C mineral water is pumped from its source, cooled to a soothing 38° C, then pumped into the pool. Admission is adult $7, senior and child $5. The pool is open in summer daily 8 a.m.-9 p.m., the rest of the year daily 9 a.m.-9 p.m. The lake itself provides many recreation opportunities, with good swimming, sailing, canoeing, and fishing for trout and coho salmon.

Lakeside **Harrison Hot Springs Hotel,** 100 Esplanade, tel. (604) 796-2244 or (800) 663-2266, is the town's most elegant accommodation, and it offers guests use of a large indoor and outdoor complex of mineral pools, complete with grassed areas, lots of outdoor furniture, and a café. Other facilities include boat and canoe rentals, sailing lessons, and a restaurant and lounge bar. Most of the 300 rooms have private balconies, many with spectacular views across the lake. Rates range $114-200. Moderate-Luxury. Within walking distance of the public hot pool and lake is **Glencoe Motel,** 259 Hot Springs Rd., tel. (604) 796-2574, which charges $60 s, $70 d. Inexpensive. The least expensive option is to camp at one of three campgrounds along the road into town or through town in lakeside **Sasquatch Provincial Park.**

Abbotsford (70 km from downtown), Chilliwack (110 km from downtown), or Hope (150 km from downtown). If you head out of the city on Hwy. 7 through Coquitlam and Pitt Meadows, it's 125 km to **Harrison Hot Springs** (see the special topic), the perfect turnaround point for a day trip.

Abbotsford and Chilliwack

If you decide to cross from Hwy. 1 to Hwy. 7 at Abbotsford, make the detour to delightful **Clayburn Village** (access is east along Clayburn Rd., which intersects with Hwy. 11 six km north of Hwy. 1), originally a company town for a local brickworks. As you'd expect, most of the neat houses are built of brick, providing a local atmosphere a world away from the surrounding modern subdivisions. Head to the local general store for delicious Devonshire tea.

It is possible to continue east through Clayburn to **Sumas Mountain Provincial Park** (ask directions at the local general store), or take Exit 95 from Hwy. 1 to Sumas Mountain Rd., then take Batts Rd., which climbs steadily up the mountain's southern slopes. From the end of this service road, it's a short climb to the 900-meter summit of Sumas Mountain, from where views extend north across the Fraser River and south across a patchwork of farmland to Washington's snowcapped Mt. Baker. From the pullout one km from the end of road, a hiking trail descends for 1.5 km to forest-encircled Chadsey Lake and a lakeside picnic area.

Farther east along the TransCanada Hwy., **Cultus Lake Provincial Park,** 11 km south of Chilliwack, holds a warm-water lake surrounded by mountains—a good spot for swimming, picnicking, or camping. The park's campground is open year-round; cost is $17 per night March-Oct., free the rest of the year.

Kilby Historic Store and Farm

This historic site, tel. (604) 796-9576, lies on the north side of the Fraser River, near the turnoff to Harrison Hot Springs, 40 km east of Mission and six km west of Agassiz (look for the inconspicuous sign close to Harrison Mills). It is off the beaten track and often missed by those unfamiliar with the area. The fascinating museum/country store, which operated until the early 1970s, is fully stocked with all the old brands and types of goods that were commonplace in the 1920s and '30s. On the two-hectare riverside grounds are farm equipment, farm animals, a gift shop, and a café serving delicious home-style cooking. It's open April-Nov. daily 11 a.m.-5 p.m.

Around the corner, you can picnic, swim, and fish at **Harrison Bay.**

Golden Ears Provincial Park

Returning to the city along Hwy. 7, the turnoff to this, the largest of Vancouver's provincial parks, is in Maple Ridge, 34 km west of Mission. From the west, it's a 38 km drive from downtown, either along Hwy. 1, then Hwy. 7, or along the more scenic Hwy. 7A, a continuation of Hastings St. that follows the shoreline of Burrard Inlet through Coquitlam. Either way, from Hwy. 7 take 232nd St. north for five km then 132nd Ave. east to access the park.

Encompassing 55,590 hectares of the Coast Mountains east of downtown Vancouver, this park extends from the Alouette River, near the suburb of Maple Ridge, north to Garibaldi Provincial Park. To get to the main facility areas, follow Hwy. 7 east out of the city for 40 km to Maple Ridge, then follow signs north. Much of the park was logged for railway ties in the 1920s, but today the second-growth montane forest—dominated by western hemlock—has almost erased the early human devastation.

The park access road follows the Alouette River into the park, ending at Alouette Lake. The river and lake provide fair fishing, but the park's most popular activity is hiking. **Lower Falls Trail** begins at the end of the road and leads 2.7 km (one-way) along Gold Creek to a 10-meter-high waterfall; allow one hour each way. Across Gold Creek, **West Canyon Trail** climbs 200 meters over 1.5 km (allow 40 minutes each way) to a viewpoint of Alouette Lake. This trail begins from the West Canyon parking lot, where you'll also find a 12-km trail along the west bank of Gold Creek to Panorama Ridge and to the summit of the park's namesake, the **Golden Ears.** The name comes from the way the setting sun reflects off the twin peaks of Mt. Blanchard. This trail gains 1,500 meters, making it an extremely strenuous hike best undertaken as an overnight trip.

A number of riverside and lakeside picnic areas line the park access road, and at road's end are two large campgrounds.

RECREATION
FUN IN THE SUN

WALKING AND HIKING

Stanley Park
Vancouver is not a particularly good city to explore on foot, but it does have one redeeming factor for foot travelers—Stanley Park, an urban oasis crisscrossed with hiking trails and encircled by a 10-km promenade that hugs the shoreline. Along the way are many points of interest (see Stanley Park in the Sights chapter), benches, and interpretive plaques pointing out historical events. Allow three hours for the entire circuit. The promenade can be walked in either direction, but those on bikes and skates must travel counterclockwise. It is *always* busy, especially in late afternoon and on weekends.

Away from the Seawall Promenade, you'll find most trails a lot less used. A good alternative to one long section of the promenade is to ascend the steps immediately north of Lions Gate Bridge to Prospect Point (and maybe stop for a snack at the café), then continue west along the Merilees Trail, which follows the top of the cliff band to Third Beach. Along the way, an old lookout point affords excellent views of Siwash Rock and the Strait of Georgia.

The isthmus of land linking the park to the rest of the downtown peninsula is less than one kilometer wide, but it's mostly taken up by Lost Lagoon. A 1.5-km trail (30-minute roundtrip) encircles this bird-filled body of water. In the heart of the park is Beaver Lake, a smaller body of water, but still alive with birds throughout summer. Trails lead into this lake from all directions, and it can easily be walked around in 20 minutes.

False Creek
From English Bay Beach, a promenade continues along English Bay to Sunset Beach and Vancouver Aquatic Centre. The small ferries that operate on False Creek, extending service as far west as the Aquatic Center, open up a number of walking combinations around False Creek. Granville Island is a good starting point.

No official trails go around the island, but if you walk east from the market, you pass a flotilla of floating houses and go through a grassed area to Lookout Hill. Continue around the island and you'll come across a small footbridge leading to the mainland. From this point, it's seven km (allow two hours) around the head of False Creek, passing Science World and the Plaza of Nations, then closely following the water to the foot of Hornby St. for the short ferry trip back across to Granville Island. A dusty detour must be made through construction work between Cambie St. and Science World; bypass this section of the trail by crossing the Cambie Street Bridge or taking to the water at Stamps Landing and catching a ferry to Science World or the Plaza of Nations.

Pacific Spirit Regional Park and Vicinity
This 762-hectare park on the Central Vancouver peninsula offers 35 km of hiking trails through a forested environment similar to that which greeted the first European settlers over 200 years ago. A good starting point is the Park Centre, tel. (604) 224-5739, which has a supply of trail maps. The entire park is crisscrossed with trails, so although getting seriously lost is impossible, taking the wrong trail and ending up away from your intended destination is easy. One good trailhead is in the southeast of the park, at the junction of King Edward and 29th Avenues. From this point, the Imperial Trail heads west through a forest of red cedar and fir, crosses Salish Creek, then emerges on Southwest Marine Dr., at a monument commemorating the journey of Simon Fraser. From this lofty viewpoint, the view extends across the Strait of Georgia. This trail is 2.8 km (allow one hour) one-way. In the same vicinity as the trailhead detailed above, at the west end of 19th Ave., a short boardwalk trail leads to Camosun Bog, home to a great variety of unique plant- and birdlife.

In the north of the park, north of Chancellor Blvd., trails lead through deep ravines and across Marine Dr. to Arcadia and Spanish Banks Beaches. Walk along these beaches then up any ravine, across Marine Dr., and along Admiral Trail, following the bluffs for a circuit that can be as short or as long as you wish.

For the more ambitious, it is possible to use the trails of Pacific Spirit Park and around Point

Grey to circumnavigate the UBC campus; 14 km roundtrip (allow 4-5 hours).

Burnaby Mountain
This high point of the city, 12 km east of downtown, is best known as the home of Simon Fraser University, but surrounding the campus is a forested wilderness laced with hiking trails. The best starting point is the day-use area at the

WHITEWATER RAFTING

Some of Canada's most exciting whitewater rafting lies right on Vancouver's back doorstep. The Fraser River and its tributaries are the most popular destinations, with commercial operators dotted throughout the region. Whichever operator you go with, and whichever river you choose to run, you'll be in for the trip of a lifetime. The mighty Fraser itself is known for its spectacular canyon and obstacles such as Hell's Gate, while the Thompson claims fame for its high water. Those looking for an extra thrill also run the Nahatlatch, another tributary of the Fraser. All companies include a great lunch (such as a salmon barbecue) and transfers, and charge around $90-100 for a full day. Companies include **Down to Earth Adventures,** tel. (604) 323-6350; **Fraser River Raft Expeditions,** tel. (604) 863-2336 or (800) 363-7238; **Hyak Rafting Adventures,** tel. (604) 734-8622 or (800) 663-7238; **Kumsheen Raft Adventures,** tel. (604) 455-2296 or (800) 663-6667; and **REO Rafting,** tel. (604) 867-9252 or (800) 736-7238.

Vancouver is also the starting point for extended river trips. These usually last one to two weeks and combine the Chilko, Chilcotin, and Fraser Rivers in an unforgettable wilderness trip through a remote tract of land north of the city. The above companies charge from $1,300 for a six-day trip, but worth considering are the trips offered by **Canadian River Expeditions,** tel. (604) 938-6651 or (800) 898-7238, website www.whistler.net/canriver, Canada's oldest rafting company. Its classic expedition is an 11-day trip that begins with a cruise up the coast from Vancouver to Bute Inlet, then a flight over the Coast Mountains to Remote Chilko Lake for the beginning of the three-river float. The cost is $2,895.

very end of Centennial Way (take E. Hastings St. out of the city, turn right onto Burnaby Mountain Parkway, then turn left onto Centennial Way). This high point is a worthy destination in itself, with views extending across Burrard Inlet to the North Shore, but it is also the trailhead for an eight-km (two-and-a-half-hour) circuit of the university campus. The first six km, along Joe's Trail, are through second-growth forest and over many small streams, while the final two km traverse campus grounds.

North Shore

The provincial parks along the North Shore contain outstanding scenery and wildlife, crystal-clear lakes and rivers, and established trails that are generally well maintained and easy to follow. (These trails are covered in the North Shore section of the Sights chapter.)

tively even terrain, quiet roads, loads of sunshine, and ever-changing scenery. For information on touring, tour operators, bicycle routes, and local clubs, contact **Cycling B.C.,** Suite 332, 1367 W. Broadway, Vancouver, BC V6H 4A9, tel. (604) 737-3034, or the **Outdoor Recreation Council of B.C.,** Suite 334, 1367 W. Broadway, Vancouver, BC V6H 4A9, tel. (604) 737-3058. The Outdoor Recreation Council also publishes a series of maps covering much of British Columbia. These maps can by purchased directly from the council or at many sporting-goods stores and bookstores.

Several local companies offer cycling tours, among them **Benno's Adventure Tours,** 3/1975 Maple St., Vancouver, BC V6J 3S9, tel. (604) 738-5105, which offers eight-day trips through B.C. and the Canadian Rockies, with bus lifts between the most spectacular sections

BICYCLING

Stanley Park is a mecca for cyclists; among its network of bike paths is the popular Seawall Promenade, which hugs the coast for 10 km (bike travel is in a counterclockwise direction). On the south side of English Bay, a cycle path runs from Vanier Park to Point Grey and the university, passing some of the city's best beaches on the way. On the north side of Burrard Inlet, hard-core mountain-bike enthusiasts tackle the rough trails of Cypress Provincial Park and Grouse Mountain.

Near the entrance to Stanley Park, where Robson and Denman Streets meet, you'll find a profusion of bike-rental shops. These include **Alley Cat Rentals,** 1779 Robson St., tel. (604) 684-5117; **Bayshore Bicycles,** at 745 Denman St., tel. (604) 688-2453, and at 1601 W. Georgia St., tel. (604) 689-5071; **Spokes Bicycle Rental,** 1798 W. Georgia St., tel. (604) 688-5141; and **Stanley Park Cycle,** 1741 Robson St., tel. (604) 608-1908. Expect to pay from $5 per hour or $15 per day for the most basic bike, $12 per hour or $36 per day for a good mountain bike.

Long-distance

Vancouver is a popular jumping-off point for long-distance cycling trips, with nearby Vancouver Island and the Southern Gulf Islands especially popular. In both cases, you'll find rela-

GOLF

Golf in Vancouver has come a long way since 1892, when a few holes were laid out across the sand dunes of Jericho Beach. Today, the city is blessed with over 50 courses, many of which are open to the public. It is often quoted that in Vancouver it is possible to ski in the morning and golf in the afternoon, and because most courses are open year-round this really is true.

For golf fans, the year's biggest event is the **Air Canada Championship** (formerly the Greater Vancouver Open), a regular stop on the PGA Tour. It is contested at the Arnold Palmer-designed Northview Golf and Country Club, in Surrey, over the first weekend of September. For ticketing information call the club at (604) 576-4653.

The Courses

There's a pitch-and-putt golf course in Stanley Park ($8) and another in Queen Elizabeth Park (also $8), but for serious golfers, the following courses provide a truer test of the game.

One the best courses open to the public is the **University Golf Course,** 5185 University Blvd., Point Grey, tel. (604) 224-1818. The course has no affiliation with its namesake, but does have a strong teaching program. The course itself features fairways lined with mature trees and plays to

6,584 yards. The clubhouse exudes old-world charm and features an adjacent golf museum. Green fees are a reasonable $35; reservations can be made up to a week in advance.

Vancouver Parks and Recreation operates three 18-hole courses on the south side of Central Vancouver: **McCleery Golf Course,** 7188 McDonald St.; **Fraserview Golf Course,** 7800 Vivian Dr.; and **Langara Golf Course,** 6706 Alberta St. (off Cambie St.). Green fees range $34-38 for 18 holes.

Water comes into play on many holes of the **Mayfair Lakes Golf Course,** 5460 No. 7 Rd., Richmond, tel. (604) 276-0505, but its most unique feature is the salmon, which spawn in its waterways. This course plays host to a stop on the Canadian Professional Tour each June but is open to the public the rest of the year, playing a challenging 6,641 yards from the back markers; green fees are from $55.

On the North Shore, **Gleneagles Golf Course** is a short nine-hole layout with ocean views. Operating on a first-come, first-served basis, green fees for nine holes are just $15. It's at 6190 Marine Dr., West Vancouver, tel. (604) 921-7353. Farther north up Howe Sound beyond Porteau Cove is **Furry Creek Golf and Country Club,** tel. (604) 922-9461 or (888) 922-9461, which is generally regarded as one of the most scenic courses in the province. Immaculately manicured, the course is bordered on one side by the driftwood-strewn beaches of Howe Sound and on the other by towering mountains. It is relatively short, at just over 6,000 yards, but water comes into play on many holes, including one where the green juts into the sound and is almost an island. On summer weekends, green fees are $90, with the price of a round decreasing to $80 midweek and as low as $55 the rest of the year. Twilight rates reduce the costs further. All rates include valet parking, a locker, power cart, tees, and a towel.

Of the many golf courses spread out along the Fraser River Valley, **Meadow Gardens Golf Course,** on the north side of the river at 19675 Meadow Gardens Way (off Hwy. 7), Pitt Meadows, tel. (604) 465-5474 or (800) 667-6758, stands out. Water comes into play on 13 holes, including the signature 18th hole, a par 5 that comprises island-only landing areas for the drive and the second shot, and then the approach is played on an island green. Adding to the fun is a course length of a scary 7,041 yards from the back markers. Facilities include a huge clubhouse featuring a restaurant with views, jacuzzis, and a sauna, and a driving range. Green fees start at $40 for 18 holes.

West Coast Golf Shuttle

The West Coast Golf Shuttle, tel. (604) 878-6800 or (888) 599-6800, transports golfers to a "course of the day" and includes hotel pick-ups, a booked tee time, green fees, club, rentals, a power cart, and even umbrellas and sunscreen for a fee of $80-150, depending on the course and day of the week.

WATER SPORTS

Swimming and Sunbathing

All of Vancouver's best beaches are along the shoreline of English Bay; 10 have lifeguards on duty through the summer months 11:30 a.m.-8.45 p.m. Closest to downtown is **English Bay Beach,** at the end of Denman Street. Flanked by a narrow strip of parkland and a wide array of cafés and restaurants, this is *the* beach for people-watching. From English Bay Beach the Seawall Promenade leads north to **Second** and **Third Beaches,** both short, secluded stretches of sand. To the south is **Sunset Beach,** most popular with families.

Swimmers take note: Even at the peak of summer, the water here only warms up to about 17° C (63° F), tops. If that doesn't sound very enticing, continue to the south end of Sunset Beach to **Vancouver Aquatic Centre,** 1050 Beach Ave., tel. (604) 665-3424. Inside is a 50-meter heated pool, saunas, whirlpools, and a small weight room. Admission is adult $5, senior $3.

On the south side of English Bay, **Kitsilano Beach** offers spectacular views back across the bay to downtown and the mountains beyond. Take a dip in the adjacent public pool, which is 137 meters long and was built in 1931. The beach and pool are an easy walk from both Vanier Park and a False Creek Ferries dock.

Canoeing and Kayaking

Granville Island is the center of action for paddlers, and the calm waters of adjacent False

VANCOUVER BEACHES

Vancouver might not be best known for its beaches, and the water is too cold for swimming most of year (but don't tell that to the 2,000-odd locals who take to the water each January for the Polar Bear Swim), but in summer the long stretches of sand that fringe the city are a hive of activity.

The best beaches are along **English Bay,** a shallow body of water between downtown and Central Vancouver. **English Bay Beach,** in the West End, has been a popular summer hangout for Vancouverites since the 1920s, when legendary Joe Fortes began his 25-year-long self-appointed role as local lifeguard. The white, sandy beach is surrounded by parkland, behind which is a crush of beachy boutiques and outdoor cafés and restaurants. To the north, along a seaside promenade, is **Second Beach,** with a large outdoor pool complex, and more secluded **Third Beach.**

On the south side of English Bay is trendy Kitsilano and **"Kits" Beach,** a mecca for sun worshippers and *the* place to be seen on a summer day. The beach extends for over half a kilometer between Arbutus and Trafalgar Streets, backed by a park dotted with trees, picnic tables, and benches. The water off Kits Beach is relatively shallow, meaning the water is warmer than on the north side of the bay. Continuing west is **Jericho Beach** (a bastardization of "Jerry's Cove"), backed by a large park. This stretch of sand gives way to **Locarno Beach** and then **Spanish Banks Beach;** the beaches become less crowded as you travel westward.

The westernmost of these beaches on Point Grey is also Vancouver's most infamous. **Wreck Beach** is a nudist hangout, where the unabashed prance around naked and nude dudes sell hot dogs and pop from driftwood concession stands. Swimming here isn't particularly good, but the beach still gets extremely busy. Access to the beach is down a steep trail from Northwest Marine Dr., near the end of University Blvd. (take Trail No. 4, 5, or 6).

In the south of city, the warm, shallow waters of Boundary Bay are surrounded by sandy beaches. **Point Roberts,** south of Tsawwassen, is a popular swimming spot, as is **Crescent Beach,** across the bay in Surrey. The actual beaches around Boundary Bay are much wider than those at English Bay, and at low tide many spots come alive with shorebirds. One particularly good birdwatching spot is **Blackie Spit;** walk up to the spit from Crescent Beach.

The coastline on the North Shore is generally steep and rocky. The beach at **Ambleside Park,** West Vancouver, is the exception. A few rocky beaches lie along Howe Sound, north of Horseshoe Bay, including **Porteau Beach,** a popular scuba diving spot.

The ocean waters around Vancouver reach a maximum temperature of 17° C midsummer, but swimming is still popular. All the beaches listed above have lifeguards on duty in summer (11:30 a.m.-8:45 p.m.). For the not-so-brave, Second Beach and Kitsilano Beach have outdoor pools where the temperature is considerably warmer than the ocean.

Creek make the perfect place to practice your skills. For the widest choice of equipment, head to **Adventure Fitness,** 1510 Duranleau St., tel. (604) 687-1528, or **Ecomarine Ocean Kayak Centre,** 1668 Duranleau St., tel. (604) 689-7575. Both rent single sea kayaks from $14 for two hours or $25 for 24 hours, and double sea kayaks and canoes from $19 for two hours, $30 for 24 hours. Both companies also teach kayaking.

The **Indian Arm** of Burrard Inlet allows for a real wilderness experience, right on the city's back doorstep. This 18-km-long fjord cuts deeply into the North Shore Range; the only development is at its southern end, where the suburb of Deep Cove provides a takeoff point for the waterway. **Deep Cove Canoe and Kayak Centre,** 2007 Rockcliff Rd., tel. (604) 929-2268, rents canoes and kayaks from $40 per day for a single kayak. If you'd prefer to take a tour, contact the two Granville Island companies listed above or **Lotus Land Tours,** tel. (604) 684-4922 or (800) 528-3531; all charge around $100 pp including lunch. **Bowen Island Sea Kayaking,** tel. (604) 947-9266, operates tours around the waters of Bowen Island, which lies at the mouth of Howe Sound. The company is based at Snug Cove, a short ferry trip from Horseshoe Bay, from where a three-hour paddle costs $50 pp and a seven-hour kayak trip to nearby uninhabited islands costs $90.

The oceanside pool at Kitsilano Beach is over 130 meters long—so there's plenty of room for everyone.

Vancouver is also a jumping-off point for longer trips. The two Granville Island companies listed above operate one or two Strait of Georgia trips each summer, while they are a specialty for **Northern Lights Expeditions,** P.O. Box 4289, Bellingham, WA 98227, tel. (360) 734-6334 or (800) 754-7402, website www.seakayaking.com. Each Northern Lights trip features three knowledgeable guides, all necessary equipment, and an emphasis on gourmet meals, such as shoreline salmon bakes, complete with wine and freshly baked breads. The six-day camping trip is US$1,095, but Northern Lights also offers the luxury of a lodge-based trip for US$1,320.

Boating and Yachting

The calm waters of False Creek and Burrard Inlet are perfect for boating and are always busy with pleasure craft. Beyond the natural harbors of Vancouver, and sheltered from the open ocean by Vancouver Island, island-dotted Strait of Georgia is a boater's paradise. Along its length are

forested coves, sandy beaches, beautiful marine parks, and facilities specifically designed for boaters—many accessible only by water. For the entire rundown on facilities for boaters, pick up a copy of the invaluable *Pacific Yachting Cruising Services Directory,* put out by *Pacific Yachting* magazine. In it are lists of charter companies, boating schools, chart and map sources, sail makers, water taxis, yacht clubs, marinas, and boater-oriented resorts for Vancouver and the entire British Columbia coastline. If you can't find one in the Visitor Info Centres, write to Special Interest Publications, Division of Maclean Hunter, Suite 900, 1130 W. Pender St., Vancouver, BC V6E 4A4.

For puttering around the inner-city waterways, rent a boat from **Stanley Park Boat Rentals,** Coal Harbour Marina, 566 Cardero St., tel. (604) 682-6257, or **Granville Island Boat Rentals,** 1696 Duranleau St., tel. (604) 682-6287. Both companies will suggest a trip to suit your boating ability and time schedule, while also providing bait and tackle and directing you to the fishing hot spots.

Yachties and yachties-to-be should head for **Cooper's Boating Centre,** 1620 Duranleau St., Granville Island, tel. (604) 687-4110, website www.cooper-boating.com, which boasts Canada's largest sailing school and also holds the country's biggest fleet for charters. For those with experience, Cooper's rents yachts ($150 per day for a Catalina 22) for a day's local sailing, or take to the waters of the Strait of Georgia on a bareboat charter (from $1,154 per week for a Catalina 27).

If you're arriving in Vancouver by boat from the U.S., contact Customs Border Services, Regional Information Unit, 333 Dunsmuir St., Vancouver, BC V6B 5R4, tel. (604) 666-0545, for information on official vessel entry points and their hours of operation.

Fishing

The tidal waters of the Pacific Northwest hold some of the world's best fishing, with remote lodges scattered along the coast catering to all budgets. And although most keen anglers will want to head farther afield for the best fishing opportunities, many top fishing spots can be accessed on a day trip from Vancouver. The five species of Pacific salmon are most highly prized by anglers. The chinook (king) salmon in particular is the trophy fish of choice. They commonly weigh over 10 kg and are occasionally caught at over 20 kg (those weighing over 12 kg are often known as "tyee"). Other salmon present are coho (silver), pink (humpback), sockeye (red), and chum (dog). Other species sought by local recreational anglers include halibut, ling cod, rockfish, cod, perch, and snapper.

A resident tidal-water sportfishing license, good for one year from 31 March, costs $22.47 ($11.77 for those 65 and over); for nonresidents of British Columbia, the same license costs $108.07, or $7.49 for a single-day license, $20.33 for three days, and $34.17 for five days. A **salmon conservation stamp** is an additional $6.42. Licenses are available from sporting stores, gas stations, marinas, and charter operators. When fish-tagging programs are on, you may be required to make a note of the date, location, and method of capture, or to record on the back of your license statistical information on the fish you catch. Read the current rules and regulations. For further information contact **Fisheries and Oceans Canada,** Station 415, 555 W. Hastings St., Vancouver, BC V6B 5G3, tel. (604) 666-6331, website www.pac.dfo-mpo.gc.ca.

The **Sport Fishing Institute of British Columbia,** tel. (604) 689-3438, website www.sportfishing.bc.ca, produces an annual magazine (free), *Sport Fishing,* that lists charter operators and fishing lodges and details license requirements.

Freshwater fishing takes place in the larger mountain lakes on the North Shore. Here you'll find stocks of rainbow trout, kokanee (a landlocked trout endemic to British Columbia), and Dolly Varden. Separate licenses are required for freshwater fishing, and as with tidal-water licenses, prices vary according to your age and place of residence. Canadian residents pay $24 for a freshwater adult license, good for one year. Nonresidents pay $41 for a one-year license, or $25 for a six-day license. For more information contact Recreational Fisheries, Ministry of Environment, Lands, and Parks, Parliament Buildings, Victoria, BC V8V 1X4, tel. (250) 387-4573, and request the *British Columbia Freshwater Fishing Regulations Synopsis.*

Scuba Diving

Scuba diving might not be the best-known recreational activity in the Vancouver area, but some of the world's most varied and spectacular cold-water diving lies off the coast in the Strait of Georgia (the legendary Jacques Cousteau once rated the strait second only to the Red Sea). Unfortunately, a plankton bloom reduces visibility considerably through the warmer months, so the best time of year for diving is winter, when the water is at its most frigid. Most winter divers slip into a six-millimeter wetsuit or a drysuit; these can be rented from most dive shops. During winter, visibility is incredible (up to 40 meters), especially offshore. Hundreds of colorful marine species live in nearby waters, and wrecks litter the seabed. At Porteau Beach, north of Horseshoe Bay, wrecks have even been placed just offshore for shore divers to enjoy. The most popular dive sites along the Strait of Georgia are along the Sunshine Coast, accessible by ferry from Horseshoe Bay.

A quick flip through the Vancouver Yellow Pages lets you know that scuba diving is alive and well in this community. The city's many scuba shops have everything you need, and they're excellent sources of information on all the best spots along Georgia Strait. They can also usually tell you who is chartering what, and when. Coming highly recommended is **Rowand's Reef Scuba Shop,** 1512 Duranleau St., Granville Island, tel. (604) 669-3483, a full-service dive shop offering rentals, sales, organized diving trips, and dive-certification courses throughout the year. Available here and in most bookstores are the diver's bibles *101 Dives from the Mainland of Washington and British Columbia* and *99 Dives from the San Juan Islands in Washington to the Gulf Islands and Vancouver Island in British Columbia,* both by Betty Pratt-Johnson, the best source of detailed diving in the strait. *Diver* magazine is another good source of local information; its scuba directory lists retail stores, resorts, charter boats, and other services.

SKIING

While Vancouver is the gateway to world-renowned Whistler/Blackcomb (see the special topic Skiing at Whistler/Blackcomb), the city boasts three other downhill ski resorts on its back doorstep. They don't offer the terrain or facilities of Whistler, and their low elevations can create unreliable conditions, but a day's skiing at any one of the three sure beats being

SKIING AT WHISTLER/BLACKCOMB

No matter what your ability, the skiing at Whistler/Blackcomb, 120 km north of Vancouver, makes for a winter holiday you won't forget in a hurry. Until the 1997-98 season, the ski area, consistently rated as North America's No. 1 ski destination, comprised two different resorts that in themselves boasted impressive statistics. Combined, they now overshadow all other North American resorts in terms of size and stature. The two lift-served mountains, Whistler and Blackcomb, are separated by a steep-sided valley through which Fitzsimmons Creek flows, with lifts converging at Whistler Village. Skiing is over 2,874 hectares (7,070 acres), comprising more than 200 groomed runs, hundreds of unmarked trails through forested areas, three glaciers, and 12 bowls. Blackcomb and Whistler Mountains are 2,284 meters and 2,182 meters high, respectively. The lift-served vertical rise of Blackcomb is 1,609 meters (5,280 feet), the highest in North America, but Whistler is only slightly lower at 1,530 meters. (When Blackcomb and Whistler operated as separate entities, they boasted North America's highest and second-highest vertical rise). In total, the resort has 32 lifts, including three gondolas, 10 quad chairlifts, six triples, one double, four T-bars, two platters, and six rope tows. The terrain is rated intermediate over 55% of the resort, with the remaining 45% split evenly between beginner and expert. Snowboarders are well catered to with four snowboard parks and numerous half pipes. The length of season is also impressive, running from November to May with the Horstman Glacier open for skiing for a few weeks of summer.

For many skiers, the resort can be overwhelming. Trail maps detail all marked runs, but they can't convey the vast size of the area. A great way to get to know the mountain is on an orientation tour; these leave throughout the day from various meeting points (ask when and where when you buy your ticket) and are free. **Whistler/Blackcomb Ski and Snowboard School,** tel. (604) 932-3434 or (800) 766-0449, is the country's largest ski school, offering a great variety of lesson packages and programs such as the Esprit, a three-day, women's only "camp" that provides instruction in a variety of disciplines.

Lift tickets are adult $59, senior and youth $50, child $29, and those under seven ski for free. For general resort information call (604) 932-3434 or (800) 766-0449; for snow reports call (604) 932-4211 or, from Vancouver, (604) 687-7507. The resort's website is www.whistler-blackcomb.com.

Staying at Whistler
Development of the ski resort has been mirrored by development along the Whistler Valley. Most accommodations are top end, but a few less-expensive choices do exist, such as **Hostelling International Whistler,** Alta Lake Rd., tel. (604) 932-5492. For anything within walking distance of the ski lifts or **Whistler Village,** expect to pay from $200 per night in winter. The easiest way to book Whistler accommodations is through **Whistler Central Reservations,** tel. (604) 664-5625 or (800) 944-7853, website www.whistler-resort.com.

Summer or winter, Vancouver locals always find a way to enjoy the great outdoors.

stuck in the hustle and bustle of the city on a cold winter's day.

Grouse Mountain

Towering above North Vancouver, the cut slopes of this ski area can be seen from many parts of the city, but as you'd expect, on a clear day views from *up there* are much more spectacular. To get there, take Capilano Rd. north from the TransCanada, following it onto Nancy Greene Way, from where a gondola lifts you up 1,000 vertical meters to the slopes. Four chairlifts and a couple of T-bars serve a vertical rise of 365 meters. Advanced skiers shouldn't get too excited about a day's skiing here—even the runs with names like Inferno and Purgatory are pretty tame. But skiing the slopes of Grouse Mountain after dark is an experience you won't soon forget. Most runs are lit and overlook the city of Vancouver, laid out in all its brilliance far below. Facilities at the resort include a rental shop, ski school, and a couple of dining choices. Lift tickets are $30 per day. For more information call (604) 986-0661; for a snow report call (604) 986-6262.

Cypress Bowl

In Cypress Provincial Park, this ski area offers about 25 runs on a vertical rise of 534 meters. Its four double chairs open a wide variety of terrain, most suited to beginners and intermediates. Spectacular views take in Howe Sound and Vancouver Island. Another highlight of Cypress Bowl is the night skiing; many runs are lit until 11 p.m. Other facilities include a rental shop, ski school, café, and lounge. Lift tickets are $35 per day. Cypress Bowl also caters to cross-country skiers; of the resort's 16 km of groomed trails, most are set around the historic Hollyburn Lodge and lit for night skiing.

To get to the ski area, take the TransCanada Hwy. 12 km west from Lions Gate Bridge and turn north on Cypress Bowl Road. If you don't feel like driving up the mountain, catch the shuttle bus that departs hourly from Cypress Mountain Sports in Park Royal Mall, West Vancouver; $8 roundtrip. Cypress Mountain Sports also rents equipment and offers an overnight repair service. For ski area and shuttle bus information, call (604) 926-5612; for a snow report call (604) 419-7669.

Seymour Ski Country

With the highest base elevation of Vancouver's three ski areas, Seymour's snow is somewhat reliable, but the area's relatively gentle terrain will be of interest only to beginning and intermediate skiers. Four chairlifts serve 20 runs and a vertical rise of 365 meters. The emphasis is on learning at this hill, and a line of instructors always awaits your business. On-hill facilities include a massive day lodge with rental shop. Lift tickets are $28 per day.

The ski area is in Mt. Seymour Provincial Park. To get there, head north off the Trans-Canada Hwy. 15 km east of the Lions Gate Bridge, following the Mt. Seymour Parkway to Mt. Seymour Road. For resort information call (604) 986-2261; for a snow report call (604) 879-3999.

SPECTATOR SPORTS

Ice Hockey

In 1911 the world's largest artificial ice rink opened in Vancouver, and just four years later Vancouver won its first and only **Stanley Cup,**

Practicing for the big time?

the holy grail of professional ice hockey. The team of today is known as the **Vancouver Canucks,** and although the glory days of Tiger Williams and Darcy Roda are long gone and the team struggles to get the best players in a U.S.-dollar-oriented market, the team is still competitive, and came close to reclaiming the Cup in 1994 when it reached the finals against the New York Rangers. In the mid-'90s, after playing at the Pacific Coliseum for 25 years, they moved to General Motors Place (known locally as "The Garage"), across from B.C. Place Stadium on Griffith Way. The season runs from October to April; ticket prices range $24-61. For more information call (604) 899-4625 or 280-4400, or check out website www.orcabay.com/canucks.

Basketball
In 1995 Vancouver was awarded a franchise with the National Basketball Association, becoming the 29th team in the NBA and the first Canadian team to join the league since 1946. The 20,000-seat General Motors Place was built specially for the team, which was named the **Grizzlies** and given a distinctive red, bronze, and turquoise color scheme. Season tickets sold out for that first season within a month, and although the team always languishes well below pre-season hype, it is still on a learning curve (don't ask local fans about the very unenviable "records" held by the team). In the meantime, basketball-mad Vancouverites get the opportunity to see the sport's biggest names demolish their home team. General Motors Place is at 800 Griffith Way. For Grizzlies information call (604) 899-4667 or 280-4400, or go online to website www.orcabay.com.grizzlies.

Football
The **B.C. Lions,** tel. (604) 589-7627 or 280-4400, website www.bclions.com, are Vancouver's Canadian Football League franchise. (American football fans might be surprised by some of the plays—the rules are slightly different than those of the NFL. And no, you're not imagining things, the playing field is larger than those used in the game's American version.) CFL teams have been competing for the Grey Cup, named for Earl Grey, a former governor-general of Canada, since 1909. In recent years, the Lions have struggled to gain a large support base, but

they continue to perform well and last won the Grey Cup in 1994. Home games are played at B.C. Place Stadium, on the south side of downtown at the corner of Robson and Beatty Streets, tel. (604) 669-2300. The season runs June-Nov.; tickets range $13.50-43.

Soccer
Vancouver's professional soccer team, the **86ers,** competes in the American Professional Soccer League throughout summer. They play against teams from across the continent and boast one of the winningest teams in all professional sport. Home games are played at Swangard Stadium, in Burnaby's Central Park. To get there, take the Kingsway out of the city to Patterson Avenue. For information and tickets call (604) 589-7627. The team's website is www.86ers.com.

Horse Racing
Thoroughbred racing takes place in Exhibition Park at **Hastings Park Racecourse,** six km east of downtown on the corner of Renfrew and McGill Streets, tel. (604) 254-1631. Full betting and a variety of dining facilities are offered. The season runs April-Oct., with the first race starting at 1:30 p.m. on weekends and 6:30 p.m. on Wednesday and Friday.

TOURS

If you don't have a lot of time to explore Vancouver on your own, or just want an introduction to the city, consider one of the many tours available—they'll maximize your time and get you to the highlights with minimum stress.

Bus Tours
Gray Line, tel. (604) 879-3363, offers a large variety of tours. The three-and-a-half-hour Deluxe Grand Tour, which includes Stanley Park, Grouse Mountain, Chinatown, Gastown, Robson Street, and English Bay, costs $40 per person. Another option with Gray Line is a downtown loop tour aboard an old English double-decker bus. You can get on and off as you please at 22 stops made on the two-hour loop. Tickets cost adult $24, senior $23, child $13 and are valid for two consecutive days. Farther afield, Gray Line has daily tours from Vancouver to

Whistler, $63, and a 12-hour tour to Vancouver Island, $102. All ticket prices include pick-ups at major downtown hotels.

More personalized tours are run by **Rockwood Adventures,** tel. (604) 926-7705. On its two-hour Stanley Park tour, guides describe local natural and human history and take you to all the best viewpoints; $24 per person. The company also offers a guided walk along the Capilano River with a visit to a fish hatchery; four hours, $38 per person.

Vancouver Trolley Company

From the main pick-up point, a trolley-shaped booth at the top end of Water St., this company operates an old-fashioned trolley through the streets of downtown Vancouver. The two-hour loop stops at 16 tourist attractions, from Stanley Park in the north to Science World in the south. Trolleys run April-Oct. daily 9 a.m.-4 p.m., coming by each stop every half hour. Tickets are adult $18, child $10. In July and August an extra loop is made, starting at 7 p.m. in Gastown, with hotel pick-ups until 7:40 p.m., then it's off on a two-hour tour through downtown, to Stanley Park, and as far away as Queen Elizabeth Gardens; adult $22, child $10. Reservations aren't necessary, but for more information call (604) 801-5515 or (888) 451-5581.

Harbor Cruises

From June to September, **Harbour Cruises,** tel. (604) 688-7246 or (800) 663-1500, offers a 70-minute tour of bustling Burrard Inlet on the paddlewheeler MV *Constitution.* Tours depart from the north foot of Denman St., Coal Harbour, three times daily; adult $15, senior and student $13. In the evening (7 p.m. departure), the paddlewheeler heads out onto the harbor for a three-hour Sunset Dinner Cruise. The cruise costs $55, which includes dinner and, if booked through Gray Line (tel. 604-879-3363), hotel transfers. This same company operates the MV *Britannia,* which departs daily at 9:30 a.m. for a cruise up Howe Sound to Squamish. This trip is best taken in conjunction with the Royal Hudson steam train (see below) for adult $77.57, senior $65.54, child $21.40, which includes transfers between the train station and Coal Harbour.

While puttering around False Creek on a small ferry is an inexpensive way to see this part of the city from water level, **False Creek Ferries,** tel. (604) 684-7781, also offers a 30-minute guided tour of the historic waterway for just $6 per person. Departures are daily 10 a.m.-5 p.m. from below Bridges Restaurant on Granville Island.

Royal Hudson

The only steam train in North America that runs a scheduled service along a main line track is the *Royal Hudson,* which departs daily from Vancouver for a day tour up to Squamish. The trip is spectacular. Squamish lies at the head of Howe Sound, and along the way the train is always in sight of the water and snowcapped peaks (sit on the left-hand side of the train on the outward journey for the best views), while on the other side the Coast Mountains rise precipitously, densely forested and with numerous waterfalls cascading down their slopes. The trip takes two hours each way, with two hours allotted in Squamish to visit the

THE REMARKABLE TERRY FOX

Vancouver-born Terry Fox is a name that is sure to come up at some point on your Canadian travels. In 1977, as a college-bound teenager, Fox lost his right leg to cancer. On 12 April 1980, after three years of training, with next to no sponsorship and little media coverage, he set off from Newfoundland on his **Marathon of Hope,** with the aim of raising money for cancer research. After running over 5,000 km in 144 days, a recurrence of the cancer forced him to stop just outside Ontario's Thunder Bay. Cancer had begun spreading to his lungs, and on 28 June 1981, aged just 22, he died. As his run had progressed, the attention had grown, and, more importantly, the donations poured in. In total, his Marathon of Hope raised $24 million, far surpassing all goals.

The legacy of Terry Fox lives on in many ways, including the Terry Fox Run, an annual fall event in many Canadian towns, and a $5 million scholarship fund. In Vancouver, the B.C. Sports Hall of Fame and Museum holds a tribute to the courage of Terry Fox, and in the adjacent **Terry Fox Plaza,** at the foot of Robson St., a pagoda-style arch made of steel, brick, and tile and topped by four lions has been erected in his honor.

local heritage park and for lunch. It departs daily mid-May to the end of September from the B.C. Rail terminal, 1311 W. 1st St., North Vancouver, tel. (604) 984-5246 or (800) 663-8238. Roundtrip fare is adult $47.50, senior $41, child $12.75. Travel in the more luxurious Parlour Car or Private Club Car is $75 pp regardless of age and includes either brunch or high tea. A train/boat package is also offered, allowing visitors to take the *Royal Hudson* in one direction and the **MV Britannia** (which cruises Howe Sound between Squamish and downtown Vancouver) in the other. The fare for the combination trip is adult $77.57, senior $65.54, child $21.40.

Flightseeing

Flightseeing tours of the city are offered by **Harbour Air,** from its seaplane base on the west side of Canada Place, tel. (604) 688-1277. A 20-minute flight is $72 pp, or include the Southern Gulf Islands and the Sunshine Coast on a two-hour flight for $189 pp. **Vancouver Helicopters,** based at a heliport on the east side of Canada Place (enter through Waterfront Station), tel. (604) 270-1484, offers a short flight for $55 pp, or fly over the heart of downtown, Stanley Park, and across to the North Shore for $195 pp. This company also offers flights from the top of Grouse Mountain.

ARTS AND ENTERTAINMENT

There's never a dull moment in Vancouver. For complete listings of all that's happening around the city, pick up the free *Georgia Strait* (weekly), or buy a copy of one of the two daily newspapers, the *Province* or the *Vancouver Sun.* Another source of information is the Vancouver Cultural Alliance's **Arts Hotline,** tel. (604) 684-2787.

Call **Ticketmaster,** tel. (604) 280-3311, website www.ticketmaster.ca, and have your credit card ready to purchase tickets for all major entertainment events.

DRINKING AND DANCING

Ever since "Gassy Jack" Deighton set up the city's first liquor outlet (a barrel of whiskey set atop a crude plank "bar") in the area that became known as Gastown, Vancouver has had its favorite watering holes. Deighton located his saloon to take advantage of a liquor ban in the adjacent company town; over 100 years later Vancouver's liquor laws are still regarded by many as antiquated. The laws *have* been relaxed, though. Until 1964, most bars had sections reserved for men only, as recently as the 1970s live entertainment was prohibited in bars, and until Expo86 no alcohol could be served on Sunday unless accompanied by food. Two important laws remain: most controversially, no alcohol can be served after 2 a.m., and no liquor store sales are allowed on Sunday.

The legal drinking age varies throughout Canada. In British Columbia it is 19. Driving drunk is a criminal offense. The provincial blood-alcohol limit is .08%.

Bars

In the historic building The Landing, at 375 Water St., **Steamworks Brewing Co.,** tel. (604) 689-2739, is the perfect place to relax with a beer from the in-house brewery. The atmosphere is casual yet stylish, and you'll have great views across Burrard Inlet. Hours are 11:30 a.m.-10 p.m. daily. In the same part of the city, but toward Chinatown, the lively **Blarney Stone** pub, 216 Carrall St., tel. (604) 687-4322, frequently resounds with rowdy impromptu Irish sing-alongs. In the same vein, across the road is the **Irish Heather,** 217 Carrall St., tel. (604) 688-9779, renowned for its Guinness. This part of downtown also holds some of the city's worst bars, but the beer is cheap and the atmosphere, well, different. The best of a bad bunch is the **Balmoral,** 159 E. Hastings, with occasional live music, and the **Grand Union,** 74 W. Hastings, where country music is blasted throughout the day and night.

In trendy Yaletown, **Bar None,** 1222 Hamilton St., tel. (604) 689-7000, has a band playing Mon.-Thurs. nights and a DJ cranking tunes on weekends; it's open daily from 8 p.m.

Toward the West End, **Joe Fortes Seafood and Chop House,** 777 Thurlow St., tel. (604) 669-1940, boasts a great bar, complete with a wide range of beers and a condensed menu from the adjacent restaurant.

Checkers, 1755 Davie St., West End, tel. (604) 682-1831, is another popular bar, this one with a distinctive checkered decor and live rock on weekends.

The small but always lively **Stamp's Landing Neighbourhood Pub** overlooks False Creek at 610 Stamp's Landing (just east of Granville Island), tel. (604) 879-0821. Aside from beer and liquor, Stamp's offers delicious tasty snacks to keep you going, live music on weekends, and great sunset views overlooking the harbor. On Granville Island itself, the **Backstage Lounge,** 1585 Johnston St., has a few outdoor tables with water views.

Across Burrard Inlet from downtown, the **Rusty Gull Neighbourhood Pub,** 175 E. 1st St. in North Vancouver, tel. (604) 988-5585, features more than a dozen locally brewed beers. Another favorite north of Burrard Inlet, **Queens Cross Neighbourhood Pub** on Upper Lonsdale at the corner of Queens Rd., tel. (604) 980-7715, is a favorite local hangout for lunch, after-work drinks, conversation, and evening meals.

Nightclubs

Nightclubs change names and reputations with regularity, so check with the free entertainment newspapers for the latest hot spots. Along with the cover charge, drink prices can be outrageous, so be prepared to overspend your budget if you plan on drinking and dancing the night away.

The city's most popular Top 40 nightclub is the **Big Bam Boo,** 1236 W. Broadway, Kitsilano, tel. (604) 733-2220. It's open Wed.-Sun. from 8 p.m. Cover charge is just $4 and drinks are reasonably priced, which attracts droves of students from the nearby UBC campus. Best known as Dick's on Dicks, **Richard's on Richards,** 1036 Richards St., tel. (604) 687-6794, competes in the same mainstream market. It's most popular with the over 30s, but is still pretty much a meat market. The best place to escape the schmoozing is the second-floor shooter bar, which has a good view back down to the dance floor.

Heading into a new millennium, **Sonar,** 66 Water St., tel. (604) 683-6695, has grown to become one of the hottest Vancouver nightspots. Many DJs are imported from London, and most nights feature the latest techno, hip hop, and house music from across the Atlantic. Apart from Sonar, downtown nightclubs are concentrated south of Granville Street. The hottest of these is **Wett Bar** (formerly MaRS), 1320 Richards St., tel. (604) 662-7077. The centerpiece is a massive dance floor featuring a hanging light system that produces incredible effects. Above this a moving re-creation of the Milky Way is projected onto the high ceiling, and below the dance floor is imbedded with thousands of lights. The video system (claimed to be the most technologically advanced in the world) includes a six-meter fiber-optic screen and effects that wouldn't seem out of place in Hollywood. At **Stone Temple,** 1082 Granville St., tel. (604) 488-1333, a DJ spins hip hop, retro, and top 40 discs nightly until 4 a.m. Denizens of the alternative-music scene might want to check out **Luv-A-Fair,** around the corner at 1275 Seymour St., tel. (604) 685-3288. A few years ago, heading to the **Rage,** 750 Pacific Blvd., tel. (604) 685-5585, *was* all the rage. It has been surpassed in popularity by the above venues, but it still cranks out music from a sound system that is generally regarded as the loudest in the city.

LIVE MUSIC AND COMEDY

Rock

The world's biggest rock acts usually include Vancouver on their world tours, and the city's thriving local rock industry supports live bands at a variety of venues. Most big-name acts play the Orpheum or Queen Elizabeth Theatres. At the classic **Roxy,** 932 Granville St., tel. (604) 331-7999, bands play rock 'n' roll music from the '60s, '70s, and '80s. It's open nightly from 7 p.m.; cover charges range $5-10. A similar venue is the **Starfish Room,** 1055 Homer St., tel. (604) 682-4171, although the acts have been more alternative recently. For bands, dancing, video, and a piano lounge head for the **Town Pump,** 66 Water St. in Gastown, tel. (604) 683-6695. It isn't the best laid-out of venues, but it attracts occasional big-name acts. The **Railway Club,** 579 Dunsmuir St., tel. (604) 681-1625, is a private club where nonmembers are welcome (at a higher cover charge) to listen to acts ranging from rock to country.

The Yale Hotel is one of Vancouver's favorite blues venues.

Jazz and Blues

The **Hot Jazz Society,** 2120 Main St., Central Vancouver, tel. (604) 873-4131, presents live jazz on a regular basis; cover charge is $6-9. The **Coastal Jazz and Blues Society,** tel. (604) 682-0706, maintains a listing of all the city's jazz and blues events.

Serious blues lovers should head to the historic **Yale Hotel,** 1300 Granville St., tel. (604) 681-9253, which has hosted some of the greatest names in the business. The hotel offers plenty of room for everyone, whether you want get up and dance or shoot pool down in the back. Sunday is the only night without live performances, although a jam session starts up about 3 p.m. on Saturday and Sunday afternoons. Drinks are expensive and a $7 cover charge is collected Thurs.-Sat. nights. The **Purple Onion,** next to the Old Spaghetti Factory at 15 Water St. in Gastown, tel. (604) 602-9442, features live jazz and blues most nights of the week. Admission is free before 9 p.m. Also downtown, the **Wedge-wood Hotel,** 845 Hornby St., tel. (604) 689-7777, features a resident blues guitarist performing nightly in the hotel's stylish lounge. No cover, but the drinks aren't cheap.

Comedy

Yuk Yuk's, 750 Pacific Blvd. S (Plaza of Nations), tel. (604) 687-5233, offers comedy nights Wed.-Saturday. Admission costs $4 on Wednesday (amateur night), $7.50 on Thursday, $14 on Friday and Saturday nights. In New West-minster, **Lafflines,** 26 4th Ave., tel. (604) 525-2262, offers a similar program and attracts acts from throughout Canada. Wednesday through Sunday, the Arts Club, tel. (604) 687-1644, hosts a TheatreSports League of improvised comedy on its New Revue Stage, Granville Island.

PERFORMING ARTS

Theater

Vancouver has theaters all over the city—for professional plays, amateur plays, comedy, and "instant" theater. One of the great joys of summer in the city is sitting around Malkin Bowl in Stanley Park watching **Theatre under the Stars,** Mon.-Sat. at 7 p.m.; $18 per person. For details of what's on call (604) 687-0174. Another summer production is **Bard on the Beach,** tel. (604) 739-0559, a celebration of the work of Shakespeare that takes place in huge, open-ended tents in Vanier Park. Tickets are well priced at just $20-25.

The **Ford Centre for the Performing Arts,** 777 Homer St., tel. (604) 844-2801, opened in November 1995 to host the biggest musical hits. Designed by renowned architect Moshe Safdie, the modern wonder features a five-story glass lobby flanked by granite walls. The trilevel theater seats over 1,800 and boasts North America's largest stage. Matinees cost from $50 while evening shows range $55-90. One-hour tours of the complex depart from the lobby Mon.-Sat. at 10 a.m.; $4 per person. A similar facility is the **Chan Centre for the Performing Arts,** on the UBC campus at 6265 Crescent Rd., tel. (604) 822-2697.

The **Arts Club,** tel. (604) 687-1644, always offers excellent theater productions at two Granville Island locations—the **New Revue Stage** and adjacent **Mainstage.** Productions range from drama to comedy to improv. Tickets run $21-35; book in advance and pick up your tickets at the door 30 minutes prior to showtime. Another venue for the Arts Club is the restored **Stanley Theatre,** on Granville Street, south of the island at 12th Avenue.

Since its inception in 1964, the **Playhouse,** 543 W. 7th Ave. in Central Vancouver, tel. (604) 665-3050, has grown to become the city's largest theater company. Seven productions are performed each year, with 8 p.m. start times and tickets ranging $31-42. Matinees (2 p.m.) cost around half the price of evening performances. Also in Central Vancouver, **Vancouver Little Theatre,** 3102 Main St., tel. (604) 876-4165, features productions by national and international companies, as well as works by up-and-coming local artists. Expect to pay $8-15.

For university productions, head out to **Frederic Wood Theatre,** on the UBC campus, tel. (604) 822-2678. Performances run throughout the academic year; admission is generally around $10.

Music and Dance

The Queen Elizabeth Theatre, in the Queen Elizabeth Complex at 630 Hamilton St., is the home of **Vancouver Opera,** tel. (604) 683-0222, and the primary venue for **Ballet British Columbia,** tel. (604) 732-5003. Tickets to the opera begin at $35 rising to $90 for the best seats, while ballet tickets range $18-45; call Ticketmaster at (604) 280-3311. The theater also hosts a variety of music recitals and stage performances.

The historic Orpheum Theatre, on the corner of Smithe and Seymour Streets, dates to 1927 and houses its original Wurlitzer organ. Now fully restored, the theater provides excellent acoustics for the resident **Vancouver Symphony,** tel. (604) 684-9100, as well as for concerts by the professional **Vancouver Chamber Choir,** tel. (604) 738-6822, the amateur **Vancouver Bach Choir,** tel. (604) 921-8012, and a variety of other musical groups.

CINEMAS

Cinemas are in all the major shopping malls and elsewhere throughout the city. Combined, **Cineplex Odeon,** tel. (604) 434-2463, and **Famous Players,** tel. (604) 681-4255, operate 20 cinemas in Vancouver. Call the respective numbers or check the two daily papers for locations and screenings. Admission to first-run screenings is about $8.

The **Paradise Theatre,** 919 Granville St., tel. (604) 681-1732, features commercial hits for the bargain-basement price of $5. If you're staying at a Robson Street or West End accommodation, head over to **Denman Place Discount Cinema,** corner of Denman and Comox Streets, tel. (604) 683-2201, for first- and second-run hits for $2.50-5. For foreign and fringe films, check out **Pacific Cinematheque,** 1131 Howe St., tel. (604) 688-8202.

IMAX

At the far end of Canada Place, the **CN IMAX Theatre,** tel. (604) 682-4629, provides spectacular movie entertainment and special effects on a five-story-high screen with wraparound surround sound. Films are generally on the world's natural wonders and last around 45 minutes, with two or three features showing each day, beginning around noon. Ticket prices range $8-11.50, or catch a double feature for a few bucks extra.

SHOPPING

Vancouver has shopping centers, malls, and specialty stores everywhere. Head to Gastown for native arts and crafts, Robson Street for boutique clothing, Granville Mall for department stores, Granville Island for everything from ships' chandlery to kids' clothing, Yaletown for the trendy clothes of local designers, E. Hastings Street for army-surplus stores and pawnbrokers, Chinatown for Eastern foods, and the junction of Main Street and 49th Avenue in Central Vancouver for Indian goods.

Before you set out, drop in at Vancouver Visitor Info Centre, 200 Burrard St., and ask for the free *Shopping Guide*. In addition to listing all the department stores and specialty shops you're likely to want to visit, the guide contains handy foldout maps of downtown Vancouver and Greater Vancouver, with all the shops and malls marked.

Gastown
Sandwiched between the many cafés, restaurants, and tacky souvenir stores along Water Street are other stores selling Vancouver's best selection of native arts and crafts. One of the largest outlets, **Hill's Indian Crafts,** 165 Water St., tel. (604) 685-4249, sells $10 T-shirts, towering $12,000 totem poles, and everything in between, including genuine Cowichan sweaters and carved ceremonial masks. Also featuring traditional native art is **Images for a Canadian Heritage,** 164 Water St., tel. (604) 685-7046.

The **Inuit Gallery of Vancouver,** 345 Water St., tel. (604) 688-7323, is in The Landing, a waterfront warehouse built in 1905 and completely restored to a stylish arcade featuring such luminaries as Polo–Ralph Lauren. The gallery exhibits the work of Inuit and northwest coast native artists and sculptors. Among the highlights are many soapstone pieces by carvers from Cape Dorset.

Down the street from Hill's Indian Crafts, **Kites on Clouds,** 131 Water St., tel. (604) 669-5677, sells hundreds of different kites, from the simplest designs to elaborate constructions priced at over $200. The **Western Canada Wilderness Committee Store,** 227 Abbott St., tel. (604) 687-2567, features environmentally friendly souvenirs including shirts, posters, and calendars. A

couple of blocks from Water St. in the Sinclair Centre is **Dorothy Grant,** 757 W. Hastings St., tel. (604) 681-0201, a clothing store named for its owner. Dorothy and her husband are renowned for their contemporary Haida-inspired designs. The **Sinclair Centre** itself is a local landmark; its four historic buildings now hold galleries, boutiques, and food outlets.

Granville Island
Arts and crafts galleries on Granville Island include **Wickaninnish Gallery,** 1666 Johnston St., tel. (604) 681-1057, selling stunning native art, jewelry, carvings, weaving, and original paintings; **Gallery of B.C. Ceramics,** 1359 Cartwright St., tel. (604) 669-5645, showcasing the work of the province's leading potters and sculptors; and **Forge and Form,** 1334 Cartwright St., tel.

Granville Island is home to a great variety of maritime-based businesses and shops.

SHOPPING FOR NATIVE ARTS AND CRAFTS

Indigenous artistry tends to fall into one of two categories: "arts" such as woodcarving and painting, argillite carving, jade and silverwork, and totem restoration (all generally attended to by the men); and "handicrafts" such as basketry, weaving, beadwork, skinwork, sewing, and knitting (generally created by the women).

Painting and woodcarving are probably the most recognized art forms of the Pacific Northwest. Throughout the city—in museums and people's homes, outdoors, and of course for sale in shops—you can see brightly colored carved totems, canoes, paddles, fantastic masks, and ceremonial rattles, feast dishes, bowls, and spoons. Fabulous designs, many featuring animals or mythical legends, are also painstakingly painted in bright primary colors on paper. You can buy limited-edition, high-quality prints of these paintings at many Indian craft outlets. They are more reasonable in cost than carvings, yet just as stunning when effectively framed.

Basketry comes in a variety of styles and materials. Look for decorative cedar-root (fairly rare) and cedar-bark baskets, still made on the west coast of Vancouver Island; spruce-root baskets from the Queen Charlotte Islands; and beautiful, functional, birch-bark baskets from the northern interior of British Columbia.

Beaded and fringed moccasins, jackets, vests, and gloves are available at most craft outlets. And all outdoorspersons should consider forking out

for a heavy, water-resistant, raw sheep-wool **Cowichan** sweater; they're generally white or gray with a black design, much in demand because they are warm, good in the rain, rugged, and last longer than one lifetime. The best place to get your hands on one is the Cowichan Valley on Vancouver Island, although you can also find them in native craft outlets in Vancouver. Expect to pay $120-200 for the real thing.

Carved argillite (black slate) miniature totem poles, brooches, ashtrays, and other small items, highly decorated with geometric and animal designs, are created exclusively by the Haida on the Queen Charlotte Islands; the argillite comes from an island quarry that can be used only by the local band, but the carvings are widely available in Vancouver. Silverwork is also popular, and some of the best is created by the Haida. Particularly notable is the work of Bill Reid, a Haida artist living in Vancouver.

(604) 684-6298, which creates and sells a variety of gold and silver jewelry.

Duranleau St. is home to many maritime-based businesses, adventure-tour operators, and charter operators. The **Quarterdeck,** 1660 Duranleau St., tel. (604) 683-8232, stocks everything from marine charts to brass shipping bells. **The Ocean Floor,** 1525 Duranleau St., tel. (604) 681-5014, sells a similar range of treasures, including seashells and model ships. To buy a sea kayak or canoe (from $1,100 secondhand), head to **Adventure Fitness,** 1528 Duranleau St., tel. (604) 687-1528, or **Ecomarine Ocean Kayak Centre,** 1668 Duranleau St., tel. (604) 689-7575. Both shops also carry related equipment, books,

and nautical charts. Before heading over to Vancouver Island, divers pick up gear at **Rowand's Reef Scuba Shop,** 1512 Duranleau St., tel. (604) 669-3483.

Department Stores, Plazas, and Malls

Despite looking pretty dowdy these days, **Granville Mall** nevertheless forms the heart of the downtown shopping precinct; the two-block stretch of Granville St. is closed to private vehicles, though buses and taxis still pass through. Here you'll find the city's largest department store, **The Bay,** 674 Granville St., tel. (604) 681-6211, a Canadian chain that evolved from the historic Hudson's Bay Company. Today the store emphasizes Canadian goods, from souvenirs to household appliances. Also on the mall, the **Pacific Centre** features 165 shops, a massive food court, and a three-story-high waterfall. In the center's southwest corner, you'll find **Oh Yes, Vancouver,** a great place to shop for colorful city souvenirs.

Across Lions Gate Bridge in West Vancouver are a couple of shopping centers worth a mention. In a scenic location at Marine Dr. and Taylor Way, **Park Royal Shopping Centre** holds almost 200 shops and three department stores. It's open seven days a week. Also on the north side of Burrard Inlet is **Lonsdale Quay Market,** the terminus of the SeaBus from downtown. This bustling center features a great fresh food market on the first floor and a range of boutiques and galleries on the second.

British Columbia's largest shopping complex, **Metrotown,** houses more than 200 shops. It's on the Kingsway in Burnaby; get there from downtown on the SkyTrain.

Outdoor and Camping Gear

A small stretch of W. Broadway, between Main and Cambie Streets, holds Vancouver's largest concentration of outdoor equipment stores. The largest of these, and the largest in British Columbia, is **Mountain Equipment Co-op,** 130 W. Broadway, tel. (604) 872-7858. Like the American R.E.I stores, it is a cooperative owned by its members; to make a purchase, you must be a member (a once-only charge of $5). The store holds a massive selection of clothing, climbing and mountaineering equipment, tents, backpacks, sleeping bags, books, and other accessories. It's open Mon.-Wed. 10 a.m.-7 p.m., Thurs.-Fri. 10 a.m.-9 p.m., Saturday 9 a.m.-6 p.m. To order a copy of the mail-order catalog, call (800) 663-2667. One block west, **Great Outdoors Equipment Co.,** 222 W. Broadway, tel. (604) 872-8872, sells a similar range of gear and has a particularly wide choice of footwear. Next door, **Helly Hansen,** 202 W. Broadway, tel. (604) 872-7858, specializes in high-quality clothing.

FESTIVALS AND EVENTS

Festivals of some description take place in Vancouver just about every month of the year. Whether it's a celebration of local or international culture, the arts, sporting events, or just a wacky long-time tradition, there's always a reason to party in Vancouver. Most of the most popular festivals are held during summer, the peak visitor season, but the rest of the year is the main season for performances by the city's dance, theater, and music companies, and not-to-be-missed events such as the Christmas Carol Ship Parade. For details and exact dates of the events listed below contact the numbers given, or visit any local tourist information center. Tickets for most major events can be booked through **Ticketmaster;** for the arts call (604) 280-3311, for sporting events call (604) 280-4400.

SPRING

Vancouver Playhouse
International Wine Festival
• When: April
• Where: Vancouver Convention and Exhibition Centre

• Contact: tel. (604) 873-3311, website www.winefest.sympatico.ca

---

PUBLIC HOLIDAYS

Vancouver celebrates 10 statutory holidays, most of which coincide with dates across the nation. Most businesses are closed on these days, but you can always find open some restaurants, pubs, and stores selling basic necessities.

The officially recognized holidays are:

New Year's Day, 1 January

Good Friday, March or April

Victoria Day, closest Monday to 24 May

Canada Day, 1 July

B.C. Day, first Monday in August

Labour Day, first Monday in September

Thanksgiving, second Monday in October

Remembrance Day, 11 November (only banks and government offices are closed)

Christmas Day, 25 December

Boxing Day, 26 December

This, one of North America's largest wine shows, takes place over 10 days in April (changing dates every year), bringing together more than 100 winemakers and 500 wines for public sampling.

Vancouver Sun Run
- When: last Sunday in April
- Where: downtown
- Contact: tel. (604) 689-9441, website www.sunrun.com

The spring sport schedule kicks off with a blast from the starter's gun for the Vancouver Sun Run, a 10-km run (or walk) through the streets of downtown that ends at B.C. Place Stadium with drinks, snacks, and entertainment for participants.

Vancouver International Marathon
- When: first Sunday in May
- Where: downtown
- Contact: tel. (604) 872-2928, website www.wi.bc.ca

One week after the annual fun run, serious runners hit the streets for this internationally accredited marathon that begins at B.C. Place Stadium and winds through the streets of downtown, then Stanley Park, before ending in Kitsilano.

Hyack Festival
- When: mid-May
- Where: New Westminster
- Contact: tel. (604) 522-6894

The streets of New Westminster come alive for nine days in the middle of May for a festival that celebrates the history of the province's one-time capital. Events include a street parade, a 21-gun salute, and fireworks.

Cloverdale Rodeo and Exhibition
- When: the third weekend of May.
- Where: Cloverdale
- Contact: tel. (604) 576-9461, website www.cloverdalerodeo.com

Rodeo isn't usually associated with Vancouver, but each May cowboys from throughout North America descend on the city for one of western Canada's biggest rodeos. All rodeo events—saddle bronc, bareback, bull riding, steer wrestling, and calf roping—and a Western trade show take place at the rodeo grounds in Cloverdale (between Surrey and Langley).

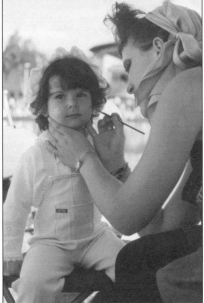

JANE AND BRUCE KING

face-painting at the Children's Festival

Vancouver International Children's Festival
- When: last week of May
- Where: Vanier Park
- Contact: tel. (604) 708-5655, website www.youngarts.ca

Generally starting during the last week of May and running for a full week is this festival for the young; it's a kid's paradise, with face painting, costumes, and fancy-hat competitions. Bring your camera! You'll need to buy tickets in advance for the special events—plays, puppetry, mime, sing-alongs, storytelling, etc.—but the rest of the fun and frivolity is free.

SUMMER

Alcan Dragon Boat Festival
- When: mid-June
- Where: False Creek
- Contact: tel. (604) 688-2382, website www.canadadragonboat.com

These dragon boat races, contested over the two middle weekends of June, attract up to 2,000 competitors from around the world. In addition to the races, a variety of cultural activities take place in the Plaza of Nations.

Bard on the Beach
- When: mid-June to late September
- Where: Vanier Park
- Contact: tel. (604) 739-0559, website www.faximum.com/bard

Throughout summer, three favorite Shakespeare plays are performed in open-ended tents, allowing a spectacular backdrop of English Bay, the city skyline, and the mountains beyond. Tickets are well priced at just $20-25.

Kitsilano Showboat
- When: late June-August.
- Where: Kitsilano Beach
- Contact: tel. (604) 734-7332

Watching amateur variety acts at the Kitsilano Showboat on a warm summer evening has been a Vancouver tradition since 1935. Today, amateur singers, dancers, and musicians take to the Showboat stage nightly, entertaining over 100,000 people through the two-month season.

Du Maurier International Jazz Festival
- When: last week of June
- Where: throughout the city
- Contact: tel. (604) 872-5200, website www.jazzfest.bc.sympatico.ca

Vancouver taps its feet to the beat of this annual jazz fest when more than 600 musicians from countries around the world gather to perform traditional and contemporary jazz at 25 venues around the city. Part of the festival is a two-day street party in historic Gastown, while other venues include Grouse Mountain and the Dr. Sun Yat-Sen Classical Chinese Garden. Get your tickets early; if you want to go to a number of events, buy a jazz pass from ticket outlets.

Canada Day
- When: 1 July
- Where: Canada Place

The first day of July is Canada's national day. The main celebrations—music, dancing, and fireworks—are held at Canada Place, but if you

head out to the **Steveston Salmon Festival** (tel. 604-277-6812) you'll come across a massive salmon barbecue.

Vancouver Folk Music Festival
- When: middle weekend of July
- Where: Jericho Beach
- Contact: tel. (604) 602-9798, website www.thefestival.bc.ca.

Summertime folk festivals draw crowds across the country, and although the Vancouver version isn't the best known, it still attracts big-name artists performing everything from bluegrass to the music of the First Nations in a beachside setting with the city skyline and mountains beyond as a backdrop. In addition to the wonderful music, the festival features storytelling, dance performances, and live theater.

Vancouver Chamber Music Festival
- When: late July
- Where: various venues
- Contact: tel. (604) 602-0363, website www.vanrecital.com

Hosted by the Orpheum Theatre and the Chan Centre, this festival presents 10 evenings of performances by chamber musicians, such as piano, cello, and violin players, from across Canada and the world.

Vancouver International Comedy Festival
- When: last week of July
- Where: Granville Island
- Contact: tel. (604) 683-0883

It's a laugh a minute during the city's annual comedy festival, which takes place over a week on Granville Island.

Mondo Pride
- When: last week of July
- Where: various venues
- Contact: tel. (604) 687-0955, website www.vanpride.org

This celebration of the gay lifestyle includes a picnic in Stanley Park, art exhibitions, a harbor cruise, and nightly parties in local nightclubs. It culminates in the Mondo Pride Parade on the first Sunday in August. The parade runs along Denman Street, ending at Sunset Beach, where there's entertainment and more partying.

World Championship Bathtub Race
- When: last Sunday in July
- Where: Kitsilano Beach
- Contact: tel. (800) 663-7337

This hilarious summer event is really one that the city of Nanaimo, on Vancouver Island, claims as its own, but this zany race only begins there—the finish line is Vancouver's Kitsilano Beach. The rules are simple: competitors fit a modified bathtub with a 7.5-horsepower outboard motor and try to navigate it as fast as possible across the 35-km stretch of Georgia Strait between Nanaimo and Kitsilano Beach. The racers are escorted by hundreds of boats of the more regular variety, loaded with people just waiting for the competitors to sink! Every bathtubber wins a prize—a golden plug for entering, a small trophy for making it to the other side of the strait, and a silver plunger for the first tub to sink!

Benson & Hedges Symphony of Fire
- When: end of July/early August
- Where: English Bay
- Contact: tel. (604) 738-4304

Year after year, Vancouver locals await with much anticipation the Symphony of Fire, the world's largest musical fireworks competition, which fills the summer sky with color over four nights. Each year, three different countries are invited to compete; each has a night to itself, putting on a display that lasts up to an hour; then on the final night, the three competing countries come together for a grand finale. The fireworks are let off from a barge moored in English Bay, allowing viewing from Stanley Park all the way to Kitsilano. Music that accompanies the displays can be heard around the shoreline; if you're away from the action tune your radio to 980 AM or 101.1 FM for a simulcast.

Abbotsford International Airshow
- When: second weekend of August
- Where: Abbotsford
- Contact: tel. (604) 852-8511

Attracting over 25,000 spectators, one of Canada's largest air shows (and voted world's best in the 1990s) is held at Vancouver's "other" airport, 70 km east of downtown in Abbotsford. The highlight is a flyby of Canada's famous Snowbirds, but there's a full program of stunt and technical flying and an on-ground exhibition of planes from all eras of aviation.

Wooden Boat Festival
- When: last weekend of August
- Where: Granville Island
- Contact: tel. (604) 688-9622, website granvilleisland.com

Wander down to the wharves of Granville Island on the last weekend of August and you'll think you've stepped back in nautical time. Wooden boat owners from along the Pacific Coast gather at the island and allow enthusiasts to view their pride and joys during this casual gathering of seafaring folk.

FALL

Molson Indy Vancouver
- When: first weekend of September
- Where: False Creek
- Contact: tel. (604) 280-4639

The CART Indy Series descends on the streets of Vancouver through the first weekend of Sep-

---

SO, IT'S RAINING OUTSIDE, BUT YOU STILL FEEL ACTIVE

Then consider heading down to **Score**, on the south side of downtown in the Plaza of Nations at 770 Pacific Blvd., tel. (604) 602-0513. This interactive indoor sports complex combines sports and games with the latest computer technology to provide entertainment for all levels of fitness. Unlimited access is $10 for the first hour, or pay $20 and "play" all day. Test your speed and accuracy with a hockey puck, shoot hoops with a sensored basket and backboard, or test your skills on an archery range. You can also play virtual golf, hitting golf balls into a screen that moves you around a course as you play; play virtual baseball at Yankee Stadium; and even go fishing via the marvels of modern technology. The complex also holds a climbing wall ($4 extra), a roller hockey rink, and a room filled with computer games for kids. It's open Sun.-Thurs. 11 a.m.-11 p.m., Fri.-Sat. 11 a.m.-1 a.m.

tember for the grand finale of the season's race schedule. The road circuit, set up on the south side of downtown along Pacific Boulevard and around the head of False Creek, is lined with cheering motor racing fans. Ticket prices for the main Sunday race are $40; events earlier in the weekend are a little cheaper.

Air Canada Championship
- When: first week of September
- Where: Northview Golf and Country Club, Surrey
- Contact: tel. (604) 576-4653, website www.pgatour.com

This 72-hole golf championship is the only western Canada stop on the regular PGA Tour. Until 1998, the event was known as the Greater Vancouver Open, and it clashed with the World Championship of Golf, which was where the best tour players were. Now, with a new name and a new date the Air Canada Championship draws the very best golfers in the world to compete on a local course.

The Fringe—Vancouver's Theatre Festival
- When: second week of September
- Where: Commercial Drive
- Contact: tel. (604) 257-0350

This large fringe theater festival schedules around 500 performances by 100 artists from around the world at indoor and outdoor stages along Commercial Drive and throughout East Vancouver.

World Championship
Sand Sculpture Competition
- When: second weekend in September
- Where: Harrison Hot Springs
- Contact: tel. (604) 796-3425, website www.harrisand.org

The world's best sand sculptors congregate on the beach at the resort town of Harrison Hot Springs, 125 km east of downtown, to create a masterpiece and claim the title of world champion (and a share of the $25,000 prize money). Each team has 100 man-hours to complete its sculpture, with the judging taking place on Sunday afternoon.

Vancouver International Film Festival
- When: mid-October
- Where: various venues

- Contact: tel. (604) 685-0260, website www.viff.org

Through the second and third weeks of October, this festival features 300 of the very best movies from around 50 countries at theaters across downtown. The festival isn't as well known as other film festivals, but it has grown to become the third largest in North America.

Vancouver International Writers Festival
- When: late October
- Where: Granville Island
- Contact: tel. (604) 681-6330

The week after movie buffs have had their fill, literary types congregate on Granville Island for a celebration of local and national literary talent. Most events are open to the public and include lectures and talks by leading writers, poets, and playwrights.

WINTER

Christmas Carol Ship Parade
- When: most of December
- Where: on the water
- Contact: tel. (604) 878-9988

For three weeks leading up to Christmas Eve, the waterways of Vancouver come alive with the sounds of the festive season. A flotilla of boats, each decorated with colorful lights, sails around Burrard Inlet, English Bay, and False Creek, while onboard carolers sing the songs of Christmas through sound systems that can clearly be heard from along the shoreline.

Festival of Lights
- When: all December
- Where: VanDusen Botanical Garden
- Contact: tel. (604) 878-9274

Through the month of December, Central Vancouver's VanDusen Botanical Garden is transformed each evening by over 100,000 lights and seasonal displays such as a nativity scene.

Polar Bear Swim
- When: 1 January
- Where: English Bay Beach
- Contact: tel. (604) 732-2304

While most normal folk spending New Year's Day recovering from the previous night's celebrations, up to 2,000 brave souls head down to English Bay Beach and go *swimming.* The tradition was started in the early 1900s by a local businessman, Peter Pantages, who took to the water every day of the year; to promote the fact that it was possible to swim year-round, he formed the Polar Bear Club. On the first day of 1920, a small group assembled at English Bay Beach dived into the frigid waters and began a tradition that continues to this day. The stupidity starts at 2:30 p.m.

Chinese New Year
• When: late January/early February
• Where: Chinatown
• Contact: tel. (604) 662-3207
The Chinese calendar is linked to the lunar New Year, which varies from late January to early February, through which time Chinatown comes alive for two weeks with a colorful parade, music, dancing, and a spectacular display of fireworks.

The Pan Pacific Hotel sits high above Canada Place.

ACCOMMODATIONS

Whether you're looking for a luxurious room in a high-rise hotel or a dingy downtown dorm, Vancouver has accommodations to suit all budgets. Before arriving, wise travelers will obtain a copy of Tourism BC's free guide, *British Columbia Accommodations,* using it to make advance reservations at their lodgings of choice. The guide lists hotels, motels, bed and breakfasts, backpacker lodges, and campgrounds. It contains no ratings, simply listings with facilities and rates. To request a copy of the guide, contact **Tourism British Columbia,** P.O. Box 9830, Stn. Provincial Government, Victoria, BC V8W 9W5, tel. (250) 387-1642 or (800) HEL-

LOBC (435-5622), website www.hellobc.com. The toll-free number (800-HELLOBC) is also a reservations hotline. Once in the city, **Vancouver Visitor Info Centre,** 200 Burrard St., tel. (604) 683-2000, is the best place to get all the accommodations information in one shot. The center maintains accommodation listings for Vancouver and the entire province and stocks a good selection of brochures provided by the lodgings. The staff will make bookings, too.

If you show up in late spring or summer without reservations, you may find all the best places, and definitely all the most reasonable, booked for the season.

HOTELS AND MOTELS

For those on a limited budget, one of the true joys of Vancouver is the number of centrally located old hotels, where rooms are furnished with nothing more than a bed and a sink and share bathroom facilities. In recent years, many have been upgraded (and are now priced according-

ly), and some, such as the old Niagara Hotel (now part of the Ramada Limited family), have been completely transformed. Vancouver's East Side once held over 10,000 of these most basic hotel rooms, and many remain along E. Hastings St., a few blocks on either side of Main Street.

ACCOMMODATIONS RATINGS CHART

To make choosing an accommodation that comes within your budget easy, all hotels and motels, bed and breakfasts, backpacker lodges, and campgrounds have been afforded a one-word "rating" in this book. The rating is based on high season (summer) double occupancy rates. In the off-season, prices will often drop to a less expensive category, as will many city hotels on weekends. The rating is only a price indication and has no bearing on the facilities offered at each establishment.

Except for campgrounds, an eight percent provincial hotel and motel tax, a two percent tourism tax, and, like the rest of Canada, the seven percent goods and services tax must be added; the latter is refundable to visitors from outside the country.

Budget: up to $60
Inexpensive: $60-90
Moderate: $90-120
Expensive: $120-150
Premium: $150-180
Luxury: $180 and up

This is Vancouver's skid row, where rooms are rented by the month and the city's down-and-outs are within stumbling distance of the nearest bar. This part of town should be avoided, especially at night. At the other end of the price spectrum, Vancouver excels. The American AA gives a five-diamond rating to less than 100 hotels in the world. Three of these are in Vancouver.

DOWNTOWN

Inexpensive

Many inexpensively priced accommodations lie in the downtown area, but only the following can be recommended.

The pick of the bunch is the old three-story **Kingston Hotel,** 757 Richards St., tel. (604) 684-9024 or (888) 713-3304, a small hotel with a European atmosphere. Most rooms share a bathroom. Amenities include a sauna, laundry, TV rental, and guest parking. Rates start at $60

s, $75 d, including a continental breakfast. Weekly and off-season rates are available.

The **Dominion Hotel,** 210 Abbott St., tel. (604) 681-6666, is in Gastown, a five-minute walk from downtown along Water Street. The old hotel dates to 1899, has a bar downstairs, and is popular with international travelers. Rooms are $70-100 s, $80-110 d, through summer, from $65 the rest of the year. All rates include breakfast.

The location of the **Patricia Hotel,** at 403 E. Hastings St., tel. (604) 255-4301, isn't the best—it's separated from downtown by infamous E. Hastings St.—but the price is right. Rooms are $52 s, $62 d, and downstairs is popular Pat's Pub.

Moderate

The largest concentration of hotels in this price category is southwest of the business district, toward Granville Island.

Best value of these is the old three-story **Burrard Motor Inn,** 1100 Burrard St., tel. (604) 681-2331 or (800) 663-0366, which charges from $80 s, $95 d for a large but simply furnished room.

Immediately to the east of Burrard Motor Inn is **Bosman's Motor Hotel,** 1060 Howe St., tel. (604) 682-3171 or (888) 267-6267, which offers rooms from $100 s, $110 d.

A few blocks farther south, and a five-minute walk to a False Creek Ferries wharf, is **Travelodge Vancouver Centre,** 1304 Howe St., tel. (604) 682-2767 or (800) 578-7878. Rooms are clean and comfortable, but this accommodation has seen better days, making the rates of $99 s, $109 d a little steep.

Expensive

Accommodations in this price range are scattered between the business district and Granville Island.

Least expensive of the city-center hotels is **Days Inn Vancouver Downtown,** 921 W. Pender St., tel. (604) 681-4335 or (800) 329-7466. The 85 rooms are small, and surrounding highrises block any views. But each room is decorated in bright and breezy pastel colors, and tea-and coffee-makers are provided; $125-185 s or d.

The 12-story **Best Western Vancouver Downtown,** 718 Drake St., tel. (604) 669-9888 or (888) 669-9888, lies at the southern end of downtown. Because the hotel opened in 1997, its 143 rooms are still relatively new, making the rates of $129 s or d, including a light breakfast, good value.

Premium

Century Plaza Hotel, 1015 Burrard St., tel. (604) 687-0575 or (800) 663-1818, offers 230 rooms, each with a kitchen. The biggest attraction is Spa at the Century, a full-service spa facility. Nightly rates are $139 s, $154 d, but weekly discounts are offered.

While guest facilities at **Ramada Limited Downtown Vancouver** are limited compared to other properties in this price category, the location is very central. As an old hotel the rooms are small, but they are well appointed and come with everything from hair dryers to Nintendo. The rates of $159-195 include a light breakfast. It's at 435 W. Pender St., tel. (604) 488-1088 or (888) 389-5888, easily recognizable by the distinctive neon sign out front.

At the elegantly furnished **Quality Hotel–The Inn at False Creek,** 1335 Howe St., tel. (604) 682-0229 or (800) 663-8474, a few rooms can be had for $130 s or d, but the one-bedroom suites,

Hotel Vancouver

each with a full kitchen, are the best value at $159 s or d.

Two blocks closer to downtown, **Holiday Inn Hotel and Suites,** 1110 Howe St., tel. (604) 684-2151 or (800) 465-4329, features an indoor pool, health club, a kids' play room, and a restaurant. Standard rooms are $149 s, $169 d, while rooms with a kitchen are $229 s or d.

Luxury

Canadian Pacific, best known for landmark accommodations like the Empress Hotel in Victoria and the Banff Springs Hotel in Banff, operates two properties in the downtown area. The copper-roofed **Hotel Vancouver,** 900 W. Georgia St., tel. (604) 684-3131 or (800) 441-1414, is the company's Vancouver flagship and a downtown landmark—you can't help but notice the distinctive green copper roof, the gargoyles, and the classic, Gothic château-style architecture of this grand old lady. The original Hotel Vancouver, which opened in 1887, was destroyed by fire in the early 1930s. The hotel was rebuilt from the ground up and reopened amid much fanfare in 1939. The 1990s saw a multimillion-dollar refit, which took eight years. Today, with its former glory restored, the Hotel Vancouver is one of Canada's grandest accommodations, from the cavernous marble-lined lobby to the high ceilings and well-sized rooms. Facilities include restaurants, a comfortable lounge, an indoor pool, saunas, a weight room, health facilities, 24-hour room service, ample parking, and a large staff to attend to your every whim. Rooms run $245-530 s or d.

The other Canadian Pacific property is the modern, 23-story **Waterfront Centre Hotel,** 900 Canada Place Way, tel. (604) 691-1991 or (800) 828-7447, across the road from Canada Place. The 489 rooms are all spacious, and over half of them enjoy stunning harbor views. Many of the artworks found throughout the hotel were specially commissioned for the property. Guest facilities include a health club, outdoor pool, and a variety of dining choices. Guests and nonguests alike can enjoy a grand Sunday brunch, with background music supplied by members of the Vancouver Symphony Orchestra. Rates are $255-285 s or d.

The 34-story **Hyatt Regency Vancouver,** 655 Burrard St., tel. (604) 683-1234 or (800) 233-1234, towers above the Royal Centre Mall.

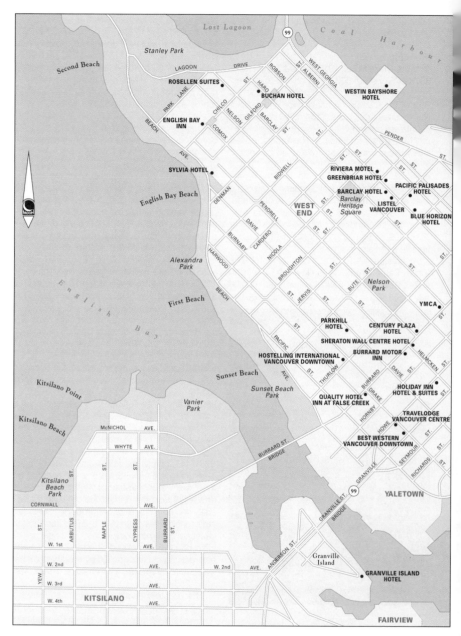

Lost Lagoon

Coal Harbour

Stanley Park

Second Beach

LAGOON DRIVE

99

WEST GEORGIA

ROBSON ST.
ALBERNI ST.

ROSELLEN SUITES

HARO

PARK LANE

BUCHAN HOTEL

WESTIN BAYSHORE HOTEL

BEACH

ENGLISH BAY INN

CHILCO
NELSON
GILFORD
BARCLAY ST.

COMOX

PENDER ST.

ST. ST.

AVE.

BIDWELL

SYLVIA HOTEL

English Bay Beach

DENMAN

RIVIERA MOTEL
GREENBRIAR HOTEL

ST.

PACIFIC PALISADES HOTEL

WEST END

BARCLAY HOTEL

Barclay Heritage Square

LISTEL VANCOUVER

BLUE HORIZON HOTEL

PENDRELL

DAVIE

ST. ST.

ST.

CARDERO

BURNABY

NICOLA

Alexandra Park

HARWOOD

BROUGHTON

BUTE

Nelson Park

English Bay

BEACH

First Beach

JERVIS ST.

ST.

ST.

YMCA

ST.

PARKHILL HOTEL

CENTURY PLAZA HOTEL

HELMCKEN

PACIFIC

SHERATON WALL CENTRE HOTEL

BURRARD MOTOR INN

Sunset Beach

HOSTELLING INTERNATIONAL VANCOUVER DOWNTOWN

THURLOW

DAVIE ST.

Kitsilano Point

Sunset Beach Park

BURRARD

DRAKE

HOLIDAY INN HOTEL & SUITES

Vanier Park

QUALITY HOTEL INN AT FALSE CREEK

HORNBY

HOWE

TRAVELODGE VANCOUVER CENTRE

Kitsilano Beach

McNICHOL AVE.

BEST WESTERN VANCOUVER DOWNTOWN

SEYMOUR ST.

RICHARDS ST.

WHYTE AVE.

BURRARD ST. BRIDGE

GRANVILLE

Kitsilano Beach Park

CORNWALL

ST.

ST.

ST.

AVE.

99

GRANVILLE ST. BRIDGE

YALETOWN

ARBUTUS ST.
MAPLE ST.
CYPRESS ST.
BURRARD ST.

W. 1st

W. 2nd

AVE.

W. 2nd AVE.

ANDERSON ST.

Granville Island

YEW ST.

W. 3rd

AVE.

GRANVILLE ISLAND HOTEL

W. 4th

KITSILANO

AVE.

FAIRVIEW

MOON

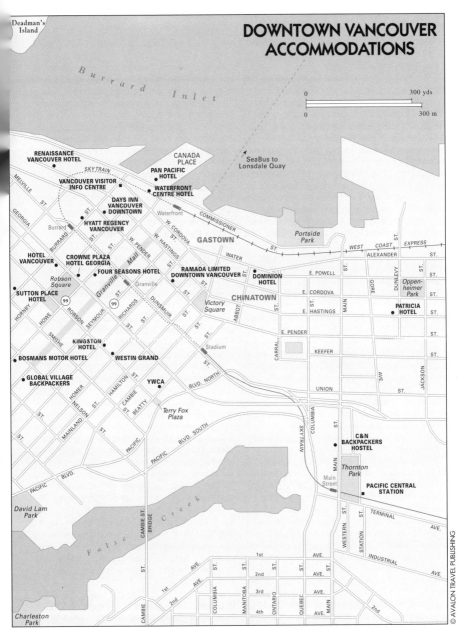

DOWNTOWN VANCOUVER ACCOMMODATIONS

Deadman's Island

Burrard Inlet

| 0 | | 300 yds |
| 0 | | 300 m |

CANADA PLACE

SeaBus to Lonsdale Quay

RENAISSANCE VANCOUVER HOTEL

SKYTRAIN

PAN PACIFIC HOTEL

VANCOUVER VISITOR INFO CENTRE

DAYS INN VANCOUVER DOWNTOWN

WATERFRONT CENTRE HOTEL

MELVILLE ST.

GEORGIA ST.

Burrard

Waterfront

COMMISSIONER ST.

HYATT REGENCY VANCOUVER

W. CORDOVA ST.

W. HASTINGS ST.

W. PENDER ST.

GASTOWN

WATER ST.

Portside Park

WEST COAST EXPRESS

ALEXANDER ST.

HOTEL VANCOUVER

CROWNE PLAZA HOTEL GEORGIA

FOUR SEASONS HOTEL

Granville Mall

Granville

RAMADA LIMITED DOWNTOWN VANCOUVER

DOMINION HOTEL

E. POWELL ST.

E. CORDOVA ST.

DUNLEVY ST.

GORE ST.

Oppenheimer Park

Robson Square

SUTTON PLACE HOTEL

HORNBY ST.

HOWE ST.

ROBSON ST.

SEYMOUR ST.

RICHARDS ST.

DUNSMUIR ST.

99

99

Victory Square

ABBOTT ST.

CHINATOWN

E. HASTINGS ST.

MAIN ST.

CARRALL ST.

PATRICIA HOTEL

JACKSON ST.

SMITHE ST.

KINGSTON HOTEL

BOSMANS MOTOR HOTEL

WESTIN GRAND

Stadium

E. PENDER ST.

KEEFER ST.

AVE.

GLOBAL VILLAGE BACKPACKERS

HOMER ST.

NELSON ST.

HAMILTON ST.

CAMBIE ST.

BEATTY ST.

YWCA

BLVD. NORTH

UNION ST.

MAINLAND ST.

Terry Fox Plaza

PACIFIC BLVD.

BLVD. SOUTH

PACIFIC

COLUMBIA ST.

SKYTRAIN

C&N BACKPACKERS HOSTEL

David Lam Park

PACIFIC BLVD.

CAMBIE ST.

BRIDGE ST.

False Creek

Main Street

MAIN ST.

Thornton Park

PACIFIC CENTRAL STATION

WESTERN ST.

STATION ST.

TERMINAL AVE.

INDUSTRIAL AVE.

Charleston Park

CAMBIE

1st AVE.

2nd AVE.

COLUMBIA ST.

MANITOBA ST.

1st AVE.

2nd AVE.

3rd AVE.

4th AVE.

ONTARIO ST.

QUEBEC ST.

MAIN ST.

2nd

© AVALON TRAVEL PUBLISHING

Needless to say, most of the 600-plus rooms have views. Guest facilities include restaurants, a lounge, an indoor pool, and a fitness center. Standard rate is $230-370 s or d, but weekend rates are considerably lower.

The historic **Crowne Plaza Hotel Georgia** lies across the road from the art gallery and is kitty-corner to the Hotel Vancouver right downtown at 801 Georgia St., tel. (604) 682-5566 or (800) 663-1111. Having recently undergone a multi-million-dollar renovation, this grand old lady has been restored to her former glory. Original oak furnishings, the oak-paneled lobby, and the brass elevator have been restored and all facilities upgraded, including a fitness center. If this is your accommodation of choice, your name will join a guest list that includes Queen Elizabeth II, Katherine Hepburn, and the Beatles. The best views are from rooms facing the art gallery. Rates start at $280 s or d but drop to $160 in winter.

One block from the city end of Robson Street is the super-luxurious, European-style **Sutton Place Hotel**, 845 Burrard St., tel. (604) 682-5511 or (800) 961-7555, which gets a precious five-diamond rating from the American AA. This, Vancouver's most elegant accommodation, features original European artworks in public areas and reproductions in the 397 rooms. Rooms are furnished with king-size beds, and guests enjoy a twice-daily maid service, complete with fresh flowers. Le Spa is an in-house spa, fitness, and health facility in the tradition of a luxurious European spa resort. Other facilities include a glass-enclosed pool, a lounge bar, and Fleuri, an up-market restaurant; from $265 per night.

Four Seasons has a reputation for the very best in comfort and service, and the Vancouver **Four Seasons Hotel**, above the Pacific Centre at 791 W. Georgia St., tel. (604) 689-9333 or (800) 268-6282, is no exception, getting a five-diamond rating from the AAA. The spacious rooms are luxuriously appointed, and guest facilities include an indoor and outdoor pool complex, a business center, and various eating establishments, including casual dining in a plant-filled atrium. Rates start at $345 s, $375 d.

For all the modern conveniences along with unbeatable city and harbor views, head for the sparkling **Pan Pacific Hotel Vancouver,** Canada Place, tel. (604) 662-8111 or (800) 937-1515 from the U.S., (800) 663-1515 from Canada.

Opened for Expo86, the Pan Pacific was the most expensive hotel ever built in western Canada at the time. Today, it has lost nothing of its original luxurious appeal—it garners a prestigious five-diamond rating from the AAA and is generally regarded as one of the world's best 100 hotels. It's part of the landmark Canada Place (the top eight floors of the 13-story complex are guest rooms), whose Teflon sails fly over busy, bustling sidewalks and a constant flow of cruise ships. The hotel lobby is up a massive escalator that begins at the city end of Canada Place. Each of the 506 rooms boasts modern furnishings and stunning views. Facilities include a pool, an extra-charge health club, the Sails Restaurant, and the Cascades Lounge. Both the restaurant and lounge offer great views. Rooms start at $445 s or d.

The **Renaissance Vancouver Hotel,** 1133 West Hastings St., tel. (604) 689-9211 or (800) 468-3571, lies two blocks west of Canada Place and offers unimpeded views across Burrard Inlet. The 439 elegantly furnished rooms feature large work and living areas, and heated floors. Other facilities include a fitness center, a pool and sundeck with mountain views, a coffee shop, a sports bar, and a restaurant. Standard rooms are $206 s, $236 d, while those facing the northern panorama of water and mountains are $236 s, $266 d.

Away from the business and shopping district is the **Sheraton Wall Centre Hotel,** 1088 Burrard St., tel. (604) 331-1000 or (800) 663-9255. No expense was spared in the construction of this stylish 35-story hostelry, which is enclosed within a glass-sided tower. Many of the furnishings were specially commissioned. Facilities include a couple of restaurants, a health club, indoor pool, and half-hectare garden. Rates for a standard room start at $240 s or d (request a higher room for better views), while corner suites, complete with marble bathrooms, are $365 per night.

In the same part of downtown as the Sheraton, the **Parkhill Hotel,** 1160 Davie St., tel. (604) 685-1311 or (800) 663-1525, offers views over a residential area to English Bay. Rooms are spacious and have private balconies, and guests have use of a pool and fitness room. Rates are $180 s, $200 d.

Vancouver's newest top-end hotel is the **Westin Grand,** which opened for the summer of 1999. It lies in the entertainment district but is still within walking distance of Granville Street Mall at 433 Robson St., tel. (604) 684-9393 or (888) 680-9393. Each of the 207 rooms is a self-contained suite, complete with a modern kitchen, a work station, two televisions, and two phone lines. Other facilities include a fitness center and an outdoor lap pool. Midweek rates range $224-369 s or d, but prices drop considerably on weekends.

ROBSON STREET

Moderate

Most accommodations on Robson Street fall into the Expensive category, but one exception is the European-style **Barclay Hotel,** 1348 Robson St., tel. (604) 688-8850. Built in the 1920s, this three-story hostelry holds 80 medium-size rooms and a stylish lobby with lounge area. Rates of $75 s, $95 d include a continental buffet breakfast, making the Barclay a good value.

Expensive

A number of accommodations on Robson Street fall into the Expensive category but do provide a lot for the money.

The **Greenbrier Hotel,** 1393 Robson St., tel. (604) 683-4558 or (888) 355-5888, looks a bit rough on the outside, but rooms have been refurbished, and each has a large living area, full kitchen, and separate bedroom. Rates are $129-169 s or d.

The **Riviera Hotel,** 1431 Robson St., tel. (604) 685-1301 or (888) 699-5222, offers similar facilities, as well as harbor or city views from the upper floors. All rooms are large and comfortably furnished; from $135 s or d.

The 214-room **Blue Horizon Hotel,** 1225 Robson St., tel. (604) 688-1411 or (800) 663-1333, is a fairly standard accommodation, but it has modern furnishings, large rooms (some with harbor views), a small pool, a fitness room, services for business travelers, and a street-level restaurant that serves good breakfasts. Rates are from $149 s or d.

Luxury

Listel Vancouver, 1300 Robson St., tel. (604) 684-8461 or (800) 663-5491, is an elegant full-service lodging with 130 luxurious rooms, a fitness room, and an indoor pool. Standard rooms are $220 s, $240 d, while rooms on the two Gallery Floors, which feature original artworks, separate bedrooms, and bay windows, are $300 s, $320 d.

Diagonally opposite the Listel is **Pacific Palisades Hotel,** 1277 Robson St., tel. (604) 688-0461 or (800) 663-1815, which is part of the Shangri-La Hotels and Resorts chain. The hotel was formerly a luxury apartment building, so each of the 223 rooms is very spacious. Don't be put off by the dull exterior or tiny lobby; the rooms are furnished in a bright and breezy style, and each has a spacious living area and is stocked with touches such as luxurious toiletries and bathrobes. Amenities include a lounge and stylish restaurant, a fitness center, large lap pool, daily newspapers, and a variety of business services. Rates are $229 s, $259 d, kitchenettes an extra $10.

The **Westin Bayshore,** 1601 W. Georgia St., tel. (604) 682-3377, is unique within the downtown peninsula in that it offers a distinctive resort-style atmosphere. It lies right on Coal Harbour and is linked to Stanley Park by a waterfront promenade. It features a large outdoor pool surrounded by outdoor furniture settings and a poolside lounge. Guests also have use of a health club. Each of the 517 rooms is luxuriously appointed and has a private balcony. Rates start at $265 s, $295 d.

WEST END

The few accommodations at the west end of downtown are near some fine restaurants, close to Stanley Park and English Bay, and a 25-minute walk along bustling Robson Street from downtown proper.

Overlooking English Bay and Vancouver's most popular beach, the **Sylvia Hotel,** 1154 Gilford St., tel. (604) 681-9321, is a local landmark sporting a brick and terra-cotta exterior covered with Virginia creeper. Built in 1912 as an apartment building, the eight-story Sylvia was the tallest building on this side of town until 1958. It went upmarket in the 1950s, with the opening of Vancouver's first cocktail bar. Today, it provides excellent value as rates range $85-170 s or d (the less expensive rooms are fairly small), with the more expensive rooms featuring fantastic views and full kitchens. The Sylvia also has a restaurant and lounge. Inexpensive.

Sylvia Hotel

Another less expensive choice is the three-story **Buchan Hotel,** in a quiet residential area at 1906 Haro St., tel. (604) 685-5354 or (800) 668-6654. Built as an apartment hotel in 1936, the Buchan's rooms are small, but the atmosphere is friendly and Stanley Park is only one block away; from $75 s, $85 d. The Buchan is a nonsmoking hotel. Inexpensive.

Right by Stanley Park is **Rosellen Suites,** 2030 Barclay St., tel. (604) 689-4807, where each of the 30 units features modern furnishings, a separate living and dining area, and a full kitchen. Rates start at $145 for a one-bedroom unit and $205 for a two-bedroom unit. Expensive.

Coast Plaza Suite Hotel at Stanley Park, 1763 Comox St., tel. (604) 688-7711 or (800) 663-1144, is actually closer to English Bay than Stanley Park, but it's a full-service hotel with 267 rooms on 35 levels. As a former apartment tower, its rooms are spacious; all have balconies and many feature kitchens. Amenities include a health club, pool, restaurants, and a nightclub. Rates are from $170 s or d. Premium.

NORTH VANCOUVER AND VICINITY

Without a doubt, the pick of accommodations on the north side of Burrard Inlet is the **Park Royal Hotel,** 540 Clyde Ave., West Vancouver, tel. (604) 926-5511. The Tudor-style accommodation sits on the banks of the Capilano River—you can fish for salmon and steelhead right on the property—and is surrounded by well-maintained gardens. Inside you'll find an English-style pub, a lounge area with fireplace, and 30 cozy rooms, each with a brass bed. Rates are a reasonable $160-285 s or d, which includes tea and coffee and a daily newspaper. Book *well* ahead to be assured of a room at this popular place. To get there from downtown, take the Lions Gate Bridge over Burrard Inlet, turn left over the Capilano River, turn right onto Taylor Way, then take the next right, Clyde Avenue. Premium.

If you don't have transportation but don't want to stay right downtown, **Lonsdale Quay Hotel,** 123 Carrie Cates Court, North Vancouver, tel. (604) 986-6111 or (800) 836-6111, is a good choice. It's above lively Lonsdale Quay Market and the SeaBus Terminal, only 12 minutes to downtown by water. Amenities include restaurants, a fitness center, a sauna and whirlpool, a nightclub with entertainment, shops, and covered parking. Rates are from $175 s, $210 d, more for harbor views. Luxury.

Less expensive is **Holiday Inn Express Vancouver North Shore,** 1800 Capilano Rd., tel. (604) 987-4461 or (800) 663-4055, where well-furnished rooms, use of an outdoor pool, and a light breakfast are included in the rates of $139 s or d. Expensive.

Horseshoe Bay Motel, 6588 Royal Ave., tel. (604) 921-7454, is right by the BC Ferries terminal, from where ferries depart for the Sunshine Coast and Nanaimo. It's within easy walking distance of numerous cafés and restaurants, and the nearby Horseshoe Bay Marina is a pleasant place for an evening stroll. Rooms are $85 s or d. Inexpensive.

SOUTH OF DOWNTOWN

Granville Island
Granville Island Hotel, 1253 Johnston St., tel. (604) 683-7373 or (800) 663-1840, attracts a trendy, fun-loving, jet-setter crowd looking for action. The hotel overlooks False Creek from Granville Island, just south of city center. Most of the elegantly furnished rooms have water views. Amenities include a jacuzzi, sauna, fitness center, restaurant, lounge, pub (always crowded in the evenings), and disco. Elsewhere on the island, within easy striking distance of the hotel, are theaters, restaurants, art galleries, shops, and a public market. Rooms run $200-220 s or d. Luxury. If you object to loud, pounding music till 2 a.m., be sure to ask for a room far from the disco.

Central Vancouver
If you have your own transportation, the lodgings south of downtown are worth consideration. They're generally less expensive than the downtown hotels, and you won't have to worry about parking. Nearby is a cluster of inexpensive restaurants, the perfect place for a budget-conscious traveler to end the day with a good meal (see West Broadway in the Food chapter).

The least expensive choices lie along the Kingsway, the main route between downtown and New Westminster. Closest of these to downtown is the **Biltmore Hotel,** 395 Kingsway, tel. (604) 872-5252 or (800) 663-5713. The rooms are small, but many have city views and there's an outdoor pool for guest use; $99 s or d. Moderate.

The old Kingsway Lodge has been renovated and is now **Days Inn Metro Vancouver,** 2075 Kingsway, tel. (604) 876-5531 or (800) 546-4792, where rooms are set around a private courtyard. Summer rates are $99-119 s or d, dropping as low as $59 the rest of the year. Moderate.

Nearby is the old **2400 Motel,** 2400 Kingsway, tel. (604) 434-2464, which charges $70-100 s or d. Inexpensive.

Holiday Inn Vancouver Centre lies on the south side of False Creek, overlooking the city and within walking distance of Granville Island at 711 W. Broadway, tel. (604) 879-0511 or (800) 465-4329. The rooms are moderately sized but well appointed, and the indoor pool complex opens to an outdoor deck with great views. Rates are $189 s, $209 d. Luxury.

Richmond (Vancouver International Airport)
The following accommodations, as well as the two in Tsawwassen, are good choices for those visitors who want to commute directly between the airport and ferry terminal without going into downtown Vancouver. All accommodations listed below offer complimentary airport shuttles.

The **Delta Pacific Resort & Conference Centre,** five km from the airport at 10251 St. Edwards Dr., tel. (604) 278-9611 or (800) 268-1133, offers a wide range of facilities, including a fitness center, large water slide, indoor and outdoor pools, tennis and squash courts, restaurants, and a couple of bars. It is also the pick-up point for Pacific Coach Line services over to Vancouver Island. Rates range $145-210 s or d. Expensive.

Holiday Inn Express Vancouver Airport, 9351 Bridgeport Rd., tel. (604) 273-8080 or (888) 831-3388, offers basic facilities, but the rooms are large and comfortably furnished. The rates of $129 s, $149 d include a large breakfast bar, which holds everything from fresh fruit to yogurt. Expensive.

In the same vicinity, **Radisson President Hotel and Suites,** 8181 Cambie Rd., tel. (604) 276-8181 or (800) 333-3333, is a sprawling complex of 184 guest rooms, a fitness center, indoor pool, and several restaurants. The rooms are spacious and well appointed, making the rates of $160-210 s or d very reasonable. Premium.

Hilton Vancouver Airport, Vancouver's first Hilton Hotel, opened late in the summer of 1999 at 5911 Minoru Blvd., tel. (604) 273-6336. It features a heated outdoor pool, a fitness center, a business center, two tennis courts, a lounge, and a restaurant. Rates start at a reasonable $160 s or d. Premium.

Close to the airport is **Delta Vancouver Airport Hotel,** 3500 Cessna Dr., tel. (604) 278-1241 or (800) 877-1133, offering a high standard of service and all the facilities of an international-style hostelry; from $300 s or d. Luxury.

The **Coast Vancouver Airport Hotel,** 1041 Southwest Marine Dr., tel. (604) 263-1555 or (800) 663-1144, is good value with large rooms, a fitness center, lounge, and restaurant; $92-130 s or d. Moderate. It lies farther from the airport (toward the city) than those detailed above but still offers airport transfers.

Also on the downtown side of the Fraser River is **Quality Inn Airport Hotel,** 725 Southeast Marine Dr., tel. (604) 321-6611 or (800) 663-6715, which charges from $99 s or d. Moderate.

Tsawwassen (BC Ferries Terminal)

The closest accommodation to the departure point for ferries to Vancouver Island is the **Best Western Tsawwassen Inn,** four km east of the terminal along Hwy. 17, tel. (604) 943-8221 or (800) 943-8221. Amenities include both an indoor and outdoor pool, a fitness center, restaurant, and complimentary ferry shuttle. Rooms are furnished simply but stylishly, and many have kitchens. Summer rates are from $110 s, $120 d, less the rest of the year. Expensive.

Halfway between the airport and ferry terminal, at the junction of Highways 17 and 99, is **Delta Town and Country Inn,** tel. (604) 946-4404, which charges from $85 s, $95 d. Moderate.

EAST OF DOWNTOWN

Burnaby

If you're coming into the city on the TransCanada Hwy., you'll find a cluster of motels in Burnaby, just west of where the highway crosses the Fraser River, including **Best Western Chelsea Inn,** 725 Brunette Ave. (take Exit 40B), tel. (604) 525-7777 or (800) 528-1234. This motel features a heated outdoor pool, jacuzzi, restaurant, laundry, and large rooms, each with a lounge and coffee-making facilities; $90 s, $100 d. Moderate.

To the south of the TransCanada Hwy., **Hol-iday Inn Metrotown,** 4405 Central Blvd., tel. (604) 438-1881 or (877) 323-1177, is part of the province's biggest shopping complex and is connected to downtown by the SkyTrain. The rooms are moderately sized and furnished with a distinct warm feeling. Rates are $155-165 d. Premium.

Also within walking distance of Metrotown, **Quality Inn Metrotown,** 3484 Kingsway, tel. (604) 433-8255, has a pool, café, restaurant, and lounge; $119 s, $129 d. Expensive.

Coquitlam

At Exit 40B, **Best Western Coquitlam Inn,** 319 North Rd., tel. (604) 931-9011 or (800) 668-3383, features rooms facing a cavernous atrium filled with plants, a pool, and a jacuzzi. Rates start at $149 s, $159 d. Premium.

Abbotsford

If you are using Vancouver's second airport, at Abbotsford, **Holiday Inn Express,** 2073 Clearbrook Rd., Clearbrook, tel. (604) 859-6211 or (800) 665-7252, is a convenient accommodation. It features a fitness center and indoor pool, and continental breakfast is included in the rates of $89 s, $99 d. Moderate.

Chilliwack

Just over 100 km from downtown, Chilliwack forms the eastern extent of Vancouver's sprawl. Take Exit 119B eastbound or Exit 120 westbound to access the following two motels.

Rainbow Motor Inn, 45620 Yale Rd., tel. (604) 792-6412 or (800) 834-5547, has basic rooms for $59 s, $69 d, or pay $5 extra for a room with a kitchenette. Inexpensive.

A step up in quality is **Holiday Inn Chilliwack,** 45920 1st Ave., tel. (604) 795-4788 or (800) 520-7555. In a quiet location overlooking a park, this motel offers 110 spacious and comfortable rooms, a fitness facility, pool, and restaurant; $129-144 s or d. Expensive.

BED AND BREAKFASTS

If you want to meet locals and prefer the idea of staying in someone's home rather than in an impersonal hotel room, stay in a bed and breakfast. B&Bs sprouted all over Vancouver just before Expo86 and today can be found all across the greater metropolitan area. Styles run the gamut—heritage homes, modern townhouses, renovated boutique hotels. Some have private baths, others shared facilities; some have swimming pools and saunas, others are on the beach or close to city attractions. Expect to pay $50-180 s, $65-210 d, including breakfast.

The **Western Canadian Bed and Breakfast Innkeepers Association,** P.O. Box 74534, 2803 W. 4th Ave., Vancouver, BC V6K 4P4, tel. (604) 255-9199, website www.wcbbia.com, represents 130 bed and breakfasts across the province, but with most in Vancouver and Victoria. The association produces an informative brochure with simple descriptions and a color photo of each property but doesn't take bookings—they must be made direct. The alternative is to book through an agency. Call and tell them what you're looking for and the price you're prepared to pay, and they'll find the right place for you. The following associations are well represented in Vancouver: **AB&C B&B of Vancouver,** 4390 Frances St., Vancouver, BC V5C 2R3, tel. (604) 298-8815 or (800) 488-1941; **All B&B Reservations,** 201-1405 Haro St., Vancouver, BC V6G 1G2, tel. (604) 683-3609; **Beachside B&B Registry,** 4208 Evergreen Ave., West Vancouver, BC V7V 1H1, tel. (604) 922-7773; **Old English B&B Registry,** 1226 Silverwood Crescent, North Vancouver, BC V7P 1J3, tel. (604) 986-5069; and **Westway Accommodation Registry,** P.O. Box 48950, Bentall Centre, Vancouver, BC V7X 1A8, tel. (604) 273-8293, for all of British Columbia. Many bed and breakfasts are listed in the *Accommodations* guide, and local information centers can also provide details.

West End

Only one block from Robson Street is **West End Guest House,** 1362 Haro St., tel. (604) 681-2889. Built at the turn of the century, this inn has been lovingly refurbished and furnished with brass beds and antiques to retain its original Victorian charm. Each of the seven rooms has a private bathroom, television, and telephone, and guests can relax either in the comfortable lounge or on the outdoor terrace. Rates start at $100 s, $160 d, which includes a full breakfast and light snacks through the day. Premium.

Toward Stanley Park and nestled among towering apartment blocks is **English Bay Inn,** 1968 Comox St., tel. (604) 683-8002, a quiet retreat from the pace of the city. The decor is stylish, in an old-fashioned way. Highlights include a lounge area with log fireplace, and a small garden out the back. Rates start at $175 s or d, and the luxurious two-room suite goes for $295. Premium.

Central Vancouver

South of False Creek you'll find a profusion of bed and breakfasts. Many lie in quiet residential areas, yet are close to public transportation.

Behind City Hall between Cambie and Yukon Streets is **Paul's Guest House,** 345 W. 14th Ave., Central Vancouver, tel. (604) 872-4753. Paul's is recommended by travelers as a friendly, clean, and comfortable place to stay. The host speaks many languages, cooks breakfast for the guests, and arranges airport transfers; rooms are from $65 s, $75 d. Inexpensive.

Pillow 'n Porridge Guest Suites, 2859 Manitoba St., tel. (604) 879-8977, only three blocks from City Hall, occupies a heritage house dating to the turn of the century. Each of the three rooms is furnished with antiques from around the world, and guests are served a hearty breakfast—with delicious porridge to start, of course. Rooms range $115-135, which includes a kitchen. Moderate.

Farther west, in the suburb of Kitsilano, is **Penny Farthing Inn,** 2855 W. 6th Ave., tel. (604) 739-9002, another heritage house with four antique-filled rooms. The least expensive room is $95 s, $110 d, while the suite, complete with mountain views, a brass bed, and separate lounge area with a television, video player, and compact disc player, is $150 s or d. Moderate.

North Vancouver and Vicinity

Close to Grouse Mountain Gondola, **Mountainside Manor,** 5909 Nancy Greene Way, North Vancouver, tel. (604) 990-9772, is a great place to unwind—especially in the outdoor hot tub. The views are spectacular, the decor modern. During summer, the four rooms are $95-145 s or d. Moderate.

Deep Cove B&B, 2590 Shelley Rd., tel. (604) 929-3932, is also in North Vancouver, not in Deep Cove as the name suggests. Set on a large property adjoining a residential area, the atmosphere is informal and relaxing. Amenities include an outdoor hot tub, lounge, and billiard table. The two guest rooms, each with private bathroom, rent for $85 s, $95 d. Moderate.

Adjoining Deep Cove's Myrtle Park, **Queen**

Anne Manor B&B, 4606 Wickenden Rd., tel. (604) 929-3239, is a modern home with a Victorian-era look, furnished with period antiques. Each of the three guest rooms has its own distinct look; the grandest is Chelsea Suite, featuring a huge canopied bed, private balcony, jacuzzi tub, and a sitting room in a turret. This room is $175 s or d, while the other two range $95-135 s or d. Moderate.

If you're prepared to spend a bit more money (and to book well ahead), **Beachside B&B,** 4208 Evergreen Ave., West Vancouver, tel. (604) 922-7773 or (800) 563-3311, is an excellent choice. Set on the waterfront at Sandy Cove (access off Marine Dr.), Beachside offers views extending across the sound to Stanley Park and the downtown skyline. Rates start at $135 s or d. Expensive.

BACKPACKER LODGES

Budget travelers enjoy many options in Vancouver for under $20 pp per night. Hostelling International (formerly the Youth Hostel Association) has undergone a radical change in direction and now appeals to all ages, and privately run "hostels" within the province fill the gaps. Either way, staying in what have universally become known as "backpackers' hostels" is an enjoyable and inexpensive way to travel through the province. Generally, you need to provide your own sleeping bag or linen, but most supply extra bedding (if needed) at no charge. Accommodations are in dormitories (two to 10 beds) or double rooms. Each also offers a communal kitchen, lounge area, and laundry facilities, while most have Internet access, bike rentals, and organized tours.

HOSTELLING INTERNATIONAL

The curfews and chores are long gone in this worldwide nonprofit organization of 5,000 hostels in 70 countries. Hostelling International—Canada operates two hostels in Vancouver, as well as 16 others scattered throughout the province. Membership isn't even compulsory anymore, although it only takes a few nights of discounted lodging to make up the difference. Other benefits of membership include discounted air, rail, and

bus travel, discounts on car rental, and discounts on some attractions and commercial activities. If you join within Canada, the membership charge is $24 annually. For more information write Hostelling International, 402-234 Abbott St., Vancouver, BC V6B 2K4, call (604) 684-7181, or surf the Internet to www.hihostels.bc.ca. The Canadian head office is at 400-205 Catherine St., Ottawa, ON K2P 1C3, tel. (613) 237-7884, website www.hostellingintl.ca.

Joining Hostelling International in your home country entitles you to reciprocal rights in Canada, as well around the world. Contact addresses include: **Hostelling International-American Youth Hostels,** Suite 840, 733 15th St. NW, Washington, DC 20005, tel. (202) 783-6161, website www.hiayh.org; **Youth Hostels Association,** Trevelyan House, St. Stephen's Hill, St. Albans, Herts. AL1 2DY, England, tel. (0172) 785-5215, website www.yha.org.uk; YHA, 422 Kent St., Sydney, NSW 2000, Australia, tel. (02) 9261-1111, website www.yha.org.au; and **Youth Hostels Association of New Zealand,** P.O. Box 436, Christchurch 1, tel. (03) 379-9970, website www.yha.org.nz.

Downtown

Opened in summer 1996, **Hostelling International Vancouver Downtown,** 1114 Burnaby St., tel. (604) 684-4565, is part of the new wave of facilities run by the world's largest and longest running network of backpacker accommodations. The complex offers a large kitchen, library, game room, and bike rentals. The dormitories hold a maximum of four beds but are small. For these beds members of Hostelling International pay $19, nonmembers $23; private rooms range $48-56 s or d. Budget.

Jericho Beach

If you don't need to stay right downtown, **Hostelling International Vancouver Jericho Beach,** 1515 Discovery St. (near the intersection of Northwest. Marine Dr. and W. 4th Ave.), Point Grey, tel. (604) 224-3208, is a good alternative choice. The location is fantastic—in scenic and safe parkland behind Jericho Beach, across English Bay from downtown and linked to extensive biking and walking trails. Inside the huge white building with snazzy blue trim are separate dorms for men and women, rooms for couples and families, a living area with television, and a kitchen. Additional amenities include a cafeteria open for breakfast and dinner (good food, reasonable prices), a handy information board, lockers, left-luggage service ($5 a bag per week), and limited free parking. Members pay $17.50 per night, nonmembers $21.50 for a dorm, or $43 and $56 respectively for a double room. Budget.

OTHER BACKPACKER LODGES

Downtown and Vicinity

Privately owned backpacker lodges in Vancouver come and go with predictable regularity. Many should be avoided, but the newest addition to the backpacker scene, **Global Village Backpackers,** 1018 Granville St., tel. (604) 682-8226 or (800) 770-7929, website www.globalbackpackers.com, is excellent in all respects. Typical of inner-city hostels the world over, rooms are small, but each has been tastefully decorated, and the communal lounge and kitchen areas serve guests well. Other facilities include public Internet access and a rooftop patio. Rates are $21.40 pp in a dormitory (maximum four beds) or $58.50-65.50 for a double. Budget.

C&N Backpackers Hostel, 927 Main St., tel. (604) 682-2441, has undergone a name change and some improvements since new owners took

over, but the rooms and kitchen are still sparse and the lounge area grubby. The location is central to Pacific Central Station, but the neighborhood is among the worst in the city after dark. Dorm beds are $12, singles $20, and doubles $28. Budget.

North Vancouver

Globetrotter's Inn, 170 W. Esplanade, North Vancouver, tel. (604) 988-2082, is across the road from Lonsdale Quay and the SeaBus Terminal (with regular ferry connections to downtown) and near restaurants, a couple of pubs, and a movie theater. Facilities include a small lounge, fully equipped kitchen, free laundry, and a pool table. Each dorm room holds a maximum of four beds. Rates for the dorm beds are $17, private rooms are $32 s, $40-45 d; weekly rates available. The office is open in summer 9 a.m.-7 p.m., shorter hours the rest of the year. At last report, the owners of Globetrotter's were planning to redevelop the site in the next couple of years, so call ahead before making the trip across Burrard Inlet. Budget.

MORE OPTIONS
FOR BUDGET TRAVELERS

YWCA Hotel

In October 1995 the YWCA opened a brand-new lodging for female travelers, couples, and families at 733 Beatty St., tel. (604) 895-5830 or (800) 663-1424. It's farther from the business core than the old Burrard Street property, but the modern facilities and choice of nearby restaurants more than compensate for the extra distance. More than 150 rooms are spread over 11 stories. Each room has a telephone, and the private rooms have televisions. Communal facilities include two kitchens, three lounges, and two laundries. Guests also have use of the nearby YWCA fitness center, which houses a pool and gym. Rooms with shared bathroom facilities are $55-68 s, $69-80 d; those with a private bathroom are $110 s or d. Inexpensive.

YMCA

Though not as modern as the YWCA, the 110-room YMCA, 955 Burrard St., tel. (604) 681-0221, enjoys a good downtown location, only two blocks from busy Robson Street and all the restaurants and nightlife. Amenities include a coin-op laundry, a small weight room, racquet-ball, sauna, and two lap pools. No cooking facilities are available, but the in-house café is open daily from breakfast to 4 p.m. Parking up the alley beside the building costs $5 for 24 hours; it's supervised during the day. Rooms, none with private bathroom, are available for men, women, and couples. Rooms are $36 s, $44 d ($3 extra per night for a television). Linen is provided and weekly rates are available. Budget.

UBC Housing and Conference Centre

Accommodations are available at the University of British Columbia, out at Point Grey, 16 km west of city center. Summer options include dorm beds, single rooms with shared bathrooms, and one- or two-bedroom suites or studio suites with private bathrooms and kitchenettes. Some suites are available year-round. A restaurant is close by, and a swimming pool, sauna, whirlpool, and tennis and fitness center are on campus; $25-62 s, $90-110 d. For further information and reservations, contact UBC Conference Centre, 5961 Student Union Blvd., tel. (604) 822-1010. Moderate.

Simon Fraser University

Although it's about 20 km east of downtown Vancouver, Simon Fraser University offers inexpensive dorm rooms to travelers in summer. The hilltop campus is known for its modern architecture and excellent city views. Single or twin fully furnished townhouse units with shared bathrooms are available May-Aug.; from $27 s, $45 d. The university is between Highways 7 and 7A in Burnaby. To get there by bus, catch no. 10 or 14 on Granville Mall (get a transfer ticket and ask the driver to tell you where to get off), then transfer to bus no. 135. Contact Housing and Conference Services, Room 212, Mc-Taggart-Cowan Hall, Burnaby, Vancouver, BC V5A 1S6, tel. (604) 291-4503. Budget.

CAMPGROUNDS

You won't find any campgrounds in the city center area, but a limited number dot the suburbs along the major approach routes. Before trekking out to any of them, ring ahead to check for vacancies. Commercial and provincial park campgrounds are listed in Tourism BC's invaluable *Accommodations* guide, available at all information centers or by calling (250) 387-1642 or (800) HELLOBC (435-5622).

North

The closest campground to inner-city attractions is **Capilano RV Park,** 295 Tomahawk Ave., North Vancouver, tel. (604) 987-4722. To get there from downtown, cross Lions Gate Bridge, turn right on Marine Dr., right on Capilano Rd., and right on Welch Street. From Hwy. 1/99 in West Vancouver, exit south on Taylor Way toward the shopping center and turn left over the Capilano River. It's about an hour walk to downtown from the campground, over Lions Gate Bridge and through Stanley Park. Although limited spots are available for tents, the park is really intended for vehicle camping and RVs. It gets crowded in summer; advance prepaid reservations are re-quired for July and August. If you want a tent site, call ahead and ask if they have any grassy areas left. A tent site runs $22; a site with electricity, water, and sewer hookups is $35. Budget.

South

Large **Richmond RV Park,** 15 km (20 minutes) south of downtown at 6200 River Rd., tel. (604) 270-7878 or (800) 755-4905, is a great place for those looking to stay in shape. It lies just across the road from the Fraser River, and atop the dike separating the river from the road is an eight-km-long footpath. The path is extremely popular with local walkers, joggers, dog exercisers, cyclists, and even seaplane and jet enthusiasts—the seaplane terminal is within sight, and the campground is just off the final flight path for Vancouver International Airport. Grassy banks and strategic benches along the path encourage quiet reflection on a bright sunny day. Tent sites are $16.50, while serviced sites range $19-28. Facilities include free showers, a coin-op laundry, and a game room. Budget.

Parkcanada RV Inns, on Hwy. 17 (take the 52nd St. exit), tel. (604) 943-5811, is convenient to the BC Ferries terminal at Tsawwassen, a 30-minute drive south of city center. The park is busy throughout summer. Amenities include a heated pool, store, laundromat, lounge, and free showers. Unserviced sites, suitable for tents, are $15; serviced sites range $18-23. Budget.

Peace Arch RV Park, 14601 40th Ave., tel. (604) 594-7009, is between the suburbs of White Rock and Delta, 10 km from Douglas Border Crossing on Hwy. 99. The well-tended facilities include a heated pool, game room, and laundry. Sites in the tenting area are $18.50 while hookups range $20-25. Budget.

East
Surrounded by Burnaby Lake Regional Park, **Burnaby Cariboo RV Park,** 8765 Cariboo Place, Burnaby, tel. (604) 420-1722, offers luxurious facilities—an indoor heated pool, jacuzzi, sundeck, an adult lounge, and much more. Sites in the walk-in tenting area cost $21 per night; hookups are $25-33. The park is 17 km east of downtown. To get there, take the Cariboo exit from the TransCanada Hwy., turn right at the first traffic light, then make the first left, then the first right into Cariboo Place. Budget.

Anmore Camplands lies on Buntzen Lake, near the head of Burrard Inlet, tel. (604) 469-2311. To get there, head north along Hwy. 7A from Exit 44 of the TransCanada Hwy., turn left onto Ioco Rd., and follow the signs. Facilities include a small heated pool, canoe and bike rentals, a barbecue area, a laundry, and a small general store. Tent sites are $24 per night, hookups $28-30.

Farther east, **Dogwood Campgrounds of B.C.,** 15151 112th Ave. (take Exit 50 north off the TransCanada Hwy., then head west on 112th Ave.), Surrey, tel. (604) 583-5585, is 35 km east of Vancouver and close to the SkyTrain station at Whalley. Hookups are $30-35. Budget.

Provincial Parks
Reserve a spot at 50 of the province's most popular provincial parks by calling BC Parks' Discover Camping hotline at (604) 689-9025 or (800) 689-9025. Reservations are taken between 15 March and 15 September, for dates up to three months in advance. The reservation fee is $6.42 per night, to a maximum of $18, and is in addition to applicable camping fees. The website is www.discovercamping.ca.

Of the provincial parks on the north side of the city, the only one with a campground is **Golden Ears,** 40 km from downtown near the suburb of Maple Ridge. To get there, take Hwy. 7 from downtown through Coquitlam and Pitt Meadows to Maple Ridge and follow the signs north on 232nd Street. The park holds almost 400 sites in two campgrounds near Alouette Lake. The campgrounds are linked by hiking trails. Facilities include hot showers, flush toilets, and a picnic table and fire ring at each site; $15.50 per night.

Traveling north on Hwy. 99 toward Whistler, **Porteau Cove Provincial Park,** 20 km north of Horseshoe Bay, offers 60 sites in a pleasant treed setting with mountain views. All sites are $15.50.

If you're traveling the TransCanada Hwy., the closest provincial park campground is at **Cultus Lake,** 100 km east of downtown and seven km south of the highway service center of Chilliwack (Exit 119). All sites are $15.50, which includes the use of hot showers.

Stanley Park's Third Beach

FOOD

Vancouver is the shining jewel in Canada's otherwise tarnished culinary crown, overcoming the country's bland reputation as a gastronomical backwater. With almost 3,000 restaurants, cafés, and coffeehouses, and as home to almost 100 cultures, this ethnic crossroads is a gourmet feast. The local specialty is Pacific Northwest cuisine (also called "fusion cuisine" by the culinarily correct), which combines fresh local produce, such as seafood and seasonal game, with Asian flavors and ingredients, usually in a healthy, low-fat way.

Most downtown restaurants open for lunch and dinner throughout the week and Saturday night only on weekends. In touristy areas such as Gastown and along Robson St. restaurants open daily for lunch and dinner, and along late-night haunts such as Davie St. many places stay open 24 hours a day. Stroll Robson St., Denman St., and W. 4th Ave. for the biggest concentrations of coffeehouses. Robson and Denman Streets also offer a cosmopolitan choice of cafés and restaurants, as does historic Gastown. For Chinese food, head to Chinatown, naturally. Restaurants throughout the city specialize in seafood; for the freshest, straight from the trawlers, head to Steveston on the city's southern outskirts.

One thing that will soon become apparent to first-time visitors is the amount of coffee consumed by the locals; specialty coffeehouses are *everywhere*. Seattle-based Starbucks Coffee Co. alone has 80 Vancouver outlets, including two sitting kitty-corner to each other on Robson Street.

DOWNTOWN DINING

CAFÉS AND CHEAP EATS

Downtown Vancouver has so many good dining options that it is a shame to eat in a food court, but like in cities around the Western world, they are a good place for a fast, reliable, and inexpensive meal. The southwest corner of the Pacific Centre (at Howe and Georgia Streets, diagonally opposite the art gallery) holds a glass-domed food court with many inexpensive food bars and seating indoors or outdoors.

Although this book purposely ignores the fast-food chains, **White Spot** is worthy of inclusion. The first White Spot restaurant opened in Vancouver in 1928, dishing up hamburgers and milkshakes. Today, 50 White Spots across the country still offer burgers—including the famous Triple O—as well as everything from pastas to stir-fried vegetables. Downtown, White Spot is at 1616 W. Georgia St., tel. (604) 681-8034.

A good place for food on the run is one of the many takeout pizza joints scattered throughout the city. While in the trendy West End a slice of pizza can cost up to $3, downtown many places charge just 99 cents a slice, and for an extra 50 cents you get a can of pop. Three of these cheapies lie along W. Pender between Granville and Richards Streets.

Two blocks up from Canada Place **Scoozis,** 808 W. Hastings St., tel. (604) 684-1009, offers dimly lit surroundings but good breakfasts for under $7. The rest of the day, it's pitas, pizzas, and main meals such as lamb chops for $14. Next door (up the hill) is **Richard and Co.,** 451 Howe St., tel. (604) 681-9885, a sparsely but stylishly furnished café where a coffee and muffin is just $2.50, soups start at $3 a bowl, and focaccia bread sandwiches are all around $5. It's open daily 7 a.m.-2 p.m.

Granville Street and Vicinity
Granville St. beyond the mall isn't exactly the culinary heart of the city, but along its rough-around-the-edges length are some of the Vancouver's best dining bargains. Don't expect too much in the way of decor from *any* of the following places, but do expect hearty portions, inexpensive prices, and in all except the infamous Elbow Room friendly service. The listings below start near Granville Mall and work their way southwest toward Granville Island.

"Quality Food, Snappy Service" is the catchcry at **The Templeton,** 1087 Granville St., tel. (604) 685-4612. Eat at the low counter or in the vinyl booths, each with a small jukebox, and enjoy traditional diner fare as well as more modern creations like veggie burgers. Breakfasts go for under $5, lunches range $5-8, and dinners are under $10.

On the same side of the street, one block toward False Creek, **Grade A Café,** 1175 Granville St., tel. (604) 669-7495, offers the classic Canadian and Chinese menu. Everything is under $10, and the daily soup, sandwich, and dessert special is just $5.

Hungry and have only a loonie? Then head to one of the cheap pizza joints down Granville Street.

Two blocks from Granville St., the **Korner Restaurant,** 1099 Richards St., tel. (604) 682-8678, is an old-style diner where the daily soup and sandwich special is a bargain at $4. It's open Mon.-Sat. 10:30 a.m.-2:30 p.m. and then reopens at 5:30 p.m. and doesn't close again until 2:30 a.m.

The **Elbow Room,** one block south of Granville St. at 560 Davie St., tel. (604) 685-3628, is a Vancouver institution where portions are huge and the prices reasonable ($7.50 for the Lumberjack breakfast), but it's the service that you'll remember long after the meal. Feel like coffee? Get it yourself. A glass of water, maybe? "Get off your ass and get it yourself" a sign declares. The waiters take no nonsense, and the constant banter from the open kitchen if not memorable is in the least unique. But it's all in good fun, and if you get abused you'll join a long list of celebrities whose photos adorn the walls. If you don't finish your meal, you must make a donation to a local charity; if it's a pancake you can't finish, you're advised to "just rub it on your thighs, because that's where it's going anyway!" The Elbow Room is open Mon.-Fri. 7:30 a.m.-3:30 p.m., Sat.-Sun. 8:30 a.m.-4 p.m., but breakfast is most popular and is served all day; Sunday morning is when the kitchen and wait staff are at their wittiest.

Continue down Davie St. from the Elbow Room and you'll spot **Steamrollers,** 437 Davie St., tel. (604) 608-0852, at street level of a residential highrise. What at first looks like just another trendy little big-city café is in fact one of Vancouver's best value eateries. The name "Steamrollers" is derived from the process of steaming tortillas, before they are rolled up as burritos around a wide variety of fillings then wrapped in tinfoil. The finished product is absolutely massive (one burrito can easily feed two people) and goes for $4-6. Steamrollers is open Mon.-Sat. 10 a.m.-8 p.m.

Around the corner is **Lui's Ville Café and Pies,** 1225 Homer St., tel. (604) 669-7437, a great little place to enjoy super-cheap cakes and pastries, or a cooked breakfast from just $3.50.

The historic **Yale Hotel,** just before the Granville Street Bridge at 1300 Granville St., tel. (604) 681-9253, is a great place to wash down a meal from one of the above eateries with a cold beer. It's been totally renovated, is a legendary blues and jazz venue, and has a large pool room.

Davie Street

The downtown end of Davie St., between Burrard and Bute Streets, holds many coffeehouses and inexpensive dining options. It is a popular after-hours haunt, with many places open 24 hours to cater to the nightclub crowd. Whether it's a slice of pizza for a buck, seafood, or sushi, you'll find it along Davie Street.

Spuntino Bakery Caffe, 1101 Davie St., tel. (604) 685-9607, is set back from its corner location with indoor and outdoor seating (complete with heat lamps). The cozy atmosphere is complemented by mellow background music, and plenty of reading material is offered. Cakes and pastries are the specialty, but the healthy sandwiches are also good. It's open daily till late.

The **Fresgo Inn,** 1138 Davie St., tel. (604) 689-1332, is a cavernous self-serve cafeteria where breakfast is bargain priced (eggs, bacon, and pancakes is just $4.50) and hamburgers cost from $3.25. Once open 24 hours, it now closes at 3 a.m. Mon.-Sat. and at midnight on Sunday.

With a full-size Cadillac mounted above the door, **Doll and Penny's,** 1167 Davie St., tel. (604) 685-3417, is hard to miss. Once inside, colorful artwork adorning purple walls is also eye-catching. Servings aren't huge, but the price is right. Cooked breakfasts cost from $4, and main meal dishes such as pasta range $7-10. Breakfast prices rise after 10 a.m., and meals from the main menu cost more after 4 p.m.

On the corner of the next intersection, at Bute St., is **Hamburger Mary's,** 1202 Davie St., tel. (604) 687-1293, a classic '50s-style diner, complete with chrome chairs, mirrored walls, and an old jukebox. Delicious hamburgers attract the crowds to Mary's; starting at $5, they aren't particularly cheap, but they come with fries, and extras such as salad are just $1. Breakfast ($5 for eggs, bacon, hash browns, and toast) begins daily at 7 a.m., and the last burgers are flipped in the early hours of the morning. Wash down your meal with one of Mary's famous milkshakes.

With bold all-black decor and mirrored walls, **The Edge,** 1148 Davie St., tel. (604) 688-3395, is where the cool cats of the local nightclubbing scene come for a late-night caffeine jolt.

Sandwiched between a florist and a hardware store beyond Jervis St. is **Zagros,** 1326 Davie St., tel. (604) 689-5999, a tiny neighborhood restaurant featuring the cuisine of Persia, as well as pizza, at bargain prices; the nightly dinner special is under $8.

For takeout, this part of town has a couple of good options. At 1091 Davie St., **Mr Pickwicks,** tel. (604) 669-7088, offers fish and chips to eat in or take out from $8. Opposite Hamburger Mary's, **Chicken on the Way,** 1226 Bute St., tel. (604) 688-9966, is a hole-in-the-wall joint where two pieces of chicken, fries, and a can of pop will set you back just $5, or choose from the Chinese menu where no dish is more than $8. Both these places also have limited seating.

Pub Grub

Two Parrots Taverna, 1202 Granville St., tel. (604) 685-9657, fills the first floor of an old hotel. The modern and colorful interior seems a little out of place at this end of town, but the food is good and there's always something on special, such as 15-cent wings on Thursday and ribs for $2 a pound on Friday.

RESTAURANTS

North American

Aqua Riva, 200 Granville St., tel. (604) 683-5599, is right beside Canada Place, and with floor-to-ceiling windows the views across Burrard Inlet are absolutely stunning. The restaurant itself is cavernous with a variety of seating arrangements, depending on the mood and the time of day. The least expensive way to enjoy the view is with a pizza baked in a wood-fired oven ($12-15), as other mains, mostly seafood, range $19-30.

As you'd expect, views are even better from the **Revolving Restaurant** atop the Harbour Centre Tower at 555 W. Hastings St., tel. (604) 689-7304. The menu features contemporary North American cuisine; diners get a free ride to the top and then can expect to pay under $20 for most mains at lunch and over $20 (up to $43 for Alaskan king crab) at dinner.

Seafood

At Canada Place is **Five Sails,** in the Pan Pacific Vancouver Hotel, tel. (604) 662-8111. It's open for dinner only, and the fabulous setting and harbor views are reflected in the prices. The menu features items as varied as a traditional Mon-

golian dish, but is mostly seafood-oriented, with highlights of locally harvested crab, salmon, sea bass, mussels, and scallops. For an appetizer, the cod chowder ($9) is an easy choice, while main dishes range $22-38. Five Sails is open daily for dinner only.

One of Vancouver's finest seafood restaurants is **A Kettle of Fish,** near the Burrard Street Bridge at 900 Pacific St., tel. (604) 682-6853. The casual decor features café-style seating and abundant greenery, while the menu swims with schools of piscatory pleasures. New England clam chowder ($5.50) is one of over 20 appetizers, while entrées such as grilled snapper ($17.50) or a seafood platter for two ($38.50) make up the main menu. It's open for lunch Mon.-Fri. and for dinner daily.

TexMex

Carlos and Bud's is near the far end of Granville St., not very convenient to downtown attractions, but in a city where tourism plays such a large role and being "seen" is so important to so many, this restaurant is unique. The young unpretentious crowds of locals linger long after business lunch hours have ended, and getting an outside table when the sun is out entails a wait at any time of day. Located in a former gas station, only the paintwork and decor have changed; even oil stains remain. Tables are spread around the two old mechanics bays and outside, on a large concrete patio where vehicles once sat awaiting repair. The tool racks and girlie posters have been ripped off the walls, replaced by a funky paint job and typical Route 66 memorabilia like gas pumps, road signage, and number plates. The menu, amusing in itself, features all the usual dishes found in Mexican restaurants throughout Canada and the States, and although not particularly cheap dishes are well presented and offer generous portions. A popular way of dining here is with a platter of finger foods and a jug of Mexican beer shared between friends. Or "lasso a waitress" and order a round of tequila, $2.50 for a shot of the "cheap shit" and $5.50 for a shot of premium. Carlos and Bud's is a little difficult to find; it's at 555 Pacific St., where it passes below Seymour St. and the beginning of the Granville Street Bridge, tel. (604) 684-5335. It's open daily from 11 a.m. until the early hours of the morning.

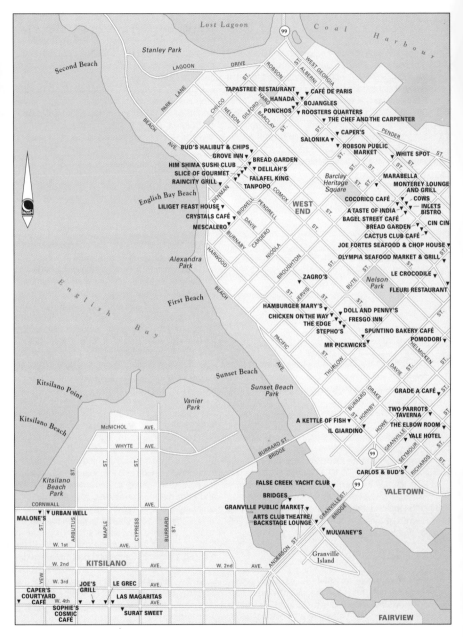

Lost Lagoon

Coal Harbour

99

Stanley Park

Second Beach

LAGOON DRIVE

WEST GEORGIA

ROBSON ST. ALBERNI ST.

PARK LANE

CHILCO NELSON GILFORD HARO BARCLAY

BEACH AVE.

TAPASTREE RESTAURANT ▼
HANADA ▼
PONCHOS ▼

▼ CAFÉ DE PARIS
▼ BOJANGLES
▼ ROOSTERS QUARTERS
▼ THE CHEF AND THE CARPENTER

PENDER ST.

▼ CAPER'S

SALONIKA ▼   ▼ ROBSON PUBLIC
                MARKET

BUD'S HALIBUT & CHIPS ▼
GROVE INN ▼
HIM SHIMA SUSHI CLUB ▼
SLICE OF GOURMET ▼
RAINCITY GRILL ▼

BREAD GARDEN ▼
▼ DELILAH'S
FALAFEL KING ▼
TANPOPO ▼

Barclay
Heritage
Square

WHITE SPOT ST.

MARABELLA ▼
MONTEREY LOUNGE
AND GRILL ▼

English Bay Beach

LILIGET FEAST HOUSE ▼

CRYSTALS CAFÉ ▼

MESCALERO ▼

DENMAN BIDWELL PENDRELL COMOX

DAVIE CARDERO NICOLA

BURNABY

HARWOOD

WEST
END

COCORICO CAFÉ ▼   ▼ COWS
                    ▼ INLETS
A TASTE OF INDIA ▼   BISTRO
BAGEL STREET CAFÉ ▼
        BREAD GARDEN ▼   CIN CIN
        CACTUS CLUB CAFÉ ▼
JOE FORTES SEAFOOD & CHOP HOUSE ▼
OLYMPIA SEAFOOD MARKET & GRILL ▼

Alexandra
Park

BROUGHTON

BEACH

First Beach

ZAGRO'S ▼

BUTE

Nelson
Park

LE CROCODILE ▼

FLEURI RESTAURANT ▼

English Bay

HAMBURGER MARY'S ▼
CHICKEN ON THE WAY ▼
THE EDGE ▼
STEPHO'S ▼

JERVIS ST.

▼ DOLL AND PENNY'S
▼ FRESGO INN

PACIFIC AVE.

MR PICKWICKS ▼

THURLOW

SPUNTINO BAKERY CAFÉ ▼
POMODORI ▼

HELMCKEN ST.

DAVIE ST.

Sunset Beach

Sunset Beach
Park

Vanier
Park

Kitsilano Point

McNICHOL AVE.

Kitsilano Beach

WHYTE AVE.

BURRARD DRAKE HORNBY HOWE GRANVILLE SEYMOUR RICHARDS ST.

GRADE A CAFÉ ▼

TWO PARROTS
TAVERNA ▼
THE ELBOW ROOM ▼
YALE HOTEL ▼

A KETTLE OF FISH ▼

IL GIARDINO ▼

BURRARD ST.
BRIDGE

99

Kitsilano
Beach
Park

CORNWALL AVE.

CARLOS & BUD'S ▼

YALETOWN

MALONE'S ▼ ▼ URBAN WELL

ARBUTUS MAPLE CYPRESS BURRARD ST.

FALSE CREEK YACHT CLUB ▼

BRIDGES ▼

GRANVILLE PUBLIC MARKET ▼

ARTS CLUB THEATRE/
BACKSTAGE LOUNGE ▼

GRANVILLE ST. BRIDGE

99

MULVANEY'S ▼

Granville
Island

W. 1st

W. 2nd

KITSILANO AVE.

W. 2nd AVE.

ANDERSON ST.

FAIRVIEW

VIEW

W. 3rd

JOE'S
GRILL

LE GREC AVE.

CAPER'S
COURTYARD
CAFÉ

W. 4th

▼ ▼ ▼ LAS MAGARITAS AVE.

SOPHIE'S
COSMIC
CAFÉ

▼ SURAT SWEET

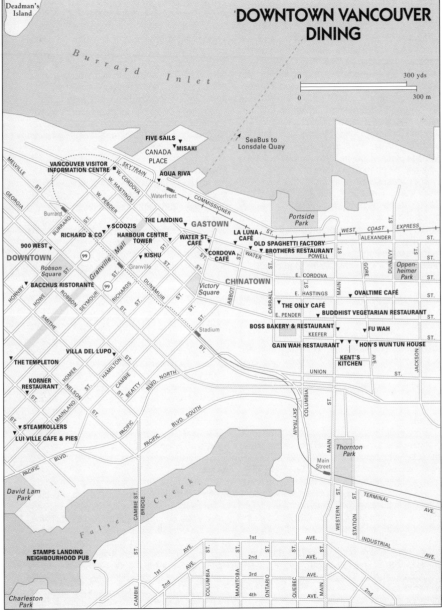

DOWNTOWN VANCOUVER DINING

Deadman's Island

Burrard Inlet

0   300 yds

0   300 m

FIVE SAILS ▼

MISAKI ▼

CANADA PLACE

SeaBus to Lonsdale Quay

VANCOUVER VISITOR INFORMATION CENTRE

AQUA RIVA ▼

Waterfront

Portside Park

SKYTRAIN

W. CORDOVA ST.

W. HASTINGS ST.

W. PENDER ST.

MELVILLE ST.

GEORGIA ST.

Burrard

COMMISSIONER ST.

THE LANDING ▼   GASTOWN

LA LUNA CAFÉ ▼

WEST COAST EXPRESS

ALEXANDER ST.

SCOOZIS ▼

RICHARD & CO ▼

HARBOUR CENTRE TOWER

WATER ST. CAFÉ ▼

CORDOVA CAFÉ ▼

WATER ST.

OLD SPAGHETTI FACTORY ▼

BROTHERS RESTAURANT ▼

POWELL ST.

GORE ST.

DUNLEVY ST.

Oppen-heimer Park

BURRARD ST.

HORNBY ST.

HOWE ST.

SEYMOUR ST.

RICHARDS ST.

HOMER ST.

HAMILTON ST.

NELSON ST.

CAMBIE ST.

BEATTY ST.

MAINLAND ST.

SMITHE ST.

900 WEST ▼

DOWNTOWN

Robson Square

99

KISHU ▼

Granville

DUNSMUIR ST.

GRANVILLE MALL

ROBSON ST.

99

BACCHUS RISTORANTE ▼

CHINATOWN

E. CORDOVA ST.

E. HASTINGS ST.

OVALTIME CAFÉ ▼

MAIN ST.

Victory Square

ABBOTT ST.

CARRALL ST.

THE ONLY CAFÉ ▼

E. PENDER ST.

BUDDHIST VEGETARIAN RESTAURANT ▼

Stadium

BOSS BAKERY & RESTAURANT ▼

KEEFER ST.

FU WAH ▼

GAIN WAH RESTAURANT ▼

HON'S WUN TUN HOUSE ▼

JACKSON AVE.

VILLA DEL LUPO ▼

KENT'S KITCHEN ▼

THE TEMPLETON ▼

UNION ST.

KORNER RESTAURANT ▼

COLUMBIA ST.

SKYTRAIN

Thornton Park

BLVD. NORTH

BLVD. SOUTH

STEAMROLLERS ▼

LUI VILLE CAFE & PIES ▼

PACIFIC ST.

Main Street

MAIN ST.

WESTERN ST.

STATION ST.

TERMINAL AVE.

PACIFIC BLVD.

David Lam Park

CAMBIE ST. BRIDGE

False Creek

INDUSTRIAL AVE.

1st AVE.

2nd AVE.

3rd AVE.

4th AVE.

COLUMBIA ST.

MANITOBA ST.

ONTARIO ST.

QUEBEC ST.

MAIN ST.

2nd AVE.

STAMPS LANDING NEIGHBOURHOOD PUB ▼

CAMBIE ST.

1st AVE.

2nd AVE.

Charleston Park

© AVALON TRAVEL PUBLISHING

Hotel Dining

Fleuri Restaurant, in the Sutton Place Hotel at 845 Burrard St., tel. (604) 682-5511, is one of Vancouver's best hotel restaurants, and you needn't spend a fortune to enjoy dining in what is generally regarded as one of the world's best hotels. Every afternoon, high tea—complete with scones and cream, finger foods, and nonalcoholic beverages—costs $17.50. The restaurant is also open for breakfast, lunch, and dinner, with a magnificent seafood buffet offered on Friday and Saturday nights. Fleuri is also regarded as having one of the city's best Sunday brunch spreads. Adjacent to the restaurant is the Gerald Lounge, the perfect spot for a pre-dinner drink.

After massive renovations to the grand old Hotel Vancouver, 900 W. Georgia St., tel. (604) 669-9378, the Timber Club, famous as a meeting place of the city's social set, reopened as **900 West,** with the same elegant feeling of days gone by. The contemporary North American menu is varied, offering everything from grilled halibut to a rack of lamb. Mains start at $26, or relax with a snack in the wine bar. It's open for lunch Mon.-Sat. and daily for dinner.

The Wedgewood Hotel's signature dining room, the **Bacchus Ristorante,** 845 Hornby St., tel. (604) 689-7777, has recently undergone renovations and now features a long bar and a cigar room. The emphasis is on Italian cuisine, but the menu relies heavily on local produce, changing with the seasons. It's open throughout the day, and afternoon tea is served daily 2-4 p.m.

Italian

Of Vancouver's many Italian restaurants, one of the most popular is **Il Giardino,** on the south side of downtown in a distinctive yellow Italian-style villa at 1382 Hornby St., tel. (604) 669-2422. The light, bright furnishings and an enclosed terrace provide the perfect ambience for indulging in the featured Tuscan cuisine. Expect to pay $12-16 for lunch entrées, $14-30 for dinner entrées. Open Mon.-Fri. noon-2:30 p.m. and Mon.-Sat. 6-11 p.m.

Of a similar high standard is **Villa del Lupo,** 869 Hamilton St., tel. (604) 688-7436, in the entertainment district. The breads and pastas are prepared daily, and mostly local fresh produce is used. Open daily for dinner.

Tucked away on the third level of a nondescript commercial building at 888 Nelson St. is **Pomodori,** tel. (604) 681-4919, a hidden gem in Vancouver's dining scene. Although the official address is Nelson St., the entrance (on Hornby St., marked only by a small banner beside a narrow stairwell that leads to the restaurant) is difficult to find. The setting is minimalistic, with all furnishings white and shades of cream. It's divided into separate sections, one furnished with couches, another with bench seating, and another with regular tables and chairs. It's open Mon.-Sat. for dinner.

French

For Vancouver's finest French cuisine, go to the small, intimate **Le Crocodile,** 909 Burrard St., tel. (604) 669-4298, named after a restaurant in the owner's homeland. The menu relies heavily on traditional French techniques and style and is complemented by an extensive wine list. Entrées range $14-22. Open for lunch Mon.-Fri. and for dinner Mon.-Sat.; make reservations for weekend dining.

Greek

Expect to wait for a table at **Stepho's,** 1124 Davie St., tel. (604) 683-2555, one of Vancouver's best-value restaurants. Locals line up here to enjoy the atmosphere of a typical Greek taverna—complete with a terra-cotta floor, blue and white tablecloths, and lots of colorful flowering plants. All the favorite Greek dishes are offered, such as souvlakis or a steak and Greek salad combination for under $8, and portions are generous. Finish off with a delicious baklava, which costs just $3, and coffee for a buck. Stepho's is open daily noon-11:30 p.m.

Asian

Many Japanese restaurants are scattered between Granville St. and Gastown, a reflection of the many English language schools concentrated in the area. They are busiest at lunchtime, when the local student population hits the streets looking for a quick and inexpensive meal, and many excellent deals can be found. **Kishu,** 538 Seymour St., tel. (604) 689-8883, is a notch above the rest in terms of decor but is typical price-wise. Lunch specials are all around $7, or try an 18-piece sushi plate and a bowl of miso soup for just $12. Open Mon.-Fri. 10 a.m.-10 p.m., Saturday noon-10 p.m., Sunday noon-8 p.m. **Misaki,** in Canada Place, tel. (604) 891-2893, offers traditional Japanese cuisine but makes use of local produce. It's not particularly cheap (expect to pay $70 for two), but the food is among the best in the city.

GASTOWN

Cafés

Gastown is the most tourist-oriented part of Vancouver, yet it has many fine eating establishments that attract locals as well as visitors. At 375 Water St., adjacent to the SeaBus terminal, is The Landing, a restored warehouse now housing elegant boutiques and a couple of good-value eateries. One option is **Pastel's,** tel. (604) 684-0176, which serves up a good $4 breakfast special and $7 Sunday brunch.

Some of Gastown's best coffee is ground and brewed at **La Luna Cafe,** 131 Water St., tel. (604) 687-5862. The café's striking yellow-and-black decor, daily papers, great coffee, and inexpensive light snacks make this a pleasant escape from busy Water Street.

Simple surroundings show off innovative artworks at **Cordova Cafe,** 307 W. Cordova St., tel. (604) 688-3440. Light meals are good value—a bowl of chili is $4, a Greek salad is $5, and the daily soup-and-sandwich special is $6.

At Gastown's busiest intersection, opposite the crowd-drawing steam clock, is **Water St. Cafe,** 300 Water St., tel. (604) 689-2832. Sidewalk tables make for good peoplewatching, while the stylish interior is well suited to a quiet meal. More of a restaurant than a café, the menu offers good pasta, chicken, and salads for around $12, and delicious specialties such as grilled Pacific salmon for a bit more.

Inexpensive Dining

The unique decor at **Brothers Restaurant,** 1 Water St., tel. (604) 683-9124, features monastery-like surroundings of wood, brick, stained glass, chandeliers, and monkish murals. Enjoy delicious soups (try the Boston clam chowder), salads, sandwiches, and a variety of entrées ($9.50-17)—all served by waiters appropriately dressed in monk attire—accompa-

nied by congregational sing-alongs and laser light shows. The daily lunch specials are good value, as are the early dinner deals available Mon.-Thurs. before 6 p.m.

The **Old Spaghetti Factory,** 53 Water St., tel. (604) 684-1288, is a family-style favorite offering lunch entrées from $6 and dinner entrées from $10, including salad, bread, dessert, and coffee. This place is worth a visit for the eclectic array of furnishings, from old lamps to a 1904 trolley car.

North American

The designers of **Raintree,** 375 Water St., tel. (604) 688-5570, have taken advantage of a historic building, The Landing, to create an elegant setting without taking away the views extending across Burrard Inlet. Exposed beams, red-brick walls, and a slate floor all give class to what was originally a warehouse. The least expensive lunch items are the pastas, which cost under $15, while seafood dishes are only a couple of dollars more. Dinner mains, ranging $20-30, take advantage of local produce, such as salmon, which is served with goat cream cheese from the Southern Gulf Islands.

CHINATOWN

For Chinese food, you can't go wrong in Chinatown, a few blocks east of the city center. Chinatown encompasses six blocks, but restaurants and fresh-produce stalls are concentrated within the two blocks bordered by Main, Keefer, Gore, and E. Hastings Streets. Within this area, look for stalls selling fish, fruit, vegetables, and other exotic goodies up Pender St. and one block either side of Pender along Gore Street. These markets are especially busy early in the morning when local restaurateurs are stocking up for the day's trade.

Dining in Chinatown offers two distinct options—traditional eateries where you'll find the locals and the larger, westernized restaurants that attract non-Chinese and a younger Chinese crowd. A perfect combination of the two is **Kent's Kitchen,** 232 Keefer St., tel. (604) 669-2237, a modern café-style restaurant where the service is fast and efficient, the food freshly prepared, and the prices incredibly low. Two specialty dishes, rice, and a can of pop make a meal that costs just $5, with more unusual dishes such as pig's feet for $3.75 including rice. The most expensive combination is a large portion of shrimp and sweet and sour pork, which along with rice and pop is $8 (and could easily feed two people).

Next door to Kent's, **Hon's Wun Tun House,** 230 Keefer St., tel. (604) 688-0871, is a large, bright, and modern restaurant that attracts a younger Chinese crowd for mostly westernized Chinese. The menu lists over 300 dishes, all under $10, and all prepared within sight of diners. Across the parkade entrance from the main restaurant is another Hon's, this one a takeout.

Tiny **Gain Wah Restaurant,** 218 Keefer St., tel. (604) 684-1740, is noted for inexpensive congee, a simple soup of water extracted from boiling rice. A bowl of congee costs $1.50, with flavorings an additional 25 cents to $2. On the main menu no dish except those containing seafood is over $10. The friendly staff will be willing to help you decide on a dish.

Around the corner from Keefer St., Gore Street is less westernized; beyond the large fish market you'll find **Fu Wah,** 555 Gore St., tel. (604) 688-8722, which has a ridiculously inexpensive dim sum menu.

A couple of other recommendations are the **Boss Bakery and Restaurant,** 532 Main St., tel. (604) 683-3860, always crowded and offering a great selection of Chinese- and Western-style pastries, and the **Buddhist Vegetarian Restau-**

EAST HASTINGS STREET

So close to the bustling tourist-filled streets of Gastown is East Hastings Street, Vancouver's very own skid row. Linking downtown to Chinatown, it draws down-and-outs from across the country for cheap hotel rooms rented by the month, dingy bars, and warm winter climate—perfect for sleeping on the streets. And although this area should *definitely* be avoided after dark, wandering its length even in daylight hours is a real eye-opener. Don't even think about staying in the hotels along here, but the restaurants are another matter. Between the pubs, pawnshops, and peepshows, there are some real bargains to be had and, well, dining in this part of the city is an experience you won't forget in a hurry.

Just 300 yards from Gastown is Vancouver's oldest restaurant, the **Only Cafe,** 20 E. Hastings St., which has been serving bargain-basement seafood for over 80 years. The decor is very 1950s, with two U-shaped counters, two duct-taped booths, and no bathrooms, but the food is always fresh and cooked to perfection. The seafood comes from the adjacent Chinatown markets, so there's always a wide variety to choose from and the fish comes deep-fried, poached, or grilled. The clam chowder is also delicious. Only Cafe is open daily 11 a.m.-8 p.m.

Beyond Main St., on the edge of Chinatown, the **Ovaltine Café,** 251 E. Hastings St. (look for the classic neon sign hanging out front), has been serving up cheap chow for over 50 years. It's a classic diner, with vinyl booths, a long counter, and a sad looking dessert rack. Breakfast servings aren't huge but start at just $3.50, and the burgers range $3.75-6. It's open 6 a.m.-midnight.

Wash down a meal from the Only Cafe with a beer at the Balmoral Hotel for a true East Hastings St. experience.

rant, 137 E. Pender St., tel. (604) 683-8816, which serves up inexpensive vegetarian food in bland surroundings.

ROBSON STREET

Linking downtown to the West End, Robson Street holds the city's largest concentration of eateries, ranging from Joe Fortes, one of Vancouver's finest seafood restaurants, to the city's Hooters franchise. In addition to a number of fine-dining restaurants, dozens of cafés sprinkle the sidewalks with outdoor tables—perfect for peoplewatching.

Cafés and Coffeehouses
It's been said that Vancouver is addicted to coffee, and walking along Robson St. it would be hard to disagree. The street harbors multiple outlets of the main coffeehouse chains, including **Starbucks** at 1099, 1100, and 1702 Robson, and **Blenz** at 345 and 1201 Robson. The listings below start closest to downtown and work their way out toward Stanley Park.

One of the best spots in all of Vancouver for coffee and a light snack is at one of the 16 **Bread Garden** cafés scattered throughout the metropolitan area. In this part of the city, the Bread Garden is half a block off busy Robson St. at 812 Bute St., tel. (604) 688-3213. It's open 24 hours a day and is always busy—so much so that patrons often need to take a number and wait for service. The coffee is great, as are the freshly baked muffins and pastries. Salads and healthy sandwiches are also available.

Back on the main drag, the **Bagel St. Cafe,** 1218 Robson St., tel. (604) 681-2711, part of a 20-strong franchise found throughout the Lower Mainland, sells a wide variety of bagels to take out or eat in.

Cows, 1301 Robson St., tel. (604) 682-2622, is a specialty ice creamery where single scoops cost from $3. A wide range of colorful Cows merchandise is also for sale (check it all out on the Cows website, www.cows.ca).

At the west end of Robson St., **Caper's,** 1675 Robson St., tel. (604) 687-5288, sells groceries for the health-conscious. Caper's also has an in-house bakery and a large café with tables spread around the balcony.

Seafood
Joe Fortes Seafood and Chophouse, 777 Thurlow St. (half a block off Robson St.), tel. (604) 669-1940, is named after one of Vancouver's best-loved heroes, a swimming coach and lifeguard at English Bay. This restaurant is a city institution and is always busy. The comfortable interior offers elegant furnishings, bleached-linen tablecloths, a rooftop patio, and an oyster bar where you can relax while waiting for your table. At lunch, the specialty grilled fish goes for $14-18. The dinner menu is slightly more expensive. Open daily for lunch and dinner, but closed each afternoon 3-5 p.m.

While the oysters at Joe's are hard to beat, those at the **Olympia Seafood Market and Grill,** just off Robson at 820 Thurlow, tel. (604) 685-0716, come pretty close. What was originally a fish market now sells cooked fish and chips, either to take out or to enjoy at the short counter. Olympia is open for lunch and dinner daily.

Robson Public Market, near the west end of Robson St., holds stalls filled with fresh produce and exotic delicacies.

North American

The menu at the **Cactus Club Cafe,** 1136 Robson St., tel. (604) 687-3278, features mostly Southwestern dishes (and a great Caesar salad), but the decor of this busy restaurant is, well, different. It's covered with cow kitsch, from the black-and-white seating to the papier-mâché cows hanging from the ceiling. Open daily noon-1:30 a.m.

One block toward Stanley Park, on the first floor of Blue Horizon Hotel, is **Inlets Bistro,** 1225 Robson St., tel. (604) 688-1411, a stylish place featuring breakfast specials for around $6 and a wide-ranging menu with entrées from $12.

European

Salonika is a modern Greek restaurant with a rooftop patio at 1642 Robson St., tel. (604) 681-8141. Some main dishes are under $10, while prawns sautéed in ouzo and garlic cost $15, but it is the platter for two that provides the best value. Moussaka, souvlaki, lamb chops, a Greek salad, rice, and pita bread is just $30.

Continuing toward Stanley Park, **The Chef and the Carpenter,** 1745 Robson St., tel. (604) 687-2700, serves up great country-French cuisine in an intimate yet relaxed atmosphere. Portions are large, but save room for the delicious desserts. Entrées range $15-19. Open weekdays for lunch and daily for dinner (reservations required).

Diners at **Marbella,** 1368 Robson St., tel. (604) 681-1175, eat from stylish tiled tables, listen to traditional music, and generally immerse themselves in the culture of Spain. The 20 tapas range $2.50-5 each, while the rest of the menu features entrées from $13. Try the Spanish-style soup at lunch. Open Tues.-Sat. for lunch, Tues.-Sun. for dinner.

At **CinCin,** 1154 Robson St., tel. (604) 688-7338, the centerpiece of the dining room is a large open kitchen, with a wood-fired oven and a rotisserie in view of diners. The specialty is pizza (from $14), but the oven is also used to cook dishes like a rack of lamb ($30) and seafood such as sea bass ($27.50). Grilled dishes are similarly priced, while pastas range $13-22. CinCin also does a wicked antipasti ($25 for two). This restaurant has been honored by dozens of awards, including for its wine list, which features over 300 choices. It's open for lunch Mon.-Sat. and daily for dinner.

In the lower level of the Pacific Palisades Hotel, the cavernous **Monterey Lounge and Grill,** 1277 Robson St., tel. (604) 684-1277, features a Mediterranean-inspired menu to suit all tastes.

East Indian

A Taste of India, 1282 Robson St., tel. (604) 682-3894, stands out along this strip of fashionable boutiques and trendy cafés. The decor—complete with plastic flowers—is nothing to write home about, but this restaurant is worth visiting for its wide selection of traditional Indian dishes at reasonable prices. Lunches are all under $10, while the most expensive dinner entrée is a prawn curry served with rice for $13. Also on the menu are kebabs, over a dozen vegetarian specialties, and dishes from the Tandoori oven. It's open daily 11 a.m.-midnight.

WEST END

Denman Street is the center of the dining action in this trendy part of downtown. Toward the English Bay end of Denman Street there is a definite seaside atmosphere, with many cafés and restaurants offering water views and attracting droves of beach-lovers in their summer wear.

Cafés and Cheap Eats

For a quick bite to eat before heading back to the beach consider the following eateries, which specialize in takeout but also put a couple of tables out on the sidewalk: **Falafel King,** 1110 Denman St., tel. (604) 669-7278, offers Greek salads and falafels from $4, while **Cafe La Cantina,** 1152 Denman St., serves pizza and pasta.

The **Bread Garden,** 1040 Denman St., tel. (604) 685-2996, is a busy café open 24 hours. Raised a few steps from street level, the long row of outdoor tables is great for peoplewatching.

One block from Denman, **Crystals Café,** 1702 Davie St., tel. (604) 682-5775, is away from the crowds and offers diners a few outdoor tables on quiet Bidwell Street.

Away from the beach, near the crest of Denman Street, a couple of older-style places have survived, offering old-fashioned service and good value. The best of these for breakfast is the **Grove Inn,** 1047 Denman St., tel. (604) 687-0557, where the breakfast special is $4 before 10 a.m.

On the same block as the Grove Inn, **Bud's Halibut and Chips,** 1007 Denman St., tel. (604) 683-0661, has been serving up battered fish and crispy fries for over 20 years. The portions are generous, and all fish comes with a massive dollop of tartar sauce. One piece of halibut and chips is just $5. If you want to eat down on the beach, the staff will happily wrap your meal in paper for you.

For chicken cooked to perfection, head over the hill to **Rooster's Quarters,** 836 Denman St., tel. (604) 689-8023, a casual eatery chockfull of chicken memorabilia. A full chicken with accompanying vegetables and fries (for two) is a reasonable $17.

At the street's north end is **Bojangles,** 785 Denman St., tel. (604) 687-3622, a small café on a busy intersection. Its few sidewalk tables and inside counters are perfect places for watching in-line skaters practice their newfound skills (or lack of them) as they leave surrounding rental shops.

Pacific Northwest

Head for the West End to find the city's finest traditional Pacific Northwest cuisine. Liliget Feast House, 1724 Davie St., tel. (604) 681-7044, serves authentic First Nations food, including oolichan in a lemon butter, bannock bread, seaweed and wild rice, watercress salad, a traditional salmon soup, seafood or caribou barbecued over an alderwood fire, and steamed fern shoots. A narrow stairway leads down to a cavernous room styled on a traditional longhouse. Cedar columns rise from the stone floor, native artwork adorns the walls, and traditional music plays softly in the background. Dining here isn't particularly cheap; most people opt for either the Potlatch Platter (seafood) or Liliget Feast Platter (game such as caribou and buffalo), which let you sample a variety of delicacies ($48.50 for two). But it's an experience you won't forget in a hurry. Open daily 5-10 p.m.

A few blocks away, you'll find contemporary Pacific Northwest cuisine at **Delilah's,** 1789 Comox St., tel. (604) 687-3424. One of Vancouver's favorite restaurants, Delilah's features an elegant setting and well-prepared dishes that take advantage of seasonal produce and locally harvested seafood. The fixed-price two-course dinner costs from $20, depending on the season; a five-course feast is also offered. Open daily for dinner.

The innovative menu and extensive by-the-glass wine list at nearby **Raincity Grill,** 1193 Denman St., tel. (604) 685-7337, have gained the restaurant numerous awards. The interior is stylish and table settings more than adequate, but it's the views across English Bay that are most impressive. The menu changes with the season but always includes seafood and various game dishes. Wednesday is the Chef's Surprise, featuring whatever the chef picked up at the local market that morning. Lunch entrées are $9-16, dinner ranges $16-26. Make reservations for dinner.

Mexican and Cajun

In a sprawling converted residence just off Denman St., **Mescalero,** 1215 Bidwell St., tel. (604) 669-2399, has high ceilings, an ocher-colored interior, and Santa Fe–style furnishings. The atmosphere is casual—the staff has a good time while still being attentive. Tapas ($6-10) are the most popular menu items, but also featured are a variety of Mexican grills; I found the chili-crusted salmon ($18) to be absolutely delicious. It's open weekdays for lunch from 11:30 a.m., on weekends from 10:30 a.m. for brunch and daily from 5:30 p.m. for dinner.

Ponchos, 827 Denman St., tel. (604) 683-7236, is an unpretentious and friendly restaurant where the walls are decorated with colorful ponchos and diners are serenaded by a guitar-playing singer between courses. The menu is extremely well priced, with hearty soups costing from $4 and combination meals for under $10. It's open Tues.-Sun. 5-11 p.m.

European

At first I was disappointed to hear that one of my favorite seafood restaurants, Flippers, had closed, but after I visited its replacement, **Tapastree Restaurant,** 1829 Robson St. (one block off Denman St.), tel. (604) 606-4680, those feelings quickly disappeared. The atmosphere here is inviting and cozy, and the service faultless. But it's the food that really shines; the tapas-only menu features a wide variety of meats, seafood, and even some vegetarian choices, all for under $10. Tapastree is open daily for dinner.

Around the corner, **Café de Paris,** 745 Denman St., tel. (604) 688-2453, is a city-style

The Fish House at Stanley Park

French bistro. Main meals range $18-25, but the daily three-course table d'hôte is best value at around $20. It's also open Mon.-Fri. for lunch and on Sunday for brunch.

Japanese
For inexpensive, no-frills Japanese food head to **Hanada,** 823 Denman St., tel. (604) 685-1136. The atmosphere is nothing special, but the service is efficient and all the traditional Japanese dishes are offered at reasonable cost, with no entrées over $13.

The contemporary **Tanpopo,** upstairs at 1122 Denman St., tel. (604) 681-7777, features a wide range of Japanese dishes, including a lunch buffet for $12 and a dinner buffet for $18.

Stanley Park
Overlooking English Bay, between Second and Third Beaches, is the **Teahouse Restaurant,** 7501 Stanley Park Rd., tel. (604) 669-3281, originally built as barracks for army troops in the 1920s. Today the building contains an intimate restaurant with elegant surroundings and a game and seafood menu making use of all the best local ingredients. Expect to pay from $12 for lunch and from $16 for dinner. Open daily.

The **Fish House at Stanley Park** lies in park-like surroundings on a rise in the southwest corner of the park, away from the crowded promenade at 2099 Beach Ave., tel. (604) 681-7275. Seating is indoors and out, the service efficient, and the food well prepared. All the usual seafood dishes are offered, as well as a few unique dishes for the adventurous. Dinner mains range $18-29, and the Fish House is open daily for lunch and dinner.

The least expensive place to eat in Stanley Park is the **Prospect Point Café,** near the south end of Lions Gate Bridge, tel. (604) 669-2737, with views extending across Burrard Inlet to the North Shore. The menu is extensive, but salmon is the specialty, with dishes starting at $15. It's open daily for lunch and dinner.

DINING IN OTHER PARTS OF THE CITY

GRANVILLE ISLAND AND VICINITY

Granville Island Market

This market, on Johnston St., bustles with locals and tourists alike throughout the day. As well as fresh meats, seafood, and fruit and vegetables, many specialty stalls are stocked with pre-packaged goodies to go. At the Burrard Inlet end of the market you'll find a variety of take-out stalls, and while there's a large expanse of indoor tables, most people head outside to enjoy their meal among the sights and sounds of False Creek. It is difficult to go past the **Stock Market** when recommending a stall to grab lunch. Starting at $3.50, the soups are absolutely mouthwatering, but it's worth the extra for a huge serving of Red Snapper Chowder for $6 (or go for the small serving for $4.50). Around the corner from the Stock Market is a stall selling good fish and chips.

Island Restaurants

On Granville Island's northern tip is **Bridges,** a distinctive yellow building at 1696 Duranleau St., tel. (604) 687-4400, with stunning water views. Getting a table at the large outdoor area usually entails a wait, and the menu features typical pub fare of hamburgers, salads, and basic seafood dishes, while the upstairs restaurant is more formal (and more expensive).

The **Backstage Lounge,** in the back of the Arts Club Theatre, Johnston St., tel. (604) 687-1354, is more of a bar than a restaurant but offers a well-priced bistro-style menu, and if you're lucky you may snag a table on the outdoor deck overlooking the water.

Next door to the theater complex, the venerable **Mulvaney's,** 1535 Johnston St., Granville Island, tel. (604) 685-6571, is the place to go for Cajun and Creole dishes. Entrées range $12-20. Open weekdays for lunch, daily from 5:30 p.m. for dinner, and on Sunday for brunch from 10 a.m.

Across False Creek

From Granville Island, hop aboard a False Creek Ferry to the foot of Hornby Street, then walk 200 meters around the seawall to the False Creek Yacht Club and the **Riley Waterfront Café,** 1661 Granville St., tel. (604) 684-3666, the least expensive place in the city to enjoy waterfront dining. Tables are inside or out, and the whole building is built over the water, allowing great views of the bustling waterway below. Prices are more reasonable than you might imagine; battered halibut and fries is $12 while pizza, burgers, pastas, and salads are all around $10.

KITSILANO

The main concentration of restaurants on the south side of False Creek is in Kitsilano, along W. 4th Ave. between Burrard and Vine Streets. This part of the city was the heart of hippiedom 30 years ago, and while most restaurants from that era are long gone, a few remain, and other, newer additions to the Central Vancouver dining scene reflect that period of the city's history. **Sophie's Cosmic Café,** 2095 W. 4th Ave. (at Arbutus St.), tel. (604) 732-6810, typifies the scene, with a definite "cosmic" look, but also providing good value (daily specials under $10). Expect a wait for Sunday breakfast. It's open daily 8 a.m.-9 p.m. **Joe's Grill,** on the next block to the east at 2061 W. 4th Ave., tel. (604) 736-6588, has survived from the 1960s serving up typical greasy spoon fare at good prices. A cooked breakfast is $4, the daily soup-and-sandwich special is just $6, the milk-shakes are to die for, and coffee refills are free. It is also open daily 8 a.m.-9 p.m.

Caper's Courtyard Café, 2285 W. 4th Ave. (at Vine St.), tel. (604) 739-6676, features food for the health-conscious, with a small outdoor eating area shaded by a couple of trees. As well as a café, Caper's holds a large fresh produce market.

Cool and Casual

Biceps and butts are the order of the day along trendy Kitsilano Beach, and when the beautiful people have finished sunning themselves they head for **Malone's,** overlooking the beach at 2202 Cornwall Ave. (at Yew St.), tel. (604) 737-

7777. Pub grub is the order of the day, with all the usual burgers and salads for $8-12, but the real reason to stop by is to soak up the atmosphere and take in the view.

On the same corner, the **Urban Well,** 1516 Yew St., tel. (604) 737-7770, has a few outdoor tables and a main underground restaurant with a healthy menu of wraps, salads, and vegetarian burgers. It's open in summer daily noon-2 a.m., closing earlier Sun.-Tues.; in winter it's closed for lunch during the week, opening at 5 p.m.

Pacific Northwest
At the **Livingroom,** 2958 W. 4th Ave., tel. (604) 737-7529, the menu may reflect modern tastes, but as a throwback to days gone by in Kitsilano, the atmosphere is typically bohemian. The owners have cleverly created a classy restaurant using retro-style furnishings, right down to mismatched plates. Mains average $16 and are accompanied by an extensive wine list. The Livingroom is open daily for dinner.

Vegetarian
A throwback to the hippie era of the 1960s is **Naam,** 2724 W. 4th Ave. (at Stephens St.), tel. (604) 738-7151, a particularly good natural-food restaurant in a renovated two-story private residence. Boasting large servings, excellent service, and an easy-going atmosphere that has become legendary, it's open 24 hours a day,

every day of the week. Veggie burgers start at $5, full meals range $6.50-10.50.

Surat Sweet, 1938 W. 4th Ave. (between Cypress and Maple Streets), tel. (604) 733-7363, needs a coat of paint, but the decor plays second fiddle to the food, which is remarkably inexpensive. The menu is entirely vegetarian and vegan—even eggs aren't used. Apart from the curries, most diners will be unfamiliar with many of the dishes, such as *bhajia,* a deep-fried potato dish covered in a coconut chutney ($6.50). Surat Sweet is open Tues.-Sat. for lunch and dinner.

Mexican
Las Margaritas, 1999 W. 4th Ave. (at Maple St.), tel. (604) 734-7117, is open for lunch (around $8) and dinner ($10-14), and boasts "mild or wild, we can add all the octane you wish." The decor is vintage south-of-the-border—white stucco walls, Mexican hats, tile floor, tile-topped tables, and an outdoor deck. It's a good place to take your taste buds for a buzz. Get some chips and salsa, throw back a couple of margaritas, and pretend you're in Mexico.

Farther west, near McDonald St., **Topanga Cafe,** 2904 W. 4th Ave., tel. (604) 733-3713, offers less expensive California-style Mexican dishes in a homely atmosphere. Most main meals are under $12, including massive chicken burritos, complete with rice, beans, and corn chips for $10.

Greek
Since moving from Commercial Dr. to fashionable Kitsilano, **Le Grec,** 2041 W. 4th Ave., tel. (604) 733-7399, has gone from strength to strength. Set back slightly from the road, the new location features a patio and live evening entertainment. The menu takes from the cuisine of countries around the Mediterranean and is well priced. The seafood chowder ($4.45) is a great starter, and from there the choices are mouthwatering, and nothing is over $15. Seafood dominates the menu, with many dishes marinated in wines and sprinkled with exotic spices, but I had the *soutzoukia*—a simple dish comprising lamb, tomato, and feta cheese formed into rolls—which costs just $6.45. Le Grec is open for lunch Tues.-Sun. and for dinner nightly.

A HIDDEN CENTRAL VANCOUVER DINING GEM

Queen Elizabeth Park is home to **Seasons in the Park** (access from Cambie St.), tel. (604) 874-8008, in a delightful park-like setting where views extend back across Central Vancouver to downtown and the mountains beyond. It is a popular spot with tour groups, but the high standard of service and quality of food attract many locals. Diners have the choice of eating in the romantic dining room or, for the very best views, in the gazebo. The seasonal menu features contemporary North American cooking, with seafood and game dishes from $18. It's open Mon.-Fri. for lunch, daily for dinner, and Sat.-Sun. for brunch.

African

One of Vancouver's few African eateries, **Nyala African Hotspot,** 2930 W. 4th Ave. (at McDonald St.), tel. (604) 731-7899, provides the opportunity to try some unique dishes without spending a fortune. *Pakora,* a dish of battered vegetables, is an Ethiopian staple, and can be combined with a variety of stir-fries for under $18 per person. Vegetarians are well catered to with all meat-free dishes under $10. On Wednesday and Sunday nights a vegetarian buffet is offered for $11. Nyala is open daily 11:30 a.m.-2 p.m. and 5-11 p.m. (until 2 a.m. Thurs.-Sat.).

WEST BROADWAY

Broadway runs parallel to 4th Ave. five blocks farther south. The restaurants listed below are farther east than those along 4th Ave. and are generally less "trendy," appealing to those looking for value. This area of town also holds many outdoor clothing and equipment shops, so if you have any money left from a shopping spree, the following are perfect choices for lunch. The easiest way to get here by public transportation from downtown is to catch the SkyTrain to Broadway then jump aboard a westbound bus. If you're after a *really* cheap meal, get off the bus at Kingsway (two blocks east of Main St., the beginning of W. Broadway) and cross the road to **Reno's,** 151 E. Broadway, tel. (604) 876-1119, an old-style restaurant where diners order at the cash register, sit at the counter or booths, and enjoy free newspapers and bottomless coffee. Cooked breakfasts are $5 and a burger and fries is just $3.50.

Asian

Nakornthai, 401 W. Broadway (at Yukon St.), tel. (604) 874-8923, specializes in the cuisine of Thailand, where many dishes are based on thick, milk-based sauces. Pork is a staple in Thai cooking, prepared here in many different ways. The restaurant itself is small but clean, well decorated, and bright and airy. It's also very inexpensive, with hearty lunch specials from just $5. Open daily for lunch and dinner.

Renowned for sushi is **Tojo's Restaurant,** 777 W. Broadway, tel. (604) 872-8050. Japanese entrées are also available; various teriyakis range $15-35.

In the strip mall at the next major intersection westbound (Oak St.), **Sami's,** 986 W. Broadway, tel. (604) 736-8330, offers westernized East Indian cooking. Considering its mall location and low prices (all mains around $10), the food here is remarkably good. It's open daily for lunch and dinner.

One block north of W. Broadway at Granville St. is **Vij's,** 1480 11th Ave., tel. (604) 736-6664, one of Vancouver's most acclaimed Asian restaurants. Vikram Vij, the East Indian owner, is a master at combining the cuisine of his homeland with the tastes of his Vancouver customers, thereby creating a unique menu that appeals to everyone. Presentation and service are of the highest standard, but it is the food that really shines. No reservations are taken, and getting a table often involves a wait, which in itself says something about a place within one block of a kilometer-long strip of other restaurants. Vij's is open Mon.-Sat. for dinner.

Farther west, toward Kitsilano, a well-recommended restaurant serving Indian and Asian dishes is **Woodlands Natural Food Restaurant,** upstairs at 2582 W. Broadway (at Trafalgar St.), tel. (604) 733-5411. Here you can get a main course for $8-10, or try the "buffet by weight," at which you fill your plate then weigh it, paying $1.80 per 100 grams. Open daily 8 a.m.-10 p.m.

Russian

Vancouver's only Russian restaurant is **Rasputin's,** 457 W. Broadway (near Cambie St.), tel. (604) 879-6675, with a welcoming atmosphere and waitpersons who understand that most diners aren't going to be familiar with many items on the menu. Borsch, a hearty beet-based soup, is the best-known Russian dish, and Rasputin's does it well. A big steaming bowl, almost a meal in itself, is $5, but the best way to sample everything (including a shot of vodka) is with The Feast, which is $25 pp.

NORTH VANCOUVER

If you've crossed Burrard Inlet on the SeaBus, visit **Lonsdale Market** for local produce, including a couple of market stalls selling seafood fresh from the trawlers. Between the market and the SeaBus terminal (near the bus interchange) is the **Lonsdale Café,** 147 Chadwick Court, tel. (604) 988-2761, with a few outdoor tables. Service is fast, and the daily lunch soup-and-sandwich special is just $5.

Lonsdale Ave., which climbs from the waterfront to the residential heart of North Vancouver, holds many eateries on its lower end. **Cheers,** 125 E. 2nd St., tel. (604) 985-9192, is a family-style restaurant where fish and chips with unlimited trips to the salad bar costs just $8. Open daily for lunch and dinner. (If you snag one of the two tables in the far left-hand corner, you'll enjoy filtered harbor views).

Seafood

On the north side of Burrard Inlet, **Salmon House on the Hill,** 2229 Folkstone Way, West Vancouver, tel. (604) 926-3212, offers a house specialty of salmon barbecued over an open alderwood pit. The intriguing interior is full of northwest coast native arts and crafts—including a dugout canoe suspended over the main dining area—and provides a great view of West Vancouver, Stanley Park, and downtown. Out front, a rhododendron garden blooms its bloomers off in May. Enjoy drinks and appetizers ($6-9) or afternoon tea and dessert ($5-6—the Chocolate Paradise is sinfully scrumptious) in the bistro bar, or a full meal in the adjoining restaurant. Lunch averages $11-18, dinner entrées run $17.50-29.50. The Salmon House is open for lunch Mon.-Sat. 11:30 a.m.-2:30 p.m., for dinner daily from 5 p.m., and for Sunday brunch 11 a.m.-2:30 p.m. Make dinner reservations unless you plan on eating at 5 p.m. or after 9 p.m. To get there, take the 21st St. Exit off Upper Levels Hwy. to Folkstone Way, then follow the signs.

VICTORIA

Victoria's Inner Harbour

INTRODUCTION

Victoria, the elegant capital of British Columbia, lies at the southern tip of Vancouver Island and is connected to Vancouver by regular and inexpensive ferry services and scheduled flights. It is possible to visit Victoria as a day trip from Vancouver, but the city has so many attractions that if you want to see *everything* you'd better give yourself at least two days.

Standing proudly at the southern tip of Vancouver Island, the fashionable city of 350,000 projects an intriguing mixture of images, old and new. Well-preserved century-old buildings line inner-city streets; ancient totem poles sprout from shady parks; restored historic areas house trendy shops, offices, and exotic restaurants; double-decker buses and horse-drawn carriages compete for summer trade; and the residents keep alive the original traditions and atmosphere of Merry Olde England.

Many people view the city for the first time from the Inner Harbour, coming in by boat the way people have for almost 150 years; on rounding Laurel Point, Victoria sparkles into view. Ferries, fishing boats, and seaplanes bob in the harbor, backdropped by manicured lawns and flower gardens, quiet residential suburbs, and striking inner-city architecture. Despite the pressures that go with city life, easygoing Victorians still find time for a stroll along the waterfront, a round of golf, or a typically English high tea.

The best way to get to know this beautiful city is on foot. All the downtown attractions are within a short walk of each other, and the more remote sights are easily reached by bus. In summer various tours are offered, giving you the choice of seeing Victoria by horse-drawn carriage, bus, boat, bicycle, limo—you name it! But if you still feel the need to have a car readily available, you'll be pleased to know that parking is plentiful just a few blocks from the Inner Harbour.

HISTORY

In 1792, Captain George Vancouver sailed through the Strait of Georgia, noting and naming Vancouver Island. But this had little effect on the many indigenous communities living along the shoreline. Europeans didn't see and exploit the island's potential for another 50 years, when the Hudson's Bay Company established control over the entire island and the mainland territory of "Columbia."

Fort Victoria

Needing to firmly establish British presence on the continent's northwest coast, the Hudson's Bay Company built Fort Victoria—named after Queen Victoria—on the southern tip of Vancouver Island in 1843. Three years later, the Oregon Treaty fixed the U.S./Canada boundary at the 49th parallel, with the proviso that the section of Vancouver Island lying south of that line would be retained by Canada. To forestall any claims that the U.S. may have had on the area, the British government went about settling the island. In 1849, the island was gazetted as a Crown colony and leased back to the Hudson's Bay Company. Gradually land around Fort Victoria was opened up by groups of British settlers brought to the island by the company's subsidiary, Puget Sound Agricultural Company. Several large company farms were developed, and

Esquimalt Harbour became a major port for British ships.

The Growth of Victoria

In the late 1850s gold strikes on the mainland's Thompson and Fraser Rivers brought thousands of gold miners into Victoria, the region's only port and source of supplies. Overnight, Victoria became a classic boomtown, but with a distinctly British flavor; most of the company men, early settlers, and military personnel firmly maintained their homeland traditions and celebrations. Even after the gold rush ended, Victoria remained an energetic bastion of military, economic, and political activity, and was officially incorporated as a city in 1862. In 1868, two years after the colonies of Vancouver Island and British Columbia were united, Victoria was made capital. Through the two world wars, Victoria continued to grow. The commencement of ferry service between Tsawwassen and Sidney in 1903 created a small population boom, but Victoria has always lagged well behind Vancouver in the population stakes.

VICTORIA IN A DAY FROM VANCOUVER

If you're in Vancouver and have just one day to visit Victoria, there are a few options, but, realistically, you should allow more time to fully explore the provincial capital. For full details of getting to Victoria, see Getting There in the Victoria Basics chapter.

Gray Line, tel. (604) 879-3363, has a 12-hour tour taking in all of Victoria's major sights, including downtown, the scenic marine drive, and Butchart Gardens, but it's a long day on the road; $102 pp includes ferry fares and downtown Vancouver hotel pick-ups.

For those with limited time, flying is a more practical option. The flights offered by **Harbour Air** depart by seaplane from beside Vancouver's Canada Place, tel. (604) 688-1277 or (800) 665-0212, website www.harbour-air.com. The least expensive tour is a fly/bus/ferry/bus combination for $120 pp (scheduled one-way fare is $90); another possibility is to fly both ways and take a bus tour that includes Butchart Gardens for $209 pp. Other companies providing a direct link between Victoria's Inner Harbour and downtown Vancouver (landing near Canada Place) include **West Coast Aiir,** tel. (250) 388-4521 or (800) 347-2222, website www.westcoastair.com,

and **Helijet Airways,** tel. (250) 382-6222 or (800) 665-4354, website www.helijet.com.

Ground transportation linking the two cities makes a day trip possible, but like the Gray Line Tour, traveling by public transportation makes for a long day. **Pacific Coach Lines,** tel. (604) 662-8074, website www.pacificcoach.com, operates a scheduled bus service between Vancouver's Pacific Central Station and downtown Victoria, via the Tsawwassen–Swartz Bay ferry. In summer the coaches run hourly 6 a.m.-9 p.m.; $25 one-way, $51 roundtrip, which includes the ferry fare. The trip takes three and a half hours.

If you're driving, the regular vehicle ferry service between Vancouver and Swartz Bay makes a day trip to Victoria easy. Ferries run across the Strait of Georgia from Tsawwassen, 30 km south of Vancouver, to the **Swartz Bay Ferry Terminal,** 32 km north of Victoria. Through summer, ferries run hourly 7 a.m.-10 p.m., the rest of the year slightly less frequently. The crossing takes 90 minutes. You can expect a wait in summer; limited vehicle reservations are accepted. One-way fares are $32 for a vehicle and $9 per passenger. For information, call **BC Ferries** at (250) 386-3431 or, within B.C., (888) 223-3779, website www.bcferries.bc.ca.

Goldstream Provincial Park

SIGHTS

INNER HARBOUR

Initially, Victoria's Inner Harbour extended farther inland; prior to the construction of the massive stone causeway that now forms the marina, the area on which the impressive Empress Hotel now stands was a deep, oozing mudflat. Walk along the lower level, then up the steps in the middle to come face-to-face with an unamused Captain James Cook; the bronze statue commemorates the first recorded British landing, in 1778, on the territory that would later become British Columbia. Above the northeast corner of the harbor is the **Victoria Visitor Info Centre,** 812 Wharf St., tel. (250) 953-2033, the perfect place to start your city exploration. Be sure to return to the Inner Harbour after dark, when the parliament buildings are outlined in lights and the Empress Hotel is floodlit.

Empress Hotel
The pompous, ivy-covered Empress Hotel was designed in 1908 by the well-known architect Francis Rattenbury, who also designed the parliament buildings, the CPR steamship terminal (now housing the wax museum), and Crystal Garden. It's worthwhile walking through the hotel lobby to gaze—head back, mouth agape—at the interior razzle-dazzle, and to watch people-watching people partake in traditional afternoon tea (see the Food chapter). Browse through the conservatory and gift shops, drool over the menus of the various restaurants, see what tours are available, and exchange currency if you're desperate (banks give a better exchange rate).

Royal British Columbia Museum
Canada's most visited museum and easily one of North America's best, the Royal British Columbia Museum, 675 Belleville St., tel. (250) 387-3701, is a must-see attraction for even the most jaded museum-goer.

Its fine Natural History Gallery displays are extraordinarily true to life, complete with appropriate sounds and smells. Come face-to-face with an ice-age woolly mammoth, stroll through

Empress Hotel

a coastal forest full of deer and tweeting birds, meander along a seashore or tidal marsh, then descend into the Open Ocean Exhibit via submarine—a very real trip not recommended for claustrophobics. The First Peoples Gallery holds a fine collection of artifacts from the island's first human inhabitants, the Nuu-chah-nulth (Nootka). Many of the pieces were collected by Charles Newcombe, who paid the Nuu-chah-nulth for them on collection sorties in the early 1900s. More modern human history is also explored here in creative ways. Take a tour through time via the time capsules; walk along a turn-of-the-century street; and experience hands-on exhibits on industrialization, the gold rush, and the exploration of B.C. by land and sea in the Modern History and 20th Century Galleries.

The main gift shop stocks an excellent collection of books on Canadiana, wildlife, history, and native Indian art and culture, along with postcards and tourist paraphernalia, while the Out of the Mist gift shop sells native arts and crafts. Next door, the tearoom is always crowded. A new addition to the museum is the **Na-**tional Geographic Theatre,** showing nature-oriented IMAX films daily 9 a.m.-8 p.m. (additional charge).

The museum is open in summer daily 9 a.m.-7:30 p.m., the rest of the year daily 9 a.m.-5 p.m. Admission is a very worthwhile adult $7, senior and child $4.

Surrounding the Museum

In front of the museum, the 27-meter-high **Netherlands Centennial Carillon** was a gift to the city from British Columbia's Dutch community. The tower's 62 bells range in weight from eight to 1,500 kilograms and toll at 15-minute intervals daily 7 a.m.-10 p.m.

On the museum's eastern corner, at Belleville and Douglas Streets, lies **Thunderbird Park,** a small green spot chockablock with authentic totem poles intricately carved by northwest coast natives.

Beside Thunderbird Park is **Helmcken House,** tel. (250) 361-0021, the oldest house in the province still standing on its original site. It was built by Dr. J.S. Helmcken, pioneer surgeon and legislator, who arrived in Victoria in 1850 and aided negotiating the union of British Columbia with Canada in 1870. Inside you'll find restored rooms decorated with period furniture, as well as a collection of the good doctor's gruesome surgical equipment (which will help you appreciate modern medical technology). The house is open in summer daily 10 a.m.-5 p.m., the rest of the year daily noon-4 p.m. Admission is adult $5, senior $4, child $3.

Parliament Buildings

Satisfy your lust for governmental, historic, and architectural knowledge all in one go by taking a free tour of the harborside Provincial Legislative Buildings, a.k.a. the parliament buildings. These prominent buildings were designed by Francis Rattenbury and completed in 1897. The exterior is British Columbia Haddington Island stone, and if you walk around the buildings you'll no doubt spot many a stern or gruesome face staring down from the stonework.

On either side of the main entrance stand statues of Sir James Douglas, who chose the location of Victoria, and Sir Matthew Baillie Begbie, who was in charge of law and order during the gold-rush period. Atop the copper-covered dome stands a gilded statue of Captain George Vancouver, the first mariner to circumnavigate Vancouver Island. Walk through the main entrance and into the memorial rotunda, look skyward for a dramatic view of the central dome, then continue upstairs to peer into the legislative chamber, the home of the democratic government of British Columbia. Free guided tours are offered every 20 minutes 9 a.m.-noon and 1-5 p.m. in summer, less frequently (Mon.-Fri. only) in winter. Tour times differ according to the goings-on inside; for current times, call the tour office at (250) 387-3046.

Laurel Point

For an enjoyable short walk from downtown, continue along Belleville Street from the parliament buildings, passing a conglomeration of modern hotels, ferry terminals, and some intriguing architecture dating back to the late 19th century. A path leads down through a shady park to Laurel Point, hugging the waterfront and providing good views of Inner Harbour en route. If you're feeling really energetic, continue to **Fisherman's Wharf Park** and the crowded marina.

Crystal Garden

Designed by Francis Rattenbury and built by Percy James, the Crystal Garden, 713 Douglas St., tel. (250) 381-1213, opened in 1925 as the largest saltwater pool in the British Empire. It held tearooms, ballrooms, and a promenade, and was the venue for flower shows, craft shows, and big-band dancing, along with swimming, of course. In 1971, rising maintenance costs forced its closure. The provincial government then bought it and turned it into a two-story conservatory.

Today's visitors will find themselves surrounded by lush greenery, flowering plants, a waterfall, and the cacophony of an enormous variety of exotic birds from South America, New Guinea, and Australia. Woodcarvings from New Guinea peek out of the lush undergrowth, coral-colored flamingos strut their stuff at a series of placid pools, and iguanas, monkeys, squirrels, wallabies, and marmosets cavort nearby. Sip afternoon tea on the humid upper floor, close your eyes, and you'll swear you're in the tropics. The garden is open daily 9 a.m.-6 p.m., till 8 p.m. in summer. Admission is adult $7.50, senior $6.50, and child $4. An English tea, served 2:15-4:15 p.m., costs extra.

Commercial Attractions

Oodles of ways to trim bulging wallets confront you in Victoria, some excellent, some routine. Along the waterfront on Belleville Street, across the road from the parliament buildings, is the former CPR steamship terminal, now the **Royal London Wax Museum,** 470 Belleville St., tel. (250) 388-4461. This building, completed in 1924, was also designed by Francis Rattenbury. The museum features around 300 wax figures direct from London. It's open daily 9:30 a.m.-6 p.m., until 9 p.m. in summer; adult $7, senior $6.25, child $3. On the water beside the wax museum, **Pacific Undersea Gardens,** 490 Belleville St., tel. (250) 382-5717, boasts more than 5,000 marine specimens in their "natural" habitat, as well as performing scuba divers and Armstrong the giant octopus. It's open in summer daily 10 a.m.-7 p.m., the rest of the year daily 10 a.m.-5 p.m. Admission is adult $7, child $5. Behind the Empress Hotel is **Miniature World,** 649 Humboldt St., tel. (250) 385-9731, another of Victoria's many commercial attractions; adult $8, child $5.

OLD TOWN

The oldest section of Victoria lies immediately north of the Inner Harbour between Wharf and Government Streets. Start by walking north from the Inner Harbour along historic Wharf Street, where Hudson's Bay Company furs were loaded onto ships bound for England, gold seekers arrived in search of fortune, and shopkeepers first established businesses. Cross the road to cobblestoned **Bastion Square,** lined with old gas lamps and decorative architecture dating from the 1860s to 1890s. This was the original site chosen by James Douglas in 1843 for Fort Victoria, the Hudson's Bay Company trading post. At one time the square held a courthouse, jail, and gallows. Today restored buildings house trendy restaurants, cafés, nightclubs, and fashionable offices.

Maritime Museum of British Columbia

At the top (east) end of Bastion Square, the Maritime Museum of British Columbia, tel. (250) 385-4222, traces the history of seafaring exploration, adventure, commercial ventures, and passenger travel through displays of dugout canoes, model ships, Royal Navy charts, figure-heads, photographs, naval uniforms, and bells. One room is devoted to exhibits chronicling the circumnavigation of the world, and another holds a theater. The museum is open daily 9:30 a.m.-4:30 p.m., until 6 p.m. in summer. Admission is adult $6, senior $5, child $4. The museum also has a nautically oriented gift shop.

Other Old Town Sights

Centennial Square, bounded by Government St., Douglas St., Pandora Ave., and Fisgard St., is lined with many buildings dating from the 1880s and '90s, refurbished in recent times for all to appreciate. Don't miss the 1878 **City Hall** (fronting Douglas St.) and the imposing Greek-style building of the Hudson's Bay Company. Continue down Fisgard St. into colorful **Chinatown,** one of Canada's oldest Chinese enclaves. It's a delicious place to breathe in the aroma of authentic Asian food wafting from the many restaurants. Chinese prospectors and laborers first brought exotic spices, plants, and a love of intricate architecture and bright colors to Victoria in the 19th century. Poke through the dark little shops along Fisgard St., where you can find everything from fragile paper lanterns and embroidered silks to gingerroot and exotic canned fruits and veggies, then cruise Fan Tan Alley, the center of the opium trade in the 1800s. Walk south along Store St. and Wharf St. back to Bastion Square.

SOUTH OF THE INNER HARBOUR

Carr House

In 1871 artist Emily Carr was born in this typical upper-class Victorian-era home at 207 Government St., tel. (250) 383-5843. Carr moved to the mainland at an early age, escaping the confines of the capital to draw and write about the British Columbian natives and the wilderness in which she lived. She is best remembered today for her painting, a medium she took up in later years. The house is open mid-May to mid-October daily 9 a.m.-5 p.m. Admission is adult $5.35, senior and student $4.25, child $3.

Beacon Hill Park

This large, hilly city park—a lush, sea-edged oasis of grass and flowers—extends from the back of the museum along Douglas Street out to cliffs

that offer spectacular views of Juan de Fuca Strait and, on a clear day, the distant Olympic Mountains. Add a handful of rocky points to scramble on and many protected pebble-and-sand beaches and you've found yourself a perfect spot to indulge your senses. Catch a sea breeze (along with numerous hang gliders, windsurfers, and kite-fliers) and gaze at all the strolling, cycling, dog-walking, and pram-pushing Victorians passing by. On a bright sunny day you'll swear that most of Victoria is here, too. The park is within easy walking distance from downtown and can also be reached by bus no. 5. For a tidbit of history, walk through the park to rocky Finlayson Point, once the site of an ancient fortified native village. Between 1878 and 1892 two enormous guns protected the point against an expected but unrealized Russian invasion.

A Scenic Coastal Drive

This route starts south of the Inner Harbour and follows the coastline all the way to the University of Victoria. If you have your own transportation, this is a "must-do" in Victoria; if you don't, most city tours take in the sights detailed below. You'll not be missing anything by taking Douglas St. south alongside Beacon Hill Park (see above) to access the coast, but it's possible to continue east along the Inner Harbour to the mouth of Victoria Harbour proper, passing the Canadian Coast Guard Base and the vehicular ferry terminals to Dallas Rd., the official start of the Scenic Drive (marked by blue signs). For the first few kilometers, the Olympic Mountains in Washington State are clearly visible across the Strait of Georgia, and many lookouts allow you to stop and take in the panorama. Beyond **Clover Point** (the best lookout point), the road hugs the coastline to Oak Bay, taking you through quiet residential areas, past small pebble beaches covered in driftwood, and into the ritzy mansion district east of downtown, where the residents have manicured gardens and sea views; they are said to live "behind the tweed curtain," because they are "so British."

Continue through the well-manicured fairways of Victoria Golf Club on Gonzales Point to **Oak Bay Marina,** where you'll find a casual café and the **Marina Restaurant** (tel. 250-598-8555), a favorite hangout for Sunday brunch. From the marina, the coastal road continues north to Cadboro Bay, home to the **Royal Victoria Yacht**

Club. The **University of Victoria** lies on a ridge above Cadboro Bay; from here head southwest along Cadboro Bay Rd. then Yates St. to get back downtown, or north take Sinclair Rd. then Mackenzie Ave. to reach Hwy. 17, the main route north up the Saanich Peninsula (see below) toward famous Butchart Gardens.

ROCKLAND AND OAK BAY

This historic part of downtown lies behind the Inner Harbour, east of Douglas Street, and is easily accessible on foot.

Christ Church Cathedral

On the corner of Quadra and Courtney Streets, Christ Church Cathedral, tel. (250) 383-2714, is the seat of the Bishop of the Diocese of British Columbia. Built in 1896, in 13th-century Gothic style, it's one of Canada's largest churches. Self-guided tours are possible Mon.-Fri. 8:30 a.m.-5 p.m. and Sunday 7:30 a.m.-8:30 p.m. In summer, the cathedral sponsors free choral recitals each Saturday at 4 p.m. The park next to the cathedral is a shady haven to rest weary feet, and the gravestones make fascinating reading.

Art Gallery of Greater Victoria

From Christ Church Cathedral, walk up Rockland Ave. through the historic Rockland district, passing stately mansions and colorful gardens on tree-lined streets. Turn left on Moss St. and you'll come to the 1889 Spencer Mansion and its modern wing, which together make up the Art Gallery of Greater Victoria, 1040 Moss St., tel. (250) 384-4101. The gallery contains Canada's finest collection of Japanese art, a range of contemporary art, Emily Carr pieces, and traveling exhibits, as well as a Japanese garden with a Shinto shrine. The Gallery Shop sells art books, reproductions, and handcrafted jewelry, pottery, and glass. Hours are Mon.-Sat. 10 a.m.-5 p.m., Thursday 10 a.m.-9 p.m., and Sunday 1-5 p.m. Admission is adult $6, senior and child $4; pay what you can on Monday.

Government House

Continue up Rockland Ave. from the art gallery to reach Government House, the official residence of the lieutenant governor, the queen's representative in British Columbia. The surrounding gardens, including an English-style garden, rose garden, and rhododendron garden, along with green velvet lawns and picture-perfect flower beds, are open to the public throughout the year.

Craigdarroch Castle

A short walk up (east) from the art gallery along Rockland Ave. and left on Joan Crescent brings you to the baronial mansion known as Craigdarroch Castle, 1050 Joan Crescent, tel. (250) 592-5323. From downtown take bus no. 11 (Uplands) or no. 14 (University) to Joan Crescent, then walk

JANE AND BRUCE KING

Craigdarroch Castle

up the hill. The architectural masterpiece was built in 1890 for Robert Dunsmuir, a wealthy Victorian industrialist and politician who died just before the building was completed. For all the nitty-gritties, tour the mansion with volunteer guides who really know their Dunsmuir, then admire at your leisure all the polished wood, stained-glass windows, period furnishings, and the great city views from upstairs. Admission and tour costs adult $7.50, child $5. Open in summer daily 9 a.m.-7 p.m., the rest of the year daily 10 a.m.-4:30 p.m.

WEST OF DOWNTOWN

Point Ellice House and Garden

Built in 1861, this restored mansion sits amid beautiful gardens on Point Ellice, less than two km from the Inner Harbour. The house's second owner, a successful entrepreneur and politician, bought the house in 1868 and entertained many distinguished guests there. Original Victorian-era artifacts clutter every nook and cranny of the interior.

The house, tel. (250) 380-6506, is open mid-May to mid-September, daily 10 a.m.-5 p.m. Admission is adult $4, senior $3, child $2. To get there from the Inner Harbour, jump aboard a **Victoria Harbour Ferry,** tel. (250) 480-0971 ($3 each way), or take Government or Douglas St. north from downtown, turn left on Bay St., and turn left again on Pleasant Street.

Craigflower Manor and Schoolhouse

Cross the Point Ellice Bridge from Point Ellice House and follow Craigflower Rd. west, turning right on Admirals Rd., to come to the site of Craigflower Farm, tel. (250) 387-4627. The farm was developed in the 1850s by the Puget Sound Agricultural Co., a subsidiary of the Hudson's Bay Company. The employment of colonists by this farm and three others helped in the area's transition from fur-trade camp to permanent settlement.

Built in 1856 with native materials, the farm's manor house was the center of social life for Victorian residents and the navy officers from Esquimalt. Step into your time machine, dial in 1860, and enter the house to discover furniture, lace bedspreads, bed warmers, cooking pots, books, and all sorts of things that belonged to the original family. An appropriately dressed guide lets you in

on all the family secrets—how they kept their food cold without a refrigerator, cooked without a microwave, and kept the entire house (except the nanny's room) warm in winter. See all the glamorous and hideous wallpaper designs that were "in" throughout the years, and much more.

Across Gorge Waterway from the farmhouse is Craigflower Schoolhouse, built in 1854-55 from lumber obtained from a steam-powered sawmill at Craigflower Farm. The men employed to build it were notoriously drunk, the evidence of which is quite obvious when you tour the interior; note the sloping door frames and tilted fireplace. Canada's oldest surviving schoolhouse, it operated 1855-1911. The single schoolroom served children from the farm and nearby district, and the upper floor provided living quarters for the teacher's family and student boarders.

Both historic sites are open in summer daily noon-4 p.m., spring and fall Thurs.-Mon. noon-4 p.m. Admission is adult $5.50, senior $4.50, children $3.50. Get there from the corner of Douglas and Yates Streets on bus no. 14, or from the Inner Harbour aboard the **Victoria Harbour Ferry,** tel. (250) 480-0971. For more information call (250) 592-5323.

Anne Hathaway's Thatched Cottage

The Stratford-upon-Avon cottage of Anne Hathaway, William Shakespeare's wife, has been recreated at 429 Lampson St., tel. (250) 388-4353; catch bus no. 24 (Munro) from downtown and return on no. 24 (Colville). The cottage is authentically furnished with 16th-century antiques. It's open for tours in summer daily 9 a.m.-7 p.m., the rest of the year daily 10 a.m.-4 p.m. Admission is adult $7, seniors and children $4.50.

Next to the cottage is the **Olde England Inn** (see the Accommodations chapter, below) and a series of Tudor-style buildings that make up an English village. If you feel like splurging, the food at the inn is excellent and oh so English. For an even bigger splurge, stay in one of the inn's antique-furnished rooms. Each one has a fireplace and a draped four-poster bed so high you need a stool to clamber up.

CFB Esquimalt Naval & Military Museum

This small museum lies within the confines of **CFB Esquimalt,** on Esquimalt Harbour west of downtown. A couple of buildings have been opened to the public, displaying naval, military, and general maritime memorabilia. Admission is free and the museum is open Mon.-Fri. 10 a.m.-3:30 p.m. To get there from downtown, take the Johnson Street Bridge and follow Esquimalt Rd. to Admirals Rd., turn north, then take Naden Way and you're on the base; follow the museum signs.

A free one-hour bus tour of the facility, taking in the oldest operating dry dock on North America's west coast, departs from downtown daily in summer. Call (250) 363-7060 for times and pick-up points.

Fort Rodd Hill National Historic Site

Clinging to a headland across the harbor entrance from CFB Esquimalt, this picturesque site at 603 Fort Rodd Hill Rd., Colwood, tel. (250) 478-5849, comprises **Fort Rodd,** built in 1898 to protect the fleets of ships in the harbor, and **Fisgard Lighthouse,** which dates to 1873. It's an interesting place to explore; audio stations bring the sounds of the past alive, workrooms are furnished as they were at the turn of the century, and the lighthouse has been fully restored and is open to visitors. The grounds are open daily 10 a.m.-5:30 p.m. Admission is adult $3, senior $2.25, child $1.50. To get there from downtown, take the Old Island Hwy. (Gorge Rd.) and turn left on Belmont Road. By bus, take no. 50 from downtown then transfer to no. 52.

While you're in the vicinity, continue down the forested road beyond the historic site turnoff to **Esquimalt Lagoon,** a haven for a great variety of birdlife. The lagoon is separated from the open water by a narrow 1.5-km-long causeway. An unpaved road leads along its length, providing access to a driftwood-strewn beach that is a popular swimming and sunbathing spot in summer.

Goldstream Provincial Park

Lying just 20 km from the heart of Victoria, this 390-hectare park straddles Hwy. 1 northwest of downtown. The park's main natural feature is the Goldstream River, which flows north into the Finlayson Arm of Saanich Inlet. Forests of ancient Douglas fir and western red cedar flank the river, while at higher elevations forests of lodgepole pine flourish.

The park's highlight event occurs in November and December, when chum, coho, and chinook salmon fight their way upriver to spawn them-selves out on the same shallow gravel bars where they were born four years previously. From the picnic area parking lot two km north of the campground turnoff, a trail leads 400 meters (10 minutes) along the Goldstream River to **Freeman King Visitor Centre,** tel. (250) 478-9414, where the life cycle of salmon is described. The center is open daily 9 a.m.-5 p.m.

Beyond the visitor center, the **Marsh Trail** leads 200 meters (five minutes) to the mouth of the Goldstream River and the head of Finlayson Arm, a great birdwatching spot. One of the park's longer hikes is the **Goldmine Trail,** which begins from a parking lot on the west side of Hwy. 1 halfway between the campground and picnic area. This trail winds two km (45 minutes) each way through a mixed forest of lodgepole pine, maple, and western hemlock, passing the site of a short-lived gold rush and coming to **Niagara Falls,** a poor relation of its eastern namesake but still a picturesque flow of water. (For details about camping in Goldstream Provincial Park, see the Accommodations chapter.)

SAANICH PENINSULA

The Saanich Peninsula is the finger of land that extends north from downtown. It holds Victoria's most famous attraction, Butchart Gardens, as well as Victoria International Airport and the main arrival point for ferries from Tsawwassen. If you've caught the ferry over to Vancouver Island from Tsawwassen, you'll have arrived at **Swartz Bay,** on the northern tip of the Saanich Peninsula; from here it's a clear run down Hwy. 17 to downtown Victoria. If you've been in Goldstream Provincial Park (see above) or are traveling down the island from Nanaimo on Hwy. 1, head north and south, respectively, to **Mill Bay,** where a ferry departs regularly for **Brentwood Bay** on the Saanich Peninsula. (Brentwood Bay is home to Butchart Gardens.) Ferries run in both directions nine times daily between 7:30 a.m. and 6 p.m. Peak one-way fares for the 25-minute-long crossing are adult $4, child $2.25, cars $12. For exact times call **BC Ferries** at (250) 386-3431.

Butchart Gardens

These delightful gardens on Tod Inlet are Victoria's best-known attraction. They're approxi-

EXPLORING THE REST OF VANCOUVER ISLAND

North of Victoria, the rest of Vancouver Island beckons many travelers. The island, the largest along North America's west coast, stretches for 450 kilometers. A magnificent chain of rugged snow-capped mountains, sprinkled with lakes and rivers and pierced by a number of deep inlets, effectively divides the island into two distinct sides: dense, rain-drenched forest and remote surf- and wind-battered shores on the west, and well-populated, sheltered, beach-fringed lowlands on the east. Combine this wilderness and excellent hiking and fishing with wilderness campgrounds, literally hundreds of bed and breakfasts, tempting seafood restaurants, and more than a smattering of indigenous art and culture along the way and you've got another entire vacation just waiting for you.

Almost every island town has an information center, and while most are seasonal, they open daily through summer. Other sources of pre-trip information are the **Victoria Tourist Info Centre,** on the Inner Harbour, tel. (250) 953-2033; **Tourism Vancouver Island,** 302/45 Bastion Square, Victoria, BC V8W 1J1, tel. (250) 382-3551, website www.islands.bc.ca; and **Tourism British Columbia,** P.O. Box 9830, Stn. Provincial Government, Victoria, BC V8W 9W5, tel. (250) 387-1642 or (800) HEL-LOBC (435-5622), website www.hellobc.com.

Heading up the Island

Island-hoppers take Hwy. 17 north up the Saanich Peninsula to Swartz Bay, jump on a ferry, and cruise the scenic **Southern Gulf Islands** (population 13,000; Salt Spring Island Tourist Info Centre, 121 Lower Ganges Rd., Ganges, Salt Spring Island, tel. 250-537-5252). The five main islands—Salt Spring, North Pender, Galiano, Mayne, and Saturna—are each populated and appeal to hikers, anglers, kayakers, and just about anyone who wants to get away from it all. You'll find bed and breakfasts and camping facilities on each of the islands, as well as restaurants and general stores.

Other explorers head north up Hwy. 1/19, which follows the Strait of Georgia all the way to the island's northern tip. The old highway has mostly been replaced by the Inland Island Highway, but to take in the best the island has to offer, stick to the old route. Along the way you'll pass sandy beaches, resorts, and old logging, mining, and fishing towns that now base their existence to a large degree on tourism.

The first major town heading north is **Nanaimo** (population 73,000; Nanaimo Visitor Info Centre, 2290 Bowen Rd, tel. 250-756-0106 or 663-7337, website wwwtourism.nanaimo.bc.ca), a historic city whose downtown core is set around a bustling harbor. The major route across the island is Hwy. 4, which crosses from the east coast just north of Nanaimo and leads through "oooh" and "aaah" mountain scenery to the relatively untamed west coast. **Port Alberni,** the only town along the way, is the departure point for the **MV *Lady Rose,*** tel. (250) 723-8313 or (800) 663-7192, a supply and passenger boat that has been serving the region for almost 60 years. The boat still delivers supplies, but is now more of a tourist attraction, cruising through spectacular Barkley Sound to the remote village of Bamfield three times weekly. Once on the west coast itself, you'll find the driftwood-littered sand and coastal rainforest of **Pacific Rim National Park** (tel. 250-726-4212). Beyond the park is the picture-perfect seaside village of **Tofino,** a base for sea kayaking and whalewatching and gateway to **Clayoquot Sound.**

Back on the east coast, from Parksville, the Inland Island Highway continues north to **Courtney** (population 20,000; Comox Valley Visitor Info Centre, 2040 Cliffe Ave., tel. 250-334-3234 or 888-357-4471, website www.vquest.com/cv.chamber), gateway to the island's major ski area, Mt. Washington. Farther north, 270 km from Victoria, is **Campbell River** (population 31,000; Campbell River Visitor Info Centre, in the main shopping mall parking lot at 1235 Shoppers Row, tel. 250-287-4636), a mecca for salmon fishers from around the world. The best fishing is not in the river, but in the Strait of Georgia, which is home to many remote sport-fishing lodges catering to the angling crowd.

Campbell River marks only the halfway point of Vancouver Island. To the west is the remote wilderness of **Strathcona Provincial Park,** while to the north lies a surprisingly large area mostly untouched by civilization—in fact, today you can still find maps of the island that fizzⅇe out above Campbell River. **Telegraph Cove** (population 30) is a highlight of northern Vancouver Island. Built over the water, the village itself is picture-postcard perfect, but it is also the base for Stubbs Island Charters, tel. (250) 928-3185, which offers an unparalleled opportunity to view orcas (killer whales) up close. The end of the road for most travelers is the fishing village of **Port Hardy** (population 5,500; Port Hardy Visitor Info Centre, 7250 Market St., tel. 250-949-7622), where BC Ferries, tel. (250) 386-3431 or, within B.C., (888) 223-3779, website www.bcferries.bc.ca, operates a passenger/vehicle ferry service to Prince Rupert.

West Coast Trail

Keen hikers head west from Victoria to Port Renfrew, the southern trailhead for the six- to eight-day West Coast Trail, regarded as one of the world's great hikes. The trail traverses a wild, untamed 77-km stretch of the island's west coast, spanning beaches, cliffs, rivers, waterfalls, and rainforest, and is always within hearing distance of the sounds of the surf. Hiking the trail requires reservations (tel. 604-663-6000 or 800-663-6000), or for general trail information and the brochure *West Coast Trail Hiker Preparation Guide* call (250) 726-7721.

ISLAND TRANSPORTATION

Traveling up Vancouver Island by public transportation is easy, but if you have your own vehicle or rent one in Victoria (see Getting Around in the Victoria Basics chapter), you get to see many off-the-beaten-track sights.

From downtown Victoria, take Douglas St. north for three km to Hwy. 1, which jogs westward through Victoria's residential suburbs before turning north and running up the east side of the island all the way to Port Hardy (520 km). It's not necessary to return to Victoria to get back to Vancouver; ferries operate between Nanaimo and Vancouver, and Comox and the Sunshine Coast, a short drive and two coastal ferry trips from Vancouver.

By Rail

VIA Rail's **E&N Railiner** (also known as the *Malahat)* is the only scheduled train service on Vancouver Island. It departs Victoria for Courtenay Mon.-Sat. at 8:15 a.m. and Sunday at noon, and departs Courtenay for Victoria Mon.-Sat. at 1:15 p.m. and Sunday at 5:15 p.m. Several stops are made along the way. This route is so scenic that many make the train trip a one-day excursion, going as far as Nanaimo and spending a few hours in the city before

returning; it's a cheap day out at under $40 for the roundtrip. Make reservations as far ahead as possible in summer, and buy your ticket the day before departure. For more information, stop in at the station, 450 Pandora Ave., tel. (250) 383-4324 or (800) 561-8630, website www.viarail.com.

By Bus

Island Coach Lines (operated by Laidlaw), tel. (250) 385-4411 or (800) 318-0818, website www.victoriatours.com, serves all of Vancouver Island from the main bus depot centrally located in downtown Victoria at 710 Douglas St. (corner of Belleville Street). The depot is small and gets extremely busy during summer; schedules are posted, as are fares. No bookings are taken, so just roll up, pay the fare, and jump aboard. Seven buses daily depart Victoria for Nanaimo, with one continuing to Tofino, three to Campbell River, and one or two to Port Hardy (depending on ferry departures from Port Hardy or Prince Rupert). Fares are calculated on "sectors" rather than exact destinations, but the fare to Nanaimo is under $20, to Tofino $51, to Campbell River $45.30, and to Port Hardy $89.60.

One of the highlights of a trip up Vancouver Island is a whalewatching trip with Stubbs Island Charters, based at Telegraph Cove.

mately 20 km north of downtown at 800 Benvenuto Dr., Brentwood Bay, tel. (250) 652-4422 or 652-5256 (recorded information).

A Canadian cement pioneer, R.P. Butchart, built a mansion near his quarries. He and his wife, Jennie, traveled extensively, collecting rare and exotic shrubs, trees, and plants from around the world. By 1904, the quarries had been abandoned, and the couple began to beautify them by transplanting their collection into a number of formal gardens interspersed with concrete footpaths, small bridges, waterfalls, ponds, and fountains. The gardens now contain more than 5,000 varieties of flowers, and the extensive nurseries test-grow some 35,000 new bulbs and more than 100 new roses every year. Go there in spring, summer, or early autumn to treat your eyes and nose to a marvelous sensual experience (many a gardener would give both hands to be able to work in these gardens). In winter, when little is blooming and the entire landscape is green, the basic design of the gardens can best be appreciated. Summer visitors are in for a special treat on Saturday nights (July and August only), when a spectacular fireworks display lights up the garden.

Also on the premises are several tearooms, restaurants, and a gift shop specializing in—you guessed it—floral items. The gardens are open every day of the year from 9 a.m., closing in summer at 8:30 p.m. and in winter at 4 p.m. Admission in summer is adult $14.50, student $7.50, child $3; admission is much lower in winter.

To get there from downtown take Hwy. 17 north to the Brentwood–Butchart Gardens turnoff, turn left on Keating Crossroad, and follow the signs. **Laidlaw,** tel. (250) 388-6534, runs a regular shuttle out to the gardens from its downtown depot at 700 Douglas St. for $4 each way, or join one of the many guided tours of Victoria that include this famous attraction. Buses no. 74 and 75 from downtown go to Brentwood Bay.

Butterfly Gardens

In the same vicinity as Butchart Gardens, Butterfly Gardens, corner of Benvenuto and W. Saanich Roads, tel. (250) 652-3822, offers you the opportunity to view and photograph some of the world's most spectacular butterflies at close range. Thousands of these beautiful creatures—species from around the world—live here, flying freely around the enclosed gardens and feeding on the nectar provided by colorful tropical plants. The gardens are open daily 10 a.m.-5 p.m.; admission is adult $7, senior $6, child $4.

Sidney

The small town of Sidney lies on the east side of the Saanich Peninsula, overlooking the Strait of Georgia. As well as being the departure point for ferries to the San Juan Islands (Washington), it's a pleasant spot to spend a sunny day exploring the colorful marina and the many outdoor cafés. From the marina, the **Sidney Harbour Cruise,** tel. (250) 655-5211, runs four tours daily around the harbor and to a couple of the inner Gulf Islands; $15 per person. The only official attraction is **Sidney Museum,** next to the marina at 9801 Seaport Place (off the end of Beacon Ave.), tel. (250) 656-2140, open in summer daily 10 a.m.-5 p.m., the rest of the year weekends only 10 a.m.-4 p.m. The highlight is a display pertaining to whales, which includes skeletons.

RECREATION

FUN IN THE SUN

Biking

For those keen on getting around by bike, it doesn't get much better than the bike path following the coastline of the peninsula on which Victoria lies. From downtown, ride down Government St. to Dallas Rd., where you'll pick up the separate bike path running east along the coast to the charming seaside suburb of Oak Bay. From there, Oak Bay Rd. will take you back into the heart of the city for a roundtrip of 20 km. You can rent bikes at **Sports Rent,** just north of downtown at 611 Discovery St., tel. (250) 385-7368; from $8 per hour, $25 per day.

Swimming and Sunbathing

The best beaches are east of downtown. At **Willows Beach,** Oak Bay, most of the summer crowds spend the day sunbathing, although a few hardy individuals brave a swim; water temperature here tops out at around 17° C (63° F).

Closer to downtown, at the foot of Douglas St., the foreshore is mostly rocky, but you can find a couple of short sandy stretches here and there. **Elk Lake,** toward the Saanich Peninsula, and **Thetis Lake,** west of downtown along Hwy. 1, are also popular swimming and sunbathing spots. **Crystal Pool,** one km north of downtown at 2275 Quadra St., tel. (250) 380-7946, has an Olympic-size pool as well as diving facilities, a kids' pool, sauna, and whirlpool.

Kayaking

Ocean River Sports, Market Square, 1437 Store St., tel. (250) 381-4233 or (800) 909-4233, website www.oceanriver.com, sells and rents kayaks and other equipment, offers kayaking courses (from $55), and organizes guided paddles in the Inner Harbour (from $55) and overnight trips through the Gulf Islands and Queen Charlotte Islands (from $155). **Sports Rent,** 611 Discovery St., tel. (250) 385-7368, rents canoes, kayaks, and a wide range of other outdoor equipment. Expect to pay about $35 per day and from $135 per week for a canoe or kayak.

Scuba Diving

Close to downtown Victoria lie a number of good dive sites, notably the Ogden Point breakwall. At the breakwall, **Ogden Point Dive Centre,** 199 Dallas Rd., tel. (250) 380-9119, offers rentals, instruction, and daily guided dives from its base, which features showers, lockers, and a café. A recommended downtown dive shop is **PSD Underwater Sports** at 2519 Douglas St., tel. (250) 386-3483.

To access the great diving in the Straits of Georgia and Juan de Fuca you'll need to charter a boat. One particularly interesting site lies in the shallow waters off Sidney, just north of Victoria, where a 110-meter destroyer escort was scuttled especially for divers. In Sidney, **Deep Cove Ocean Sports,** 10990 Madrona Dr., tel. (250) 656-0060, rents equipment and organizes charters out to the wreck.

Whalewatching

The whalewatching hot spots on Vancouver Island are Tofino for gray whales and Telegraph Cove for orcas, but operators also offer whale-watching day trips out of Victoria's Inner Harbour, April-October. Both resident and transient whales are sighted, along with sea lions, porpoises, and seals. Trips last two to three hours, are generally made in sturdy inflatable boats, and cost $65-85 pp. Operating from the Ocean Pointe Resort, **Seacoast,** tel. (250) 383-2254 or (800) 386-1525, has an onboard naturalist, while **Luda Marine,** tel. (250) 812-6003, and **Prince of Whales,** tel. (250) 383-4884 or (888) 383-4884, can also be recommended. **Sea Quest Adventures,** tel. (250) 656-7599 or (888) 656-7599, is based in Sidney, on the Saanich Peninsula, and offers orca-watching cruises on the Strait of Georgia. The waters here are calmer than those experienced from trips departing the Inner Harbour.

Tours

The classic way to see Victoria is from the comfort of a horse-drawn carriage. Throughout the day and into the evening **Victoria Carriage Tours,** tel. (250) 383-2207, has single-horse carriages lined up along Menzies St. awaiting passengers; a 15-minute tour to James Bay costs $25, or take a 60-minute Royal Tour for $90.

Big red double-decker buses are as much a part of the Victoria tour scene as horse-drawn carriages. These are operated by **Gray Line,** tel. (250) 388-6539 or (800) 663-8390, from beside the Inner Harbour along Belleville Street. There are many tours to choose from, but to get yourself oriented while also learning some city history, take the 90-minute Grand City Drive Tour. It departs from Belleville Street every half hour 9:30 a.m.-4 p.m.; adult $14, child $7. The most popular of Gray Line's other tours is the one to Butchart Gardens ($36.75, including admission price).

Victoria Harbour Ferry, tel. (250) 480-0971, offers boat tours of the harbor and Gorge Waterway. The company's funny-looking boats each seat around 20 passengers and depart regularly 10 a.m.-10 p.m. from below the Empress Hotel. The 45-minute loop tour allows passengers the chance to get on and off at will; adult

$14, senior $12, child $5, or travel just pieces of the entire loop for $3 per sector. You can also take to the waters of the Inner Harbour and beyond in a motorized replica of a Nuu-chah-nulth cedar canoe. The 90-minute trip costs adult $25, child $10, while the three-hour trip is adult $35, child $15. For all the details call **Blackfish Wilderness Expeditions** at (250) 216-2389.

ARTS AND ENTERTAINMENT

Victoria lacks the wild nightlife scene of neighboring Vancouver, but a large influx of summer workers keeps the bars busy and a few nightclubs jumping during the busy season. The city does have more than its fair share of British-style pubs, and you can usually get a good meal along with your pint of lager. The magazine *Monday,* website www.monday.com, offers a comprehensive arts and entertainment section.

Theater
Dating to 1914 and originally called the Pantages Theatre, the grand old **McPherson Playhouse** (known lovingly as the "Mac" by local theater goers) went through hard times during the 1990s but has seen a recent revival of fortunes and now hosts a variety of performing arts. It's in Centennial Square, at the corner of Pandora Ave. and Government Street. The Mac's sister theater, the **Royal Theatre,** across downtown at 805 Broughton St., hosts stage productions and a variety of musical recitals. For schedule information and tickets at both theaters call (250) 386-6121. While the main theater season runs Oct.-April, the **Victoria Summer Theatre** keeps the Mac full through the warmer months. Three usually humorous productions run on a rotating schedule nightly. Tickets cost $22.50, or combined with dinner at a local restaurant from $38. Performing arts on a smaller scale can be appreciated at the **Belfry Theatre,** 1291 Gladstone St., tel. (250) 385-6815, which offers live theater Oct.-April; tickets cost $22 per person.

Music and Dance
Pacific Opera Victoria, tel. (250) 385-0222 or 382-1641, performs three productions each year (usually through the winter months) in the McPherson Playhouse. Tickets run $20-65. The

Victoria Operatic Society, tel. (250) 381-1021, presents opera year-round; call for current schedule.

At the free Symphony Splash on the first Sunday of August, the **Victoria Symphony Orchestra** performs on a barge moored at the Inner Harbour. This kicks off the performing-arts season, with regular performances through to May at the Royal Theatre and other city venues. Tickets range $15-28. For details call (250) 385-9771 or the box office at (250) 385-6515.

Bars
Victoria's many English-style pubs usually feature a wide variety of beers, congenial atmosphere, and inexpensive meals. The **Strathcona Hotel,** 919 Douglas St., tel. (250) 383-7137, is Victoria's largest entertainment venue, featuring 10 bars, including one serving a magnificent rooftop patio and the Sticky Wicket, an English bar. Converted from an old warehouse to a pub is **Swans Hotel,** 506 Pandora St., tel. (250) 361-3310, which brews its own beer. As well as being a dining hot spot, it has a nonsmoking section and is decorated with original art. This popular hangout for local businesspeople gets busy weeknights 5-8 p.m. Open daily from 11 a.m. A few blocks farther north and right on the water is the **Harbour Canoe Club,** 450 Swift St., tel. (250) 361-1940, which is equally popular with the downtown crowd and has a great patio. Also offering magnificent water views is **Spinnakers Brew Pub,** across the Inner Harbour from downtown at 308 Catherine St., tel. (250) 386-2739. A casual atmosphere, modern decor, and great food make this place well worth the diversion. This was Canada's first in-house brew pub, and it continues to produce its own beers, including the popular Spinnakers Ale. It's open daily 11 a.m.-2 p.m. Farther from downtown, relax with an ale or two at the British-style **James Bay Inn,** 270 Government St., tel. (250) 384-7151.

Nightclubs and Live Music Venues
Most of Victoria's nightclubs double as live music venues attracting a great variety of acts. **Legends on Douglas,** in the Strathcona Hotel, 919 Douglas St., tel. (250) 383-7137, comes alive with live rock 'n' roll some nights and a DJ spinning the latest dance discs on other nights. In the same hotel, **Big Bad John's** is the city's main

country music venue. **Liquid,** 15 Bastion Square, tel. (250) 385-2626, was formerly Harpo's, a legendary live-music venue. The new club continues the tradition with a lineup of jazz, blues, and rock but also dance music. Nearby in the Wharfside complex, **Uforia,** 1208 Wharf St., tel. (250) 381-2331, with bright lights and a large dance floor, is the most popular dance-only club. Attracting a similar crowd, but for more progressive music, is the **Drawing Room,** 751 View St., tel. (250) 920-7797.

Victoria boasts several good jazz venues. The best of these are the **Millennium Jazz Club,** downstairs in the Swans Hotel at 1605 Store St., tel. (250) 360-9098, and **Hermann's Jazz Club,** 753 View St., tel. (250) 388-9166. **Steamers,** 570 Yates St., tel. (250) 381-4340, is a jazz and blues venue, but it also draws acts as diverse as Celtic and rock 'n' roll.

SHOPPING

Victoria is a shopper's delight. Most shops and all major department stores are generally open Mon.-Sat. 9:30 a.m.-5:30 p.m. and stay open for late-night shopping Thursday and Friday nights until 9 p.m. The touristy shops around the Inner Harbour and along Government Street are generally open Sunday. Government Street is the main strip of tourist and gift shops. The bottom end, behind the Empress Hotel, is where you'll pick up all those tacky T-shirts and such. Farther up the street are more stylish shops, such as **James Bay Trading Co.,** 1102 Government St., tel. (250) 388-5477, which specializes in native arts from coastal communities; **Hill's Indian Crafts,** 1008 Government St., tel. (250) 385-3911, selling a wide range of authentic native souvenirs; **Northern Passage Gallery,** 1020 Government St., tel. (250) 381-3380, for pottery, paintings, jewelry, and glassblown sculptures; and **Cowichan Trading,** 1328 Government St., tel. (250) 383-0321, featuring Cowichan sweaters. Traditions continue at **Rogers Chocolates,** 913 Government St., tel. (250) 384-7021, which is set up like a candy store of the early 1900s, when Charles Rogers first began selling his homemade chocolates to the local kids.

In Old Town, the colorful, two-story **Market Square** courtyard complex was once the haunt of sailors, sealers, and whalers, who came ashore looking for booze and brothels. Shops here specialize in everything from kayaks to condoms. Walk out of Market Square on Johnson Street to find camping-supply stores and the excellent **Bosun's Locker,** 580 Johnson St., tel. (250) 386-1308, filled to the brim with nautical goodies. Follow Store St. north from Market Square to find a concentration of arts and crafts shops along Herald Street.

Malls line all routes into the city. Besides those at the malls, Victoria's largest downtown department store is **The Bay,** 1701 Douglas Street.

FESTIVALS AND EVENTS

TerrifVic Jazz Party
- When: third week of April
- Where: downtown
- Contact: tel. (250) 953-2011

The first of Victoria's many music-related festivals takes place in April, when performers from around the world come together at various venues. Call for a schedule.

Luxton Pro Rodeo
- When: third weekend in May
- Where: Luxton Fairgrounds
- Contact: tel. (250) 478-4250

As well as the rodeo, this event includes a midway, a display of antique farm equipment, and a dance. The Luxton Fairgrounds are north of downtown Victoria.

Swiftsure International Yacht Race
- When: last weekend of May
- Where: Inner Harbour

Inner Harbour comes alive as the finishing point for this yachting event through local waterways.

ICA FolkFest
- When: end of June
- Where: throughout Victoria
- Contact: tel. (250) 388-4728

For eight days from the last Sunday in June, this festival features contemporary and traditional jazz at venues throughout the city in addition to an arts and crafts market. The best part is that entry to most performances is free. Call for details.

Victoria Fringe Festival
• When: August
• Where: throughout the city
• Contact: tel. (250) 383-2663 (Intrepid Theatre)
Running all August is a celebration of fringe theater with over 50 companies performing at venues throughout the city. All tickets are under $10.

Victoria Summer Theatre
• When: late June to September
• Where: McPherson Playhouse
• Contact: tel. (250) 386-6121

This theater event spans weeks rather than days. For details contact the McPherson Playhouse.

Symphony Splash
• When: first Sunday in August
• Where: Inner Harbour
The local symphony orchestra performs from a barge moored in the Inner Harbour to masses crowded around the shore in this unique festival.

Luxton Fall Fair
• When: first weekend of September
• Where: Luxton Fairgrounds
This fair highlights the island's agricultural roots with fun events and machinery displays. The fairgrounds are north of downtown Victoria.

ACCOMMODATIONS
HOTELS AND MOTELS

DOWNTOWN

Finding a room in Victoria can be difficult during the summer months, when gaggles of tourists compete for a relative paucity of motel rooms. All the best lodgings are in smaller boutique hotels offering only a few dozen rooms. Most of the major worldwide hotel chains are not represented downtown—the city has no Four Seasons, Hilton, Hotel Inter-Continental, Hyatt, Marriott, Radisson, or Regent. In the off season, rooms are discounted up to 50%, but again, occupancy rates are high as Canadians flock to the country's winter hot spot. All things considered, you'd be wise to make reservations as far ahead as possible, no matter what time of year you plan to visit. Bookings can be made direct or through the **Victoria Tourist Info Centre** at (250) 953-2022 or (800) 663-3883.

Inexpensive

Just one block from the Inner Harbour and kitty-corner to the bus depot is the old **Crystal Court Motel,** 701 Belleville St., tel. (250) 384-0551, with 60 park-at-the-door-style motel rooms, half with kitchenettes. As you'd expect with any accommodation falling into this price category in such a prime position, the rooms are fairly basic; from $77 s, $86 d.

In the same vicinity, but farther from the harbor, is the 100-year-old **Cherry Bank Hotel,** across Douglas St. in a quiet location at 825 Burdett Ave., tel. (250) 385-5380 or (800) 998-6688. Aside from a choice of rooms in either the original or new wing, the hotel offers a bar and lounge, and a restaurant known for excellent ribs. The rooms have no TV or phone. High-season rates are from $70 s, $78 d, including a cooked breakfast.

The centrally located **Hotel Douglas,** 1450 Douglas St., tel. (250) 383-4157 or (800) 332-

9981, is another old hotel, this one five stories tall and with 75 refurbished rooms. Guests have use of a coin laundry, and downstairs is a 24-hour café and quiet bar. Rooms with shared bathroom are $60 s, $80 d, while larger rooms with their own bathroom facilities are $85 s, $95 d.

On the northern outskirts of the city center, **Traveller's Inn Downtown,** 1850 Douglas St., tel. (250) 381-1000 or (888) 254-6476, charges $70 s, $80 d for a moderately sized room, which includes a light breakfast. Its advertised winter rate is $29 s, $39 d—the least expensive in the city. Part of the same local chain is **Traveller's Inn on Douglas,** 710 Queens St., tel. (250) 370-1000 or (888) 753-3774, a few blocks farther north. It, along with the other Traveller's Inn properties (website www.travellersinn.com), offers the same rates and the same winter discounts.

Moderate

In the heart of the city center, the six-story 1913 **Strathcona Hotel,** 919 Douglas St., tel. (250) 383-7137 or (800) 663-7476, attracts a younger crowd—as well as 86 guest rooms, it holds 10 bars, including a couple of the city's most popular drinking holes. Rooms are sparsely furnished but clean and comfortable. In summer, rates are $89 s, $99 d, but the rest of the year they are reduced considerably.

Away from the water, but still just one block from Douglas St., is the 1876 **Dominion Hotel,** 759 Yates St., tel. (250) 384-4136 or (800) 663-6101, Victoria's oldest hotel. Millions of dollars have been spent restoring the property with stylish wooden beams, brass trim and lamps, ceiling fans, and marble floors reliving the Victorian era. Yet staying at the Dominion is still reasonable. Advertised rates are $114 s, $118 d, but special deals are generally offered, such as accommodation and a three-course dinner for $99 d.

Around the southern end of the Inner Harbour (close to the ferry terminals), the **Admiral Motel,** 257 Belleville St., tel. (250) 388-6267, has clean and comfortable rooms, each with a small kitchen. Throw in friendly hosts, and you have good value at $89 s, $105 d.

Dating to 1907 and once home to artist Emily Carr, **James Bay Inn,** 270 Government St., tel. (250) 384-7151 or (800) 836-2649, is five blocks from the harbor and within easy walking distance of all city sights and Beacon Hill Park.

Some rooms have private baths and color TV, and the popular pub downstairs serves hearty breakfasts; $105-130 s or d.

Every time I visit Victoria I expect to see that the old **Surf Motel** has been demolished. But it's still there, still offering priceless ocean and mountain views for a reasonable $95 s, $105 d. It's located south of the Inner Harbour at 290 Dallas Rd. (take Oswego Rd. from Belleville St.), tel. (250) 386-3305.

Expensive

Right at harborside is the four-story **Days Inn on the Harbour,** 427 Belleville St., tel. (250) 386-3451 or (800) 665-3044; $130-200 s or d.

In the oldest section of downtown, surrounded by the city's best dining and shopping opportunities, is the **Bedford Regency,** 1140 Government St., tel. (250) 384-6835 or (800) 665-6500, featuring 40 luxuriously appointed rooms restored to their 1930s' art deco glory. Rates start at $135 s, $150 d, while the most luxurious suites feature fireplaces and jacuzzi tubs for $215 s or d.

On a quiet residential street behind the parliament buildings is **Holland House Inn,** 595 Michigan St., tel. (250) 384-6644, a boutique hotel dating to 1934 that has been restored in a casual yet elegant style. Each of the 10 antique-filled rooms has a four-poster bed and private bath. Rooms range $145-250, which includes a delicious cooked breakfast.

Premium

The **Swans Suite Hotel,** 506 Pandora Ave., tel. (250) 361-3310 or (800) 668-7926, is part of a restaurant/pub complex that was originally a waterfront grain storehouse. Each of the 29 split-level suites holds a loft, full kitchen, dining area, and bedroom. The furnishings are simple and casual, but the rates of $169-179 s or d are still great value. In the off season these same rooms are under $100 per night.

The **Laurel Point Inn,** 680 Montreal St., tel. (250) 386-8721 or (800) 663-7667, sits on a point of land jutting into the Inner Harbour three blocks west of Government Street. Each of the 200 rooms has a water view and private balcony. Amenities include an indoor pool, beautifully landscaped gardens, a sauna, and a small gym; from $190 s or d.

The next lodging around the harbor, but still within easy walking distance of downtown, is **Coast Victoria Harbourside Hotel,** 146 Kingston St., tel. (250) 360-1211 or (800) 663-1144. This hotel dates to the mid-1990s, so furnishings are new and modern. The least expensive rooms, $180 s or d, have views and small balconies, but for an extra $40 you get a much larger room with a wide balcony.

Across the Inner Harbour from downtown, offering stunning city views, is the luxurious **Ocean Pointe Resort,** 45 Songhees Rd., tel. (250) 360-2999 or (800) 667-4677. Opened in 1992, this hotel offers all the services of a spa resort with the convenience of downtown just a short ferry trip away. Facilities include a large health club, indoor glass-enclosed pool, spa and massage services, tennis, lounge, and restaurant. Rates for the 250-odd rooms range from $154 to over $500 for the biggest suites.

Luxury

Completely restored in 1989, the grand old **Empress Hotel,** 721 Government St., tel. (250) 384-8111 or (800) 441-1414, is Victoria's best-loved accommodation. Covered in ivy and with only magnificent gardens separating it from the Inner Harbour, it's also in the city's best location. Designed by Francis Rattenbury in 1908, the Empress is another of the grand Canadian Pacific hotels. Rooms aren't particularly large, but each is filled with Victorian period furnishings and antiques. The least expensive rooms start at $305, but for a harbor view expect to pay from $385. Rates are reduced considerably outside of summer. Parking is extra.

The **Magnolia Hotel & Suites,** 623 Courtney St., tel. (250) 381-0999 or (877) 624-6654, is a European-style boutique hotel just up the hill from the harbor. The 66 rooms are each elegantly furnished and feature a large bathtub with separate shower stall, down duvets, and a work area. Rates start at $190 s or d.

If it's modern luxury you prefer over old-world excellence, consider the **Harbour Towers Hotel,** 345 Quebec St., tel. (250) 385-2405 or (800) 663-5896, one block from the harbor. The 185 rooms each have a private balcony and are well appointed and spacious. Most also have water views. Guests have use of an indoor pool and fitness room. Rates start at $179 s, $199 d.

OTHER PARTS OF THE CITY

Esquimalt

Across the Johnson Street Bridge from downtown is the suburb of Esquimalt. The **Olde England Inn,** 429 Lampson St., tel. (250) 388-4353, provides accommodations on the grounds of Anne Hathaway's Cottage, a tourist attraction. The grounds are delightful and boast an excellent restaurant, but on busy days the crowds are bad. Rooms are furnished in period style but aren't particularly large; from $85 s, $95 d. Moderate.

Farther West

The alternative to taking Hwy. 1 out of the city is to travel along Gorge Rd. (Hwy. 1A), where you'll find a string of well-priced motels. The least expensive is the **Fountain Inn,** 356 Gorge Rd. E, tel. (250) 385-1361, which charges $50 s, $55 d for the simply decorated rooms. Budget. Much more comfortable is the **Canterbury Flag Inn,** 310 Gorge Rd. E, tel. (250) 382-2151 or (800) 952-2151, featuring a pool, restaurant, and rates from $85 s, $95 d. In the same vicinity, **Days Inn Victoria Waterway,** 123 Gorge Rd. E, tel. (250) 386-1422, has 95 large rooms, each with a kitchen. Rates start at $109 s, $119 d. Moderate.

From these accommodations, Hwy. 1A continues its westward crawl through the suburb of View Royal and around the head of Esquimalt Harbour to Langford, where it rejoins Hwy. 1. Here, the **Westwind Plaza Hotel,** 741 Goldstream Ave., tel. (250) 478-8334 or (888) 228-6622, dates from the days when Hwy. 1A was the main route out of the city. Today's travelers overnighting here enjoy in-house facilities such as a café, restaurant, and pub but best of all the Inexpensive rates of $60 s, $68 d.

Malahat

This small community is strung out along the main route up the island 25 km from downtown Victoria, making it a good place to spend the night for those who want to get an early start on northward travel. **Malahat Oceanview Motel,** Hwy. 1, tel. (250) 478-9231, offers rooms with views from private balconies; $55 s, $65 d. Inexpensive. For a splurge, consider **Aerie Resort,** 600 Ebedora Lane, tel. (250) 743-7115, high above the waters of Saanich Inlet and surrounded by well-manicured gardens and interesting hiking trails. Each of the 23 rooms features a king-size bed, private balcony, jacuzzi, lounge with fireplace, and luxurious bathroom. The resort also has an indoor pool, outdoor hot tub, tennis courts, and a restaurant. Rates start at $185 s or d including breakfast. To get there take the Spectacle Lake Provincial Park turnoff from Hwy. 1, then take the first right and follow the winding road up to the resort. Luxury.

Saanich Peninsula

Highway 17, the main route between downtown Victoria and the BC Ferries terminal at Swartz Bay, holds many motels suited to travelers arriving at or departing from the airport or ferry terminal. **Western 66 Motel,** flanking the highway at 2401 Mt. Newton Cross Rd., tel. (250) 652-4464 or (800) 463-4464, has a large variety of affordable rooms, complimentary coffee in the lobby each morning, and a family restaurant on the premises; $55 s, $70 d. Inexpensive. At the same intersection is **Quality Inn Waddling Dog,** 2476 Mt. Newton Cross Rd., tel. (250) 652-1146 or (800) 567-8466, styled as an old English guesthouse complete with an English pub; $99 s, $109 d. Moderate.

On the road into downtown Sidney is **Cedarwood Motel,** 9522 Lochside Dr., tel. (250) 656-5551. The rooms are fairly standard, but the setting is glorious, highlighted by a garden with outdoor seating overlooking the Strait of Georgia. Rates start at $89 s, $95 d. Moderate.

Dunsmuir Lodge, 1515 McTavish Rd., tel. (250) 656-3166 or (800) 255-4055, is a bit off the beaten track, but it provides clean and comfortable modern accommodations in a bushland setting with distant ocean views. Guests have use of a restaurant and two cozy lounges. Rooms start at $89 s, $99 d, while the suites are a reasonable $109 s, $129 d. Expensive.

BED AND BREAKFASTS

Victoria's bed and breakfasts are even more abundant than tour operators in the height of the season—over 300 at last count. Prices range from reasonable to outrageous. Check the brochures at the Visitor Info Centre, but if you're looking for something specific you may want to contact the **Western Canadian Bed and Breakfast Innkeepers Association,** P.O. Box 74534, 2803 W. 4th Ave., Vancouver, BC V6K 4P4, tel. (604) 255-9199, website www.wcbbia.com, and request a brochure. This association doesn't take bookings, though. For these call one of the following agencies, all of which are well represented in Victoria: **AB&C B&B of Vancouver,** 4390 Frances St., Vancouver, BC V5C 2R3, tel. (604) 298-8815 or (800) 488-1941; **All B&B Reservations,** 201-1405 Haro St., Vancouver, BC V6G 1G2, tel. (604) 683-3609, for southwestern British Columbia; **All Seasons Bed and Breakfast Agency,** 9858 5th St., Suite 101, Sidney, BC V8L 2X7, tel. (250) 655-7173; **Beachside B&B Registry,** 4208 Evergreen Ave., West Vancouver, BC V7V 1H1, tel. (604) 922-7773; or **Westway Accommodation Registry,** P.O. Box 48950, Bentall Centre, Vancouver, BC V7X 1A8, tel. (604) 273-8293. Otherwise, you can't go wrong staying at one of the personally selected places below.

Downtown

Overlooking the Inner Harbour is **Gatsby Mansion B&B,** 309 Belleville St., tel. (250) 388-9191 or (800) 563-9656, a magnificent 20-room bed and breakfast dating to 1897. The house has been elegantly restored, with stained-glass windows, a magnificent fireplace, lots of exposed wood, crystal chandeliers under a gabled roof, and antiques decorating every corner. Afternoon tea is served in a comfortable lounge area off the lobby, and the restaurant has a nice veranda. Through summer rooms are $195-305, while the rest of year rates range $105-205 s or d. Luxury.

A few blocks back from the Inner Harbour is **Andersen House Bed and Breakfast,** 301 Kingston St., tel. (250) 388-4565. Built late last century for a retired sea captain, the house features large high-ceilinged rooms all overlooking the garden. Rates start at $145 s, $155 d. Premium.

In the same residential area of downtown is **Haterleigh Bed and Breakfast,** 243 Kingston St., tel. (250) 384-9995. Beautifully restored to its

Gatsby Mansion B&B is a great accommodation in an even better location.

early 1900s' glory, each of the six rooms features a luxurious bathroom; from $210 s or d. Luxury.

Beacon Hill Park and Vicinity

Dashwood Manor, 1 Cook St., tel. (250) 385-5517 or (800) 667-5517, a 1912 Tudor-style heritage house on a bluff overlooking Juan de Fuca Strait, enjoys a panoramic view of the entire Olympic mountain range. The 14 rooms are elegantly furnished, and host Derek Dashwood will happily recount the historic details of each room. Rates range from $145 s or d up to $285 for the Oxford Grand, which holds a chandelier, stone fireplace, and antiques. Expensive.

Around the corner from Dashwood Manor is **Ambleside Bed and Breakfast,** 1121 Faithful St., tel. (250) 383-9948, a 1920s' heritage home with two light and bright guest rooms; from $95 s, $105 d. Moderate.

Rockland and Oak Bay

In the quiet residential area of Rockland, **Craigmyle B&B Inn,** 1037 Craigdarroch Rd.,

tel. (250) 595-5411 or (888) 595-5411, is a beautiful old home full of character, comfortable furnishings, and lots of original stained-glass windows. It's within walking distance of the city and stands directly in front of Craigdarroch Castle. Rooms include singles, doubles, and family suites, all with bathrooms. A comfy living room with a TV, a bright sunny dining area, and friendly owners make this a real home-away-from-home. Rates are $70 s, $85-90 d. Inexpensive.

A few blocks farther out is **Renouf House,** 2010 Stanley Ave., tel. (250) 595-4774, a 1912 home offering budget-priced bed and breakfast accommodations. Rooms sharing a bathroom are $35 s, $55 d, while those with bathroom en suite are $50 s, $70 d. Budget.

East of Government House in the suburb of Oak Bay, the Tudor-style, vintage 1912 **Oak Bay Guest House,** 1052 Newport Ave., tel. (250) 598-3812 or (800) 575-3812, offers 11 antique-filled rooms, each with a private balcony and a bathroom. A lounge area off the main lobby holds a small library, as well as tea- and coffee-making facilities. Rates of $135-170 s or d include a delicious four-course breakfast. Expensive.

North of Downtown

Heritage House, 3808 Heritage Lane, tel. (250) 479-0892, a beautiful 1910 mansion surrounded by trees and gardens, sits in a quiet residential area near Portage Inlet, five km northwest of city center. Friendly owners Larry and Sandra Gray have lovingly restored the house to its former glory. Guests choose from several outstanding rooms, one with a view of Portage Inlet from a private veranda. The three bathrooms are shared. Enjoy the large communal living room and a cooked breakfast in the elegant dining room. It's very busy in summer but quieter Nov.-April. Reservations are necessary year-round. Rooms vary in size and furnishings but all are the same cost, $125 s or d. Expensive. Heritage Lane is not shown on any Victoria maps; from city center, take Douglas St. north to Burnside Rd. E (bear left off of Douglas). Just across the TransCanada Hwy., Burnside makes a hard left (if you continue straight instead you'll be on Interurban Rd.). Make the left turn and continue down Burnside to just past Grange Road. The next lane on the right is Heritage Lane.

BUDGET ACCOMMODATIONS

Budget travelers are well catered to in Victoria, and while the accommodation choices in the capital are more varied than in Vancouver, there is no one backpacker lodge that stands out above the rest.

BACKPACKER LODGES

Hostelling International
In the heart of downtown Victoria's oldest section is **Hostelling International Victoria,** 516 Yates St., tel. (250) 385-4511. The totally renovated hostel enjoys a great location only a stone's throw from the harbor. Separate dorms and bathroom facilities for men and women are complemented by two fully equipped kitchens, a large meeting room, lounge, library, game room, travel services, and an informative bulletin board. Members of Hostelling International pay $16 per night, nonmembers $20; private rooms range $42-50 s or d. Budget.

Other Backpacker Lodges
A new addition to the backpacker scene in Victoria is **Ocean Island Backpackers Inn,** a few blocks from downtown at 791 Pandora Ave., tel. (250) 385-1788 or (888) 888-4180. It's in a restored 1893 residence, with guests having the use of kitchen facilities, a laundry, and a computer for Internet access. There's also plenty of space to relax, such as a reading room, music room, and television room. Dorm beds are $16 pp while private rooms are $20 pp. The owners will make pick-ups from the bus depot. Budget. In the same general direction but farther out (a 20-minute walk from the harbor) is **Victoria Backpackers Lodge,** 1418 Fernwood Rd., tel. (250) 386-4471, which provides cooking and laundry facilities, free coffee, bicycle rentals, and parking. A dorm bed is $14, a private room is $40 s, $45 d. Budget.

If you have your own transportation, **Selkirk Guest House,** 934 Selkirk Ave., tel. (250) 389-1213, is a good choice. This family-run accommodation is in an attractive historic home on the south side of the Gorge Waterway just under three km from downtown (cross the Johnson Street Bridge from downtown and take Craigflower Rd.). It has all the usual facilities, as well as a hot tub and pleasant gardens. Cost is $18 for a dorm bed or $35 s, $40 d. Budget.

OTHER OPTIONS

YWCA
A few blocks east of the harbor, the **YMCA/YWCA of Victoria,** 880 Courtney St., tel. (250) 386-7511, offers exercise facilities for both sexes, but the accommodation is for women only. The small, clean rooms share bathrooms. No cooking facilities are available, but the ground-floor café is good (it's usually crowded at lunchtime). Rates are $37 s, $49 twin. Budget.

University of Victoria
When University of Victoria students leave on summer vacation, their campus dormitory rooms become available to travelers. The rooms are sparse, and each has one or two single beds with shared bathroom and kitchen facilities. Rates are $38-75 s, $50-90 twin, which includes linen and a full breakfast. The rooms are at the corner of Sinclair and Finnerty Roads; for details call Housing and Conference Services at (250) 721-8396. Budget.

CAMPGROUNDS

West
Closest camping to downtown is **Fort Victoria RV Park,** 340 Island Hwy., tel. (250) 479-8112, six km northwest of city center on Hwy. 1A. This campground provides hookups (no official tent sites), free showers, laundry facilities, and opportunities to join charter salmon-fishing trips. During the summer, sites are $28. Budget. A little farther west is **Thetis Lake Campground,** 1938 Hwy. 1 (take the Thetis Lake exit), tel. (250) 478-3845, featuring pleasant shaded sites, coin-operated showers, and laundry facilities. It adjoins Thetis Lake Park, which is crisscrossed by hiking trails and holds one of the city's fa-

vorite swimming and sunbathing spots. Unserviced sites are $18, hookups $18-22. Budget.

North Along Hwy. 1

Continuing west from the two campgrounds detailed above, Hwy. 1 curves north through **Goldstream Provincial Park** (19 km from downtown) and begins its long journey north. The southern end of the park holds 161 campsites scattered around an old-growth forest—it's one of the most beautiful settings you could imagine close to a capital city. The campground offers free hot showers but no hookups. Sites are $17.50 per night. Good hiking trails and many other recreational opportunities are available in the area. Budget.

In Malahat, seven km farther north along Hwy. 1, is **KOA Victoria West,** tel. (250) 478-3332 or (800) 562-1732. Facilities include free showers, an outdoor pool, laundry, store, and game room. Unserviced sites are $22, hookups $24-28, and Kamping Kabins from $46. Budget.

Saanich Peninsula

If you're coming from or heading for the ferry terminal, consider staying at **McDonald Provincial Park,** near the tip of the Saanich Peninsula 31 km north of the city center. Facilities are limited (no showers or hookups); campsites are $11.50 per night. Budget. Also on the peninsula, halfway between downtown Victoria and Sidney, is **Island View Beach RV Park,** Homathko Dr., tel. (250) 652-0548, right on the beach three km east of Hwy. 17. Sites are $20-25 and you'll need quarters for the showers. Budget.

Victoria's Chinatown

FOOD

Coffeehouses and Cafés
Murchies, 1110 Government St., tel. (250) 381-5451, is a large coffeehouse on Victoria's busiest downtown street. It has all the usual choices of coffee concoctions as well as light snacks. Continuing away from the harbor, and across the road, is the **Electric Juice Café,** 1223 Government St., tel. (250) 380-0009. Here you'll find a huge selection of fruit and vegetable juices mixed to your liking and with the option of adding extras such as ginseng and bee pollen. At the foot of Bastion Square, a cobbled pedestrian mall, quiet **Paradiso,** 10 Bastion Square, tel. (250) 920-7266, serves a range of coffees, pastries, and muffins. In Old Town, **Willies Bakery,** 537 Johnson St., tel. (250) 381-8414, is an old-style café offering cakes, pastries, and sodas, with a quiet courtyard in which to enjoy them. Across the road, on the second story of Market Square, 560 Johnson St., the **Bavarian Bakery,** tel. (250) 388-5506, also sells a wide range of bakery delights. Farther north along the waterfront is the "arty" part of downtown; in the **Capital Iron** store

are a small concession stand and a few tables offering water views.

While tourists flock to the cafés and restaurants of the Inner Harbour and Government St., Douglas St. remains the haunt of lunching locals. A throwback to days gone by is **Cross' Quality Meats,** 1312 Douglas St., tel. (250) 384-2631, an old-style butcher's shop where you can get a coffee and muffin to go for $1.50. Dating to a similar era is **John's Place,** just off Douglas St. at 723 Pandora Ave., tel. (250) 389-0711, which has been serving hungry locals since the late 1940s. The walls are decorated with movie posters, old advertisements, and photos of sports stars, but this place is a lot more than just another greasy-spoon restaurant. The food is good, the atmosphere casual, and the waitresses actually seem to enjoy working here. It's breakfast, burgers, salads, and sandwiches through the week, but weekend brunch is busiest, when there's nearly always a line spilling onto the street. This part of town is home to all the more modern coffeehouses also, including **Blenz** at 1328 Douglas St., **Company's Coming** at 670 Fort St., and **Starbucks** at 801 Fort Street.

Casual Dining

Right across from the information center, and drawing tourists like a magnet, is **Sam's Deli,** 805 Government St., tel. (250) 382-8424. Many places nearby have better food, but Sam's boasts a superb location and cheerful atmosphere. The ploughman's lunch, a staple of English pub dining, costs $8, while sandwiches range $4.50-7 and salads are all around $6. Open daily 7:30 a.m.-10 p.m.

Wharfside Eatery, 1208 Wharf St., tel. (250) 360-1808, is a bustling waterfront restaurant with a maritime theme and family atmosphere. Behind a small café section and a bar is the main dining room, where many tables have water views. The menu features soups, salads, pizza from a wood-fired oven, a variety of meat dishes, and fresh local seafood. Sunday brunch, $8-10, is very popular. In the same complex, **Nasty Jacks,** 1208 Wharf St., tel. (250) 360-1808, is named for a South Seas pirate who spent the 1860s in Victoria. It's open all day, every day; breakfasts start at $5, but the café is best known for Nasty Stacked Sandwiches from $6.

In Old Town, the small **Sour Pickle Cafe,** 1623 Store St., tel. (250) 384-9390, comes alive with funky music and an enthusiastic staff. The menu offers bagels from $1.60, full cooked breakfasts from $5.50, soup of the day $3, healthy sandwiches $5-6.50, and delicious single-serve pizza for around $7.50. Open Mon.-Fri. 7:30 a.m.-4:30 p.m.

Away from the tourist-clogged streets of the Inner Harbour, right at sea level, is **Barb's Place,** on Fisherman's Wharf at the end of Saint Lawrence St., tel. (250) 384-6515. The specialty is fish and chips to go, but the seafood chowder is also good. Open daily from 8 a.m.

Empress Hotel Dining

Afternoon tea is served just about everywhere in Victoria—it's a local tradition—but the most popular place to indulge is the **Empress Hotel,** 721 Government St.; it's also the dressiest affair (no jeans, shorts, tennis shoes, etc.)—keep in mind that you're taking part in one of the oldest Victorian rituals. It is served in three different areas of the hotel, including the most traditional location,

the Lobby, and in the elegant Empress Room; still, it's so popular that reservations are necessary for the 1 p.m., 2:30 p.m., and 4 p.m. sittings. Sample English honey crumpets, homemade scones with cream and jam, sandwiches, Empress cakes, and an Empress blend tea for $30 per person.

For a sit-down lunch and an excuse to eat in the Empress Hotel, head to the **Bengal Lounge,** which serves meals Mon.-Sat. 11 a.m.-6:30 p.m. Prices range from $6.50 for soup to $9.50 for open sandwiches and $12-18 for main courses. The Empress's less formal **Garden Cafe** serves light meals daily 7 a.m.-9:30 p.m. The Empress Room is the hotel's most formal restaurant (and the most expensive; mains *start* at $30), dishing up Pacific Northwest cuisine in an elegant setting. Reservations are necessary only for afternoon tea and dining in the Empress Room; for these call (250) 384-8111.

Seafood

Victoria's many seafood restaurants come in all forms. Fish and chips is a British tradition and is sold as such at **Old Vic Fish & Chips,** in a heritage-listed building at 1316 Broad St., tel. (250) 383-4536; open Mon.-Thurs. 11 a.m.-7 p.m., Fri.-Sat. 11 a.m.-8 p.m. **Chandlers** is on the main strip of tourist-catching restaurants along the waterfront at 1250 Wharf St., tel. (250) 385-3474, but is generally regarded as Victoria's finest seafood restaurant. It's open daily for lunch and dinner, with mains at dinner ranging $16-28. North beyond the Johnson Street Bridge (just past Market Square) is the **Fowl & Fish Café,** 1605 Store St., tel. (250) 361-3150. Starters include a creamy oyster chowder and seafood tapas for $5-8, while most main dishes including salmon and halibut are under $20. It's open for dinner only from 5 p.m. daily.

Pub Meals

Right in the heart of downtown is the **Elephant and Castle,** corner Government and View Streets, tel. (250) 383-5858. This English-style pub features exposed beams, oak paneling, and traditional pub decor. A few umbrella-shaded tables line the sidewalk out front. All the favorites, such as steak and kidney pie and fish and chips, range $7-14. Open daily for lunch and dinner.

Across from the waterfront is **Swans Hotel,**

TWO OUT OF TOWN SPLURGES

The following two restaurants are out of town but well worth the drive. Both also provide accommodations.

Sooke Harbour House
One of Vancouver Island's finest dining experiences can be had at Sooke Harbour House, 34 km west of downtown at 1528 Whiffen Spit Rd., tel. (250) 642-3421, in a magnificent setting atop a seaside bluff. Originally a private residence, three of its largest rooms have been converted to a restaurant. Most dishes feature seafood, prepared to perfection with vegetables and herbs picked from the surrounding garden. Dinner entrées range $16-30. Open daily from 5:30 p.m.; make reservations before driving out.

Aerie Resort
The restaurant at the Aerie Resort, 25 km north from downtown Victoria on Ebedora Lane (off Hwy. 1), Malahat, tel. (250) 743-7115, is equally popular with those looking for a splurge. In a delightful setting, surrounded by forest and grazing wildlife, diners are treated to French cuisine, elegant atmosphere, and service that oozes professionalism. Main courses are around $25-30, and a seven-course feast is offered for $55 per person. Open daily 5-10 p.m.

506 Pandora St., tel. (250) 361-3310, an English-style pub that brews its own beer and serves delicious food. As well as the typical pub pews, the hotel has covered a section of the sidewalk with a glass-enclosed atrium. The **James Bay Inn,** 270 Government St., tel. (250) 384-7151, also serves up typical English pub food at reasonable prices. Look for traditional dishes such as kippers and poached eggs for breakfast, ploughman's lunches, and roast beef with Yorkshire pudding or steak and kidney pie in the evening; dinner entrées start at $9.50.

While all the above pubs exude the English traditions for which Victoria is famous, **Spinnakers Brew Pub,** 308 Catherine St., Esquimalt, tel. (250) 386-2739, is in a class by itself. It was Canada's first in-house brew pub, and it's as popular today as when it first opened. The crowds come for the beer, but also for great food

served up in a casual, modern atmosphere. It's open daily from 11 a.m.

Ribs
The **Cherry Bank Hotel Rib House,** 825 Burdett Ave., tel. (250) 385-5380, provides plenty to see and do while you wait for your ribs, seafood, or chicken. The restaurant springs to life as the honky-tonk piano player starts pounding out one old-fashioned tune after another and the air fills with voices, hands clapping, feet tapping, and tables and chairs jiving. The food is excellent; main courses run $10-19 and come with salad, potato, vegetable, and garlic bread. Open daily for lunch and dinner, with early-bird specials Mon.-Fri. 5-6 p.m.

Vegetarian
Green Cuisine, in Market Square on Johnson St., tel. (250) 385-1809, takes the vegetarian theme to the fullest, with a vegan menu that uses no oils, sugars, or refined flours. A small buffet is offered, but the regular menu provides many choices, from chili to fruit juices. Open daily.

Mexican
On the waterfront side of Market Square is **Cafe Mexico,** 1425 Store St., tel. (250) 386-1425. The atmosphere is very casual, with Mexican paraphernalia hanging everywhere and loud music playing. A large buffet lunch is served Mon.-Fri. from 11:30 a.m. The regular menu is extensive, ranging from $2.50 salsa dips to $11-15 gourmet dishes.

Italian
One of the most popular restaurants in town is **Pagliacci's,** 1011 Broad St., tel. (250) 386-1662, known for hearty Italian food, homemade bread, great desserts, and loads of atmosphere. Small and always busy, the restaurant attracts a lively local crowd; you'll inevitably have to wait for a table during the busiest times. Pastas range $10-14. This is also one of the few late-night restaurants in Victoria; open daily 11:30 a.m.-midnight. A jazz trio plays Wed.-Sun. nights.

The **Herald Street Caffe,** 546 Herald St., tel. (250) 381-1441, is also good, with a menu comparable to Pagliacci's but more extensive. Housed in a heritage building in Old Town, the atmosphere is casual, with artworks adorning the walls and flowering plants everywhere. Open Wed.-Sat. for lunch and daily for dinner.

Along a narrow sidestreet among boutiques and galleries is **Vin Santo,** 620 Trounce Alley, tel. (250) 480-5560. While small and intimate, this bistro-style restaurant has a floor-to-ceiling glass front for watching the parade of people walking past. The Northern Italian cuisine makes good use of local produce. Most lunch entrées are under $10, while dinner ranges $12-18. Open daily.

Other European Restaurants

A good place to go for Greek food, and live entertainment on weekends, is **Periklis Greek Restaurant,** 531 Yates St., tel. (250) 386-3313. Main courses range $12-25, and almost anything can be happening on the floor—from exotic belly dancers to crazy Greek dancing. For a more subdued atmosphere, head to **Millos,** 716 Burdett Ave., tel. (250) 382-4422, which also presents belly dancing some nights. Beyond the west end of Belleville St. is **Pablo's Dining Lounge,** 225 Quebec St., tel. (250) 388-4255, a long-time Victorian favorite serving a variety of European cuisines. Atmosphere in the Edwardian house is relaxed yet intimate, and the dishes are all well-prepared and well-presented. Entrées range $15-26. Open daily from 5 p.m.

The **Garlic Rose Café,** 1205 Wharf St., tel. (250) 384-1931, offers a Mediterranean-inspired menu (lots of herbs are used) with seating out front, inside, and upstairs. Dinner mains start at $15, but the daily specials include a starter for around the same price. **Med Grill,** 100 Yates St., tel. (250) 360-1660, features Pacific Northwest produce cooked with southern European techniques. The menu is short, with one dish of each meat offered, including a delicious steamed salmon dish ($21) hard for seafood lovers to pass up.

Chinese

Victoria's small Chinatown surrounds a short, colorful strip of Fisgard St. between Store and Government Streets. Near the top (east) end of Fisgard is **QV Cafe and Bakery,** 1701 Government St., offering inexpensive western-style breakfasts in the morning and Chinese delicacies the rest of the day. One of the least expensive places in the area is **Wah Lai Yuen,** 560 Fisgard St., tel. (250) 381-5355, a large, simply decorated, well-lit restaurant with fast and efficient service. The wonton soups (from $3) are particularly good, or try the hearty chicken hot pot ($8) or scallops and broccoli ($13.50). Open daily 10 a.m.-9 p.m.

Named for the Chinese province renowned for hot and spicy food, **Hunan Village Cuisine,** 546 Fisgard St., tel. (250) 382-0661, offers entrées ranging $8-15. It's open Mon.-Sat. for lunch and daily for dinner. Down the hill a little is **Don Mee Restaurant,** 538 Fisgard St., tel. (250) 383-1032, specializing in the cuisine of Canton. Entrées run about $7 each, while four-course dinners for two or more diners are a good deal at under $15 per person. Open Mon.-Fri. for lunch, daily for dinner.

A few blocks from Chinatown and just off Douglas St. is **Lotus Pond,** 617 Johnson St., tel. (250) 388-7387, a no-frills vegetarian Chinese restaurant. It's open Mon.-Sat. 11 a.m.-8 p.m.

BASICS

Pacific Central Station

VANCOUVER BASICS
GETTING THERE

AIR

Vancouver International Airport
Vancouver International Airport (YVR) is on Sea Island, 15 km south of Vancouver city center, tel. (604) 276-6101, website www.yvr.ca. It is Canada's second busiest airport, handling over 12 million passengers annually. From the airport, connections can easily be made throughout the city by shuttle bus, regular public transportation, or taxi.

A new $500 million, open-plan **International Terminal** opened in May 1996. Level 2 is for arrivals, Level 3 for departures (the check-in area for U.S.-bound flights is Concourse E). Each level holds an information booth, currency exchange facilities, ATM machines, duty-free shops, gift shops, newsstands, a post office, cafés, and restaurants. Car rental and shuttle services all have outlets on the arrivals level.

Scattered around the new terminal are many pieces of stunning art: a five-meter-high cedar carving of a Salish couple extending a traditional native welcome greets arriving passengers, while on Level 3 you'll find a large bronze sculpture of a canoe by Haida artist Bill Reid.

Linked to the international terminal by a concourse, the original airport now functions as the **Domestic Terminal.** Level 2 handles all arrivals and holds an information booth, car rental agencies, ATMs, and a variety of shops and restaurants. Level 3 is for departures.

Airlines
Canadian Airlines, tel. (604) 279-6611 or (800) 465-3611 (800-426-7000 from the U.S.), is one of the world's largest airlines, serving five continents. It offers direct flights to Vancouver from all major North American cities, including Calgary, Toronto, Montreal, Seattle, Los Angeles, San Francisco, Reno, Las Vegas, Phoenix, Chica-

go, Boston, Washington, Dallas/Fort Worth, New York, Atlanta, and St. Louis. From Europe, Canadian flies direct from London to Vancouver, and from Paris, Frankfurt, and Rome via Toronto. From Australia and the South Pacific, Canadian operates in alliance with Qantas, which flies passengers to Honolulu, where they change to Canadian for the flight to Vancouver and onward connections. Asian cities, served by Canadian in conjunction with Malaysian Airlines, include Bangkok, Kuala Lumpur, Hong Kong, Taipei, Nagoya, Beijing, and Tokyo. Canadian's flights originating in the South American cities of Santiago, Buenos Aires, Sao Paulo, and Rio de Janeiro are routed through Toronto.

Air Canada, tel. (604) 688-5515 or (800) 776-3000, also offers flights from all major Canadian and U.S. cities to Vancouver. The only Air Canada nonstop international flights to Vancouver originate in London. All other European flights are routed through Toronto. Flights from Asia and the South Pacific are routed through Honolulu or a U.S. west coast city.

Canada 3000, tel. (604) 609-3000, offers scheduled flights to Vancouver from Edmonton, Calgary, Winnipeg, Toronto, and Montreal. Between October and April Canada 3000 has "scheduled" charter flights from New Zealand and Australia to Vancouver. These are the cheapest trans-Pacific flights offered by any air-line (from CAD$999 roundtrip), but many restrictions apply and legroom is minimal.

WestJet, tel. (604) 606-5525 or (800) 538-5696, is another budget-priced airline, with specials advertised year-round. Its hub is the airport at Abbotsford, 72 km east of downtown, which receives flights from regional centers throughout British Columbia as well as from Calgary, Edmonton, Saskatoon, Regina, and Winnipeg.

Other international airlines serving Vancouver include: **American Airlines, British Airways, Cathay Pacific, Continental, Delta, Horizon Air, Japan Air Lines, KLM, Korean Air, Lufthansa, Singapore Airlines,** and **United Airlines.**

For onward travel connections, contact **Air BC,** tel. (604) 688-5515 or (800) 776-3000, or **Canadian Regional,** tel. (604) 279-6611 or (800) 465-3611, both flying to destinations throughout western Canada; **North Vancouver Air,** tel. (604) 278-1608 or (800) 228-6608, serving Vancouver Island and Powell River; and **Pacific Coastal Airlines,** tel. (604) 273-8666, flying daily between Vancouver and Powell River. From Coal Harbour, on Burrard Inlet, **Harbour Air,** tel. (604) 688-1277 or (800) 663-4267, and **West Coast Air,** tel. (604) 606-6888 or (800) 347-2222, have scheduled floatplane flights to Victoria's Inner Harbour, and **Baxter Aviation,** tel. (604) 683-6525 or (800) 661-5599, offers a similar service to Nanaimo.

DEPARTURE TAXES

The federal government imposes a tax of seven percent of the ticket price plus $6 to a maximum of $55 on all flights departing Canada for the United States. For all other international destinations, the departure tax is set at $55. These taxes are generally included in the ticket purchase price, but it pays to ask when booking.

Additionally, all passengers departing Vancouver must pay an **Airport Improvement Fee.** The "fee" on flights destined for all points within British Columbia and the Yukon is $5, elsewhere in North America it's $10, and on all other international flights it's $15. Pay the fee at the vending machines or at the desk beside the security check.

Airport Transportation

The **YVR Airporter,** tel. (604) 946-8866 or (800) 668-3141, leaves Level 2 of both terminals every 30 minutes between 6:30 a.m. and 11:30 p.m. daily, shuttling passengers along three routes between the airport and more than 40 downtown accommodations and Pacific Central Station. The one-way fare is adult $10, senior $8, child $5, with a slight discount offered for a roundtrip purchase. Buy tickets from the driver or from the ticket offices on the arrival levels of both terminals.

To get to downtown by public transport, jump aboard bus no. 100 (Midway Connector) on Level 3 (basic fare $2.25) and get off at 70th St. and Granville, then take bus no. 20 (Vancouver) to downtown.

A cab from the airport to downtown takes from 25 minutes and runs around $35.

CUTTING FLIGHT COSTS

I n today's topsy-turvy world of air travel, the first step in getting to Vancouver is to find yourself a travel agent who takes the time to call around, does some research to get you the best fare, and helps you take advantage of any available special offers or promotional deals. The next best attack is to call the airlines in person (in the U.S. most have toll-free telephone numbers) and compare fares; ask if they have any specials. Always ask for the best price they have for the time of year you wish to travel. Also look in the travel sections of major newspapers—particularly in the Sunday editions—where budget fares and package deals are frequently advertised. The Internet is another good place to start searching out the cheapest fares. The website **Travelocity** (www.travelocity.com) displays airline schedules and their published fares.

Many cheaper tickets have strict restrictions regarding changes of flight dates, lengths of stay, and cancellations. A general rule: The cheaper the ticket, the more restrictions. Most travelers today fly on APEX (advance-purchase excursion) fares. These are usually the best value, though some (and, occasionally, many) restrictions apply. These might include minimum and maximum stays, and nonchangeable itineraries (or hefty penalties for changes); tickets may also be nonrefundable once purchased. Within Canada, **Travel Cuts** and **Flight Centre**, both with offices in all major cities, consistently offer the lowest airfares available. Within the U.S., one of the largest consolidators is **Unitravel,** tel. (800) 325-2222. In London, **Trailfinders,** 194 Kensington High St., London W8 7RG, tel. (071) 938-3232, always has good deals to Canada and other North American destinations.

When you have found the best fare, open a **frequent flyer** membership with the airline—**Canadian Airlines** has a very popular reward program that makes rewards very obtainable.

Airport Parking

A covered concourse links both the domestic and international terminals to a multistory, short-term parking lot. Parking costs $4 per hour to a maximum of $20 per day. Many companies offer long-term parking within a few kilometers of the airport. **Park 'N Fly,** Miller Rd., tel. (604) 270-9476, charges $52 per week, $138 per month. For general airport parking information, call (604) 276-6104.

RAIL

In 1886, the first CPR train rolled into Vancouver, forging a link to the outside world and spurring the city's growth beyond everyone's wildest dreams. By the 1990s, though, rail travel had lost much of its appeal, thanks to drastically reduced airfares. Today, however, improved service, a refitting of carriages, a competitive pricing structure, and the luxurious privately operated Rocky Mountaineer have helped trains regain popularity in western Canada.

The Vancouver terminus of all VIA Rail services and the Rocky Mountaineer is **Pacific Central Station,** two km southeast of downtown at 1150 Station St., a $7 cab ride or a five-minute SkyTrain trip from Canada Place. Inside the station you'll find a currency exchange, cash machines, lockers, a newsstand, information boards, and a McDonald's restaurant. Pacific Central Station is also the long-distance bus depot.

VIA Rail

Government-run VIA Rail provides passenger-train service right across Canada. The **Canadian** is a thrice-weekly service between Toronto and Vancouver via Winnipeg, Saskatoon, Edmonton, Jasper, and Kamloops. Service is provided in two classes of travel: **Economy** features lots of legroom, reading lights, pillows and blankets, and a Skyline Car complete with bar service, while **Silver and Blue** is more luxurious, featuring sleeping rooms, daytime seating, all meals, a lounge and dining car, and shower kits for all passengers.

Passes and Practicalities: If you're traveling to Vancouver from any eastern province, the least expensive way to travel is on a **Canrailpass,** which allows unlimited travel anywhere on the VIA Rail system for 12 days within any given 30-day period. During high season (1 June-15 Oct.) the pass is $589; the rest of the year it's $379. Even if you plan limited train travel the pass is an excellent deal; the regular Toronto-Vancouver one-way fare alone is $570.31. VIA Rail has recently cooperated with

Amtrak to offer a North American Rail Pass, with all the same seasonal dates and discounts as the Canrailpass. The cost is CAD$919, US$643 for a high season pass. For Amtrak information call (800) 872-7245.

On regular fares, discounts of 25-40% apply to travel in all classes Oct.-June. Those over 60 and under 25 receive a 10% discount that can be combined with other seasonal fares. Students receive a 50% discount year-round. Check for advance-purchase restrictions on all discount tickets.

Pick up a train schedule at any VIA Rail station or call (800) 561-8630 within western Canada; in other Canadian locations contact your local VIA Rail station. In the U.S. call any travel agent. The VIA Rail website, www.viarail.com, provides route, schedule, and fare information as well as links to towns and sights en route. Other general sales agents include Walshes World, 4 Davies St., Surrey Hills, NSW, Australia, tel. (02) 9319-6624; Walshes World, 2nd Floor, Dingwall Building, 87 Queen St., Auckland, New Zealand, tel. (09) 379-3708; Canada Reise Dienst, Rathausplatz 2, 22926 Ahrensburg, Germany, tel. 04102-8877-0; Long-Haul Leisurail, P.O. Box 113, Peterborough PE3 8HY, Cambridgeshire, England, tel. (0733) 33-5599.

B.C. Rail

The primary function of this government-owned company is as a carrier of freight, but it also operates the **Cariboo Prospector,** a passenger service that runs between the northern British Columbia city of Prince George and Vancouver. If you're traveling to Vancouver from northern latitudes this train trip is a scenic alternative to bus travel and makes an interesting loop if you've traveled north via the ferry system. The one-way fare for the 14-hour trip from Prince George is $194, which includes meals. The route traveled is via Williams Lake, Lillooet, and Whistler (the latter two make an interesting day trip from Vancouver), with trains terminating on the north side of Burrard Inlet at 1311 W. 1st

St., North Vancouver, tel. (604) 984-5246 or (800) 663-8238.

Rocky Mountaineer

Rocky Mountaineer Railtours, tel. (604) 606-7245 or (800) 665-7245, website www.rockymountaineer.com, runs a luxurious rail trip to Vancouver from Banff or Calgary and Jasper, through the spectacular interior mountain ranges of British Columbia. Travel is during daylight hours only so you don't miss anything. Trains depart in either direction in the morning (every second or third day), overnighting at Kamloops. One-way travel in Signature Service, which includes light meals, nonalcoholic drinks, and Kamloops accommodations costs $610 pp from either Banff or Jasper and $670 from Calgary. GoldLeaf Service is the ultimate in luxury. Passengers ride in a two-story glass-domed car, eat in a separate dining area, and stay in Kamloops' most luxurious accommodations. GoldLeaf costs $1,110 from Banff or Jasper to Vancouver and $1,210 from Calgary. During value season (May and the first two weeks of October), fares are reduced $100.

BUS

All long-distance bus services terminate at **Pacific Central Station,** two km southeast of downtown at 1150 Station St. (see Rail, above).

Greyhound

Traveling by bus to Vancouver is easy with Greyhound, tel. (604) 482-8747 or (800) 661-8747, website www.greyhound.ca. From the thousands of depots throughout North America, you can go just about anywhere you desire. Reservations are not necessary—just turn up when you want to go, buy your ticket, and kick back. As long as you use your ticket within 30 days, you can stop over wherever the bus stops and stay as long as you want. The company offers Trans-Canada Highway service from Toronto, Winnipeg, Regina, and Calgary (Alberta), through

Kamloops to Vancouver, as well as a more southerly route from Calgary through Cranbrook and the Kootenays to Vancouver. Greyhound buses also link Vancouver to Seattle and the northern cities of Prince George, Prince Rupert, and Whitehorse.

When calling for information, ask about any special deals—sometimes Greyhound offers excursion fares to certain destinations that save you money if you buy a roundtrip ticket; other times it offers good prices if you buy your ticket a month in advance. The **Domestic Canada Pass** is valid on all Greyhound routes in Canada. It is sold in periods of seven days ($223.13), 15 days ($294.25), 30 days ($401.25), and 60 days ($508.25). It must be purchased seven days in advance and is nonrefundable. You can buy the pass at any bus depot. For more information, call (800) 661-8747. In the U.S. the pass can be bought from most travel agents. Outside of North America it is sold as the **International Canada Pass** with a similar pricing structure except that there is a low season with a 25% discount that runs mid-September to mid-June.

Other Bus Lines
Quick Shuttle, tel. (604) 940-4428 or (800) 665-2122, operates a regular bus service to Pacific Central Station and major downtown Vancouver hotels from downtown Seattle (US$31 one-way) and SeaTac Airport (US$38 one-way).

Pacific Coach Lines, tel. (604) 662-8074, website www.pacificcoach.com, provides a handy link from Victoria, on Vancouver Island, to Vancouver. Buses depart downtown Victoria every couple hours 6 a.m.-9 p.m., heading to Swartz Bay for the ferry trip across to Tsawwassen then dropping passengers at the Delta Pacific Resort for connections to the airport ($30.50 one-way, $59 roundtrip) before terminating at Pacific Central Station ($25 one-way, $51 roundtrip). The time to either destination is around three and a half hours, and the ferry fare is included in the price.

Pacific Central Station is also the terminus for **Maverick Coach Lines,** tel. (604) 662-8051, with services to Vancouver from Nanaimo ($31.43) on Vancouver Island, along the Sunshine Coast as far north as Powell River ($37.61), and from Whistler ($18.56) via Squamish.

Bigfoot Adventure Tours, tel. (604) 278-8224 or (888) 244-6673, offers a leisurely bus trip between Vancouver and Calgary via Banff. A different route is taken in each direction, and the pace is leisurely, with time spent at major natural attractions en route and one night spent in dormitory accommodations near Salmon Arm. Specifically designed for budget travelers, the trip leaves three times a week throughout summer and costs just $99 one-way. **Moose Run Adventure Tours,** tel. (604) 944-3007 or (888) 388-4881, website www.mooserun.com, is a similar setup; through summer buses make a continuous 10-day loop between Vancouver, Whistler, Kamloops, Jasper, Banff, Revelstoke, and Kelowna. You can get on and off wherever you please (and jump aboard the next bus as it passes through) or bond with the crowd and spend the 10 days together for $350 (transportation only).

FERRY

Two main ferry systems ply the west coast of British Columbia: government-run BC Ferries and the Alaska Marine Highway, with the former docking at two points within Vancouver city limits. For most readers of this book, the following information is more of a concern for onward travel, but a couple of interesting combinations can be used in getting to Vancouver via ferry.

From Washington State
Many scheduled ferry services cross over the international border from Washington State to British Columbia, but all terminate on Vancouver Island. From the island, though, it's just another short hop across the Strait of Georgia to Vancouver with BC Ferries (see below). For details, contact the *Victoria Clipper,* tel. (206) 448-5000, (250) 382-8100, or (800) 888-2535, a fast passenger-only service connecting Seattle's Pier 69 with Victoria; the *Royal Victorian,* tel. (206) 625-1880 or (250) 480-5555, which carries both passengers and vehicles between Seattle's Pier 48 and Victoria; and **Washington State Ferries,** tel. (206) 464-6400 or (250) 381-1551, for passenger and vehicle service between Anacortes and Sidney, 30 km north of Victoria. If you're traveling up the east coast of Washington State to Vancouver and want to bypass the built up corridor between Tacoma and the interna-

INSIDE PASSAGE CRUISES

Wander down to Canada Place at any time during summer, and chances are you'll see a cruise ship taking on or dropping off passengers and being restocked for its next trip north along the Inside Passage. Alaska is the world's third most popular cruising destination (behind the Caribbean and the Mediterranean), and Vancouver is the main southern start and finish point for these trips, handling over 300 sailings and 700,000 passengers during the short May-Sept. summer season. Canada Place was designed especially for cruise ships, but as these boats increase in size the holding capacity of Canada Place has diminished, and some now dock at Ballantyne Cruise Terminal, a renovated cargo pier east of Canada Place.

A cruise along the Inside Passage may be less expensive than you imagined, and although this form of travel isn't for everyone, it provides the unique opportunity to travel through one of the world's most spectacular landscapes surrounded in luxury. The best place to start planning a cruise is at your local travel agent, or call the cruise lines direct.

Companies include: **Holland America-Line Westours,** tel. (800) 426-0327, which has been cruising the Inside Passage since the 1940s and offers a wide range of itineraries that link up with other arms of the company operating throughout Alaska; **Princess Cruises,** tel. (800) 7746-2377, offering luxury reminiscent of days gone by; and **Carnival,** tel. (800) 327-9501, attracting a younger party crowd. Another good source of pre-trip planning is *Porthole,* tel. (800) 776-7678, website www.porthole.com, a magazine dedicated to the cruise industry.

tional border, consider heading out to Port Angeles on the Olympic Peninsula, from where the **MV *Coho,*** tel. (206) 457-4491 or (250) 386-2202, makes a twice daily crossing to Victoria.

Alaska Marine Highway
The Alaska Marine Highway operates an extensive network of ferries through Alaska's Inside Passage and along the British Columbia coast. Although these ferries don't stop at Vancouver, their main southern terminus is just 70 km away at Bellingham, in Washington State. Due to international border regulations, the only Canadian port of entry used by the ferry system is Prince Rupert in northern British Columbia. For Alaska Marine Highway schedules and reservations, call (907) 465-3940 or (800) 642-0066, website www.akferry.com. Make all reservations as far in advance as possible.

From the southeast Alaskan town of Ketchikan, an alternative to the nonstop two-day trip to Bellingham is to catch an Alaska Marine Highway ferry to Prince Rupert then a BC Ferries vessel to Port Hardy, at the northern tip of Vancouver Island, from where it's a scenic drive down to Nanaimo or Victoria for the short hop across the Strait of Georgia to Vancouver. This is a great way to include Vancouver Island and Vancouver in your northern itinerary without backtracking and at a very similar cost.

B.C. Ferries

Chances are, if you travel onward from Vancouver, at some stage of your Canadian adventure you'll use the services of BC Ferries, tel. (250) 386-3431 or (888) 223-3779 (toll-free in B.C.), website www.bcferries.bc.ca, which has a fleet of 40 vessels serving 46 ports, including **Horseshoe Bay,** on the North Shore, and **Tsawwassen,** south of the airport.

From Tsawwassen, ferries run regularly across the Strait of Georgia to the Vancouver Island centers of Swartz Bay (32 km north of Victoria) and Nanaimo. To get to the terminal from downtown by car, follow Hwy. 17 south—in summer this road gets crazy with traffic. On weekends and holidays, the one-way fare on either route is adult $9, vehicle $32, motorcycle $16, bicycle $2.50, canoe and kayak $4; rates for motor vehicles are slightly lower on weekdays. In high season (June-Sept.), the ferries run about once an hour 7 a.m.-10 p.m. The rest of the year they run a little less frequently. The crossing takes around 90 minutes. Expect a wait in summer, particularly if you have an oversized vehicle (each ferry can accommodate far fewer large vehicles than standard-size cars and trucks). Limited reservations are accepted.

The other ferry route from Vancouver is between Horseshoe Bay and Nanaimo, on Vancouver Island. Horseshoe Bay is on the north side of Burrard Inlet, a 20-minute drive northwest of downtown. You don't save any money on this route—the fares are the same as above—and the wait is often longer. This is also the departure point for ferries to the Sunshine Coast.

GETTING AROUND

TRANSLINK

Translink, tel. (604) 521-0400, website www. translink. bc.ca, operates an extensive network of **bus, SkyTrain,** and **SeaBus** routes that can get you just about anywhere you want to go within Vancouver. The free brochure *Discover Vancouver on Transit* is available from all city information centers and is an invaluable source of information. The brochure includes details of many attractions and how to reach them by public transportation.

On weekdays between 5:30 a.m. and 6:30 p.m. the city is divided into three zones, and fares vary $1.50-3 for each sector (Zone 1 encompasses all over downtown and Central Vancouver; Zone 2 covers all the North Shore, Burnaby, New Westminster, and Richmond; and Zone 3 extends to the limits of the Translink system). At other times (including all weekend), travel anywhere in the city costs $1.50 one-way. A **DayPass** costs $6 and allows unlimited travel for one day anywhere on the Translink system. Pay the driver (exact change only) for bus travel or purchase tickets from machines at any SkyTrain station or SeaBus terminal. Buses run to all corners of the city between 5 a.m. and 2 a.m. every day of the year. Transfers are valid for 90 minutes of travel in one direction. Throughout summer, a free Translink bus runs around Stanley Park.

SkyTrain is a computer-operated (no drivers) light-rail transit system that runs along 28 km of elevated track from downtown Vancouver through New Westminster and over the Fraser River to Surrey. It stops at 20 stations along its 37-minute route. The four city-center stations are underground but are clearly marked at each street entrance.

The SeaBus passenger ferry scoots across Burrard Inlet every 15-30 minutes, linking downtown Vancouver to North Vancouver in just 12 minutes. The downtown terminus is Waterfront Station, beside Canada Place and a five-minute walk from the Vancouver Visitor Info Centre. The terminal in North Vancouver is at Lonsdale Quay, from where you can catch Translink buses to most North Shore sights.

West Coast Express

Primarily a commuter service for residents living along the Fraser Valley, this relatively new rail service terminates at Waterfront Station, with service extending as far east as Mission ($15 roundtrip). Other stops are made at Port Moody, Coquitlam, Port Coquitlam, and Pitt Meadows. For further information call (604) 683-7245.

Disabled Passengers

Translink's **HandyDART** buses provide door-to-door wheelchair-accessible service for about the same price you'd pay on regular buses. You'll need to book in advance at (604) 430-2692. Many other city buses are equipped with wheelchair lifts, and all SkyTrain stations as well as the SeaBus and West Coast Express are fully wheelchair accessible. The best source of further information is the *Rider's Guide to Accessible Transit,* available by calling (604) 540-3400.

CAR

An excellent public transit system makes up for the fact that Vancouver isn't the world's most driver-friendly city, especially downtown, where congestion is a major problem, particularly during rush hour. West Georgia St. is a particular trouble spot, with traffic from all directions funneling onto Lions Gate Bridge to cross to the North Shore. Many downtown streets are one-way and lack left-turn lanes, adding to the congestion. On a larger scale, Vancouver lacks any real express-ways, meaning a tortuous trip through downtown to get anywhere on the North Shore.

Downtown Parking

Downtown metered parking costs $1 per hour but is often difficult to find during business hours. Most shopping centers have underground parking, and a few multistory parking lots are scattered throughout the city core (including between Water and Cordova Streets, Gastown; access from either side). These cost from $2.50 per hour and from $12 per day, with discounts for full-day parking for early arrivals. Throughout the residential areas of downtown, parking in many streets is designated for permit-holding residents only—look for the signs or expect to be towed.

Car Rental

All major car rental companies are represented in Vancouver, and while in many cases the vehicles are stored away from downtown, delivery to your accommodation is complimentary. Most companies also have desks at the airport. In any case, try to book in advance, especially in summer, to get your vehicle of choice. Expect to pay from $55 a day for a small economy car.

Major rental companies include: **Avis,** tel. (800) 879-2847, website www.avis.com; **Budget,** tel. (800) 268-8900, website www.budget.com; **Discount,** tel. (800) 263-2355, website www.discountcar.com; **Dollar,** tel. (800) 800-4000, website www.dollarcar.com; **Enterprise,** tel. (800) 325-8007; **Hertz,** tel. (800) 263-0600, website hertz.com; **National Tilden,** tel. (800) 227-7368, website www.nationalcar.com; and **Thrifty,** tel. (800) 367-2277, website www.thrifty.com. Cheaper used cars are available from only $39 a day plus 15 cents a kilometer from Rent-a-wreck, tel. (604) 688-0001 or (800) 327-0116. **Lo Cost,** tel. (604) 689-9664, website www.locost.com, also offers good deals, especially for longer rentals.

Vancouver is home to many companies specializing in campervan rentals, including **Cruise Canada,** tel. (604) 946-5775 or (800) 327-7799; **C.C. Canada Camper RV Rentals,** tel. (604) 327-3003; and **Go West,** tel. (604) 987-5288 or (800) 661-8813. In summer, expect to pay from $130 per day for your own home-on-wheels

Driving in Canada

United States and International Driver's Licenses are valid in Canada. All highway signs give distances in kilometers and speeds in kilometers per hour. Unless otherwise posted, the maximum speed limit on the highways is 100 kph (62 mph).

Use of safety belts is mandatory, and motorcyclists must wear helmets. Infants and toddlers weighing up to nine kilograms (20 pounds) must be strapped into an appropriate children's car seat. Use of a child car seat for larger children weighing 9-18 kilograms (20-40 pounds) is required of British Columbia residents and recommended to nonresidents. Before venturing north of the 49th parallel, U.S. residents should ask their vehicle insurance company for a Canadian Non-resident Inter-provincial Motor Vehicle Liability Insurance Card. You may also be asked to prove vehicle ownership, so carry your vehicle registration form. If you're involved in an accident with a B.C. vehicle, contact the nearest Insurance Corporation of British Columbia (ICBC) office, tel. (800) 663-3051.

If you're a member in good standing of an automobile association, take your membership card—the Canadian AA provides members of related associations full services, including free maps, itineraries, excellent tour books, road- and weather-condition information, accommodations reservations, travel agency services, and emergency road services. For more information write British Columbia Automobile Association, 999 W. Broadway Ave., Vancouver, BC V5Z 1K5, tel. (604) 268-5600.

Note: Drinking and driving (with a blood-alcohol level of .08% or higher) in B.C. can get you imprisoned for up to five years on a first offense and will cost you your license for at least 12 months.

TAXI, BOAT, AND BIKE

Taxi
Cabs are easiest to catch outside major hotels or transportation hubs. Fares in Vancouver are a uniform $2.10 flag charge plus $1.35 per kilometer. Trips within downtown usually run under $10. The trip between the airport and downtown is $35-40. A 15% tip to the driver is expected. Major companies include: **Black Top,** tel. (604) 731-1111; **Van-**couver **Taxi,** tel. (604) 871-1111; and **Yellow Cab,** tel. (604) 681-1111 or (800) 898-8294.

A number of wheelchair-accommodating taxicabs are available from Vancouver Taxi. The fares are the same as regular taxis.

Boat
Apart from the SeaBus (see Translink, above), the only other scheduled ferry services within the city are on False Creek. Two private companies, **False Creek Ferries,** tel. (604) 684-7781, and **Aquabus,** tel. (604) 689-5858, operate on this narrow waterway. From the main hub of Granville Island, ferries run every 15 minutes to the foot of Hornby St., and under the Burrard Street Bridge to the Aquatic Center (at the south end of Thurlow St.) and Vanier Park (Vancouver Museum). Every 30-60 minutes both companies also run down the head of False Creek to Stamps Landing, the Plaza of Nations, and Science World. Fares range $2-4.50 each way, with discounts for seniors and kids; schedules are posted at all docking points.

Bicycle
Downtown Vancouver is not particularly bicycle friendly, but nearby areas such as Stanley Park and the coastline west of Kitsilano are perfect places for pedal power. The main concentration of rental shops surrounds the corner of Robson and Denman Streets, two blocks from Stanley Park. Expect to pay from $5 per hour or $15 per day for the most basic bike and $12 per hour or

Traveling around False Creek is made easy by small ferries that link all points.

$36 per day for a good mountain bike. Most of the shops also rent in-line skates and tandem bikes. **Alley Cat Rentals,** 1779 Robson St., tel. (604) 684-5117, is the least expensive place to rent, but you can also try: **Bayshore Bicycles,** at 745 Denman St., tel. (604) 688-2453, and at 1601 W. Georgia St., tel. (604) 689-5071; **Spokes Bicycle Rental,** 1798 W. Georgia St., tel. (604) 688-5141; or **Stanley Park Cycle,** 1741 Robson St., tel. (604) 608-1908.

SERVICES

VISAS AND OFFICIALDOM

Entry for U.S. Citizens
United States citizens and permanent residents need only present some form of identification that proves citizenship and/or residency, such as a birth certificate, voter-registration card, driver's license with photo, or alien card (essential for nonresident aliens to reenter the U.S.). It never hurts to carry your passport as well.

Other Foreign Visitors
All other foreign visitors must have a valid passport and may need a visa or visitor permit depending on their country of residence and the vagaries of international politics. At present, visas are not required for citizens of the U.S., British Commonwealth, or Western Europe. The standard entry permit is for six months, and you may be asked to show onward tickets or proof of sufficient funds to last you through your intended stay. Extensions ($60 per person) are available from the Department of Citizenship and Immigration offices in Vancouver and Victoria.

Employment and Study
Anyone wishing to work or study in Canada must obtain authorization *before* entering the country. Authorization to work will only be granted if no qualified Canadians are available for the work in question. Applications for work and study are available from all Canadian embassies and must be submitted with a nonrefundable processing fee. The Canadian government has a reciprocal agreement with Australia for a limited number of **holiday work visas** to be issued each year. Australian citizens under the age of 26 are eligible; contact your nearest Canadian embassy or consulate. For general information on immigrating to Canada call **Immigration Canada,** tel. (604) 666-2171.

Entry by Private Aircraft or Boat
If you're going to be entering Canada by private plane or boat, contact Customs in advance for a list of official ports of entry and their hours of operation. Write Revenue Canada, Customs Border Services, Regional Information Unit, 333 Dunsmuir St., Vancouver, BC V6B 5R4, or call (604) 666-0545.

An Air Facilities Map is available from the **British Columbia Aviation Council,** 303/5360 Airport Rd. South, Richmond, BC V7B 1B4, tel. (604) 278-9330, e-mail bcac@dowco.com.

Customs
You can take the following into Canada duty-free: reasonable quantities of clothes and personal effects, 50 cigars and 200 cigarettes, 200 grams of tobacco, 1.14 liters of spirits or wine, food for personal use, and gas (normal tank capacity). Pets from the U.S. can generally be brought into Canada, with certain caveats. Dogs and cats must be over three months old and have a rabies certificate showing date of vaccination. Birds can be brought in only if they have not been mixing with other birds, and parrots need an export permit because they're on the endangered species list.

Handguns, automatic and semiautomatic weapons, and sawn-off rifles and shotguns are not allowed into Canada. Visitors with firearms must declare them at the border; restricted weapons will be held by Customs and can be picked up on exit from the country. Those not declared will be seized and charges may be laid. It is illegal to possess any firearm in a national park unless it is dismantled or carried in an enclosed case. Up to 5,000 rounds of ammunition may be imported but should be declared on entry.

On reentering the U.S., if you've been in Canada more than 48 hours you can bring back up to US$400 worth of household and personal items, excluding alcohol and tobacco, duty-free. If you've been in Canada less than 48 hours, you may bring in only up to $200 worth of such items duty-free.

For further information on all Customs regulations write Revenue Canada, Customs and Excise, Public Inquires Unit, 333 Dunsmuir St., Vancouver, BC V6B 5R4, tel. (604) 666-0545.

MONEY

All prices quoted in this handbook are in Canadian dollars and cents unless otherwise noted.

Canadian currency is based on dollars and cents, with 100 cents equal to one dollar. Coins come in denominations of one, five, 10, and 25 cents, and one and two dollars. The 11-sided, gold-colored, one-dollar coin is known as a

---

CURRENCY EXCHANGE

The Canadian dollar lost value against the greenback through the second half of the 1990s but held steady through 1999. It currently trades at roughly US$1 per CAD$1.45. On the Internet, check current exchange rates at www.rubicon.com/passport/currency/currency.html.

Current exchange rates (into CAD$) for other major currencies are:

AUS$1 = 94 cents
DM1 = 80 cents
EURO = $1.70
HK$10 = $2.01
NZ$1 = 84 cents
UK£ = $2.50
¥100 = $1.28

Currency other than U.S. dollars can be exchanged at most banks, airport money-changing facilities, and at the following foreign exchange brokers: **Custom House Currency Exchange** is in The Landing at 375 Water St., tel. (604) 482-6000. Also downtown is **Currencies International,** 1016 W. Georgia St., tel. (604) 608-0381. **Thomas Cook Foreign Exchange** operates a small money-changing facility in the lobby of the Pan Pacific Vancouver Hotel, Canada Place, tel. (604) 641-1229, as well as in the Pacific Centre and in Burnaby's Metrotown.

"loonie" for the bird featured on it. The unique two-dollar coin is silver with a gold-colored insert. The most common notes are $5, $10, $20, and $50. A $100 bill does exist but is uncommon.

The safest way to carry money is in the form of traveler's checks from a reputable and well-known U.S. company such as American Express, Visa, or Bank of America; those are also the easiest checks to cash. Cash only the amount you need when you need it. Banks offer the best exchange rates, but other foreign-currency exchange outlets are available. It's also a good idea to start off with a couple of traveler's checks in Canadian dollars so you're never caught without *some* money if you don't make it to a bank on time.

Visa and MasterCard credit cards are also readily accepted in Vancouver. By using credit cards you eliminate the necessity of thinking about the exchange rate—the transaction and rate of exchange on the day of the transaction will automatically be reflected in the bill from your credit-card company.

Costs
The cost of living in Vancouver is among the highest of any North American city. For visitors traveling with U.S. dollars the cost of visiting Vancouver has decreased in recent years as the Canadian dollar has lost value against the almighty greenback. By planning ahead, traveling outside of the busy summer period, and being prepared to stay in a budget-priced accommodation it is possible to visit Vancouver quite comfortably on less than $100 a day.

Tipping charges are not usually added to your bill. You are expected to add a tip of 15% to the total amount for waiters and waitresses, barbers and hairdressers, taxi drivers, and other such service providers. Bellhops, doormen, and porters generally receive $1 per item of baggage.

Taxes
Canada imposes a seven percent **goods and services tax (GST)** on most consumer purchases. The provincial government imposes its own seven percent tax (PST) onto everything except groceries and books. So when you are looking at the price of anything, remember that the final cost you pay will include an additional 14% in taxes.

Nonresident visitors can get a rebate for the GST they pay on short-term accommodations and on most consumer goods bought in the country and taken home. Items not included in the GST rebate program include: gifts left in Canada, meals and restaurant charges, campground fees, services such as dry cleaning and shoe repair, alcoholic beverages, tobacco, automotive fuels, groceries, agricultural and fish products, prescription drugs and medical devices, and used goods that tend to increase in value, such as paintings, jewelry, rare books, and coins.

The rebate is available on services and retail purchases that total at least $100 and were paid for within 60 days prior to your exit from the country. Rebates can be claimed any time within one year from the date of purchase. You'll need to include with your claim all receipts and vouchers that prove the GST was paid. Most visitors apply for the rebate at duty-free shops (also called Visitor Rebate Centres) when exiting the country. The duty-free shops can rebate up to $500 on the spot. For rebates over $500, you'll need to mail your completed GST rebate form directly to Revenue Canada, Customs and Excise, Visitors' Rebate Program, Ottawa, ON K1A 1J5. You can also submit rebate forms for amounts less than $500 directly to Revenue Canada. Rebate checks from Revenue Canada are issued in Canadian funds. For more info, call toll-free from anywhere in Canada (800) 668-4748; from outside Canada phone (902) 432-5608.

HEALTH

Vancouver, and Canada in general, is a healthy place. To visit, you don't need to get any vaccinations or booster shots. And when you arrive you can drink the water from the faucet and eat the food without worry.

AIDS and other venereal and needle-communicated diseases are as much of a concern here as anywhere in the world today. Take exactly the same precautions you would at home—use condoms, and don't share needles.

It's a good idea to get health insurance or some form of coverage before heading to Canada if you're going to be there for a while, but check that your plan covers foreign services. Hospital charges vary from place to place but can start at around $1,000 a day, and some facilities impose a surcharge for nonresidents. Some Canadian companies offer coverage specifically aimed at visitors.

If you're on medication take adequate supplies with you, and get a prescription from your doctor to cover the time you will be away. You may not be able to get a prescription filled at Canadian pharmacies without visiting a Canadian doctor, so don't wait till you've almost run out. If you wear glasses or contact lenses, ask your optometrist for a spare prescription in case you break or lose your lenses, and stock up on your usual cleaning supplies.

Emergency Services

For emergencies call 911. For medical emergencies contact **St. Paul's Hospital,** 1081 Burrard St., tel. (604) 682-2344, which has an emergency ward open 24 hours a day, seven days a week. Other major hospitals are: **Vancouver Hospital,** 899 W. 12th Ave., tel. (604) 875-4111; **Lions Gate Hospital,** 231 E. 15th St., tel. (604) 988-3131; or **B.C. Children's Hospital,** 4480 Oak St., tel. (604) 875-2345. **Seymour Medical Clinic,** 1530 W. 7th Ave., tel. (604) 738-2151, is open 24 hours. For emergency dental help, call the **AARM Dental Clinic,** tel. (604) 681-8530 or 683-5530, or the 24-hour clinic at Burnaby, tel. (604) 524-3674. For the **RCMP** call (604) 264-3111.

Visitors with Disabilities

For information on travel considerations for the physically handicapped, contact the **Canadian Paraplegic Association,** 780 Southwest Marine Dr., Vancouver, BC V6P 5Y7, tel. (604) 324-3611. In general, disabled visitors are well cared for, with most major hotels taking disabilities into consideration. Vancouver's public transit system, Translink, has buses that provide door-to-door wheelchair-accessible service for about the same price you'd pay on regular buses (call 604-430-2692 for bookings), and the SkyTrain and SeaBus are wheelchair accessible. **Vancouver Taxi,** tel. (604) 871-1111, has wheelchair-accommodating cabs.

COMMUNICATIONS AND MEASUREMENTS

Postal Services

Canadian **postage stamps** must be used on all mail posted in Canada. First-class letters and postcards within Canada are 46 cents, to the U.S. 55 cents, to foreign destinations 90 cents. Prices increase along with the weight of the mailing. You can buy stamps at post offices, automatic vending machines, most hotel lobbies, the airport, Pacific Central Station, many retail outlets, and some newsstands. Vancouver's **main post office** is at 349 W. Georgia St., tel. (604) 662-5725. It's open Mon.-Saturday. **Postal Station A,** 757 W. Hastings St., and the branch at **Bentall Centre,** 595 Burrard St., are also open on Saturdays.

Visitors can have their mail sent to them c/o General Delivery, Main Post Office, Vancouver, BC, Canada. The post office will hold the mail for two weeks then return it to the sender.

Telephones

The **area code** for Vancouver and the lower mainland, including the Sunshine Coast, as far north as Whistler, and east to Hope, is **604.** (The rest of British Columbia, including all of Vancouver Island, is 250). This prefix must be dialed for all long-distance calls. The country code for Canada is 1, the same as the United States. Toll-free numbers have the 800, 888, or 877 prefix, and may be good for British Columbia, Canada, North America, or, in the case of major hotel chains and car rental companies, will work worldwide.

To make an international call from Vancouver, dial the prefix 011 before the country code or dial 0 for operator assistance.

Public phones accept five-, 10-, and 25-cent coins; local calls are 35 cents and most long-distance calls cost at least $2.50 for the first minute. The least expensive way to make long distance calls from a public phone is with a **phonecard.** These are available from convenience stores, newsstands, and gas stations.

The **Public Calling Centre,** 470 W. Cordova St., tel. (604) 687-2040, is designed especially for visitors. From its private booths you can call anywhere in North America for 50 cents a minute or anywhere in the world at posted, discounted rates; pay by cash or credit card. The center can also be used for sending and receiving faxes.

Public Internet Access

Digital U is out of downtown at 1595 W. Broadway (corner Fir St.; walk up the hill from Granville Island), tel. (604) 731-1011, but it's the city's best Internet café, with very fast connections, 21-inch monitors, booth stations (for two people), computers for regular work and loaded with games. Rates range $8-11 per hour. It's open Mon.-Fri. 9 a.m.-midnight, Sat.-Sun. 10 a.m.-midnight. The most central of all public Internet access terminals is the **Cyber Booth,** lobby of Canada Place, where a credit card will get you as long as you need on the Net. Other downtown locations with public Internet access include **Internet Coffee,** 1104 Davie St., tel. (604) 682-6668, and **The Byte Place,** 1636 Robson St., tel. (604) 683-2688. Both charge $2.50 for 15 minutes and then 11 cents per minute.

Time and Measurements

Vancouver is in the **Pacific time zone,** the same as Los Angeles, one hour before mountain time and three hours before eastern time.

Canada is officially on the **metric system,** though you still hear everyone talking in pounds and ounces, miles, and miles per hour (see the metric conversion chart in the back of this book).

Business Hours

Shops throughout the city are generally open Mon.-Fri. 9 a.m.-5 p.m. and Saturday 9 a.m.-1 p.m. Major malls stay open all weekend. If you're in a city or large town, you can always find a store open for essentials, as well as restaurants and fast-food outlets. Most **banks** are open Mon.-Fri. 10 a.m.-3:30 p.m.

PHOTOGRAPHY

One-hour film processing is offered by dozens of outlets throughout Vancouver. Two of the most reliable are **London Drugs,** with branches throughout Greater Vancouver (call 604-872-8114 for the location nearest to you) and **Lens and Shutter,** which has an outlet in the lower level of the Pacific Centre. For high-quality color-print film processing and overnight slide developing, take your precious films to **Totemcolor,** 119 E. 1st St., North Vancouver, tel. (604) 986-2271.

Don't be put off by the dowdy exterior of **Leo's Cameras,** on Granville Mall at 1055 Granville St., tel. (604) 685-5331; it holds a massive se-

lection of new and used cameras and photographic equipment.

If you're in Vancouver with a video camera or in fact any electrical appliance from another country, you should be able to find parts, plugs, and adapters at **Foreign Electronics,** 111 W. Broadway, Central Vancouver, tel. (604) 879-1189.

INFORMATION

Many organizations make planning a trip to Vancouver easy. In the first instance, contact the provincial tourist office, **Tourism British Columbia,** P.O. Box 9830, Stn. Provincial Government, Victoria, BC V8W 9W5, tel. (250) 387-1642 or (800) HELLOBC (435-5622), website www.hellobc.com. As well as being a great source of tourist information, the agency produces the invaluable *Accommodations* guide and a road map of British Columbia.

Vancouver falls within the Vancouver, Coast, and Mountains Tourism Region, one of six such regions throughout the province ("Coast" means the Sunshine Coast and "Mountains" means Whistler and vicinity). Contact #250/1508 W. 2nd Ave., Vancouver, BC V6J 1H2, tel. (604) 739-0823 or (800) 667-3306, e-mail info@coastandmountains.bc.ca, website www.coastandmountains.bc.ca.

Once in Vancouver, you'll want to visit one of **Tourism Vancouver**'s 17 information centers (known as Visitor Info Centres) scattered around the city, including right downtown, at the airport, and along all major arteries (see below). This organization also maintains an excellent website, perfect for pre-trip planning. It's at www.tourism-vancouver.org.

INFORMATION CENTERS

Downtown
The city's main information center is **Vancouver Visitor Info Centre,** just up from Canada Place at 200 Burrard St., tel. (604) 683-2000, website www.tourism-vancouver.org. The specially trained staff provides free maps, brochures, and public transportation schedules; books sightseeing tours; and makes accommodations reservations. The center is open May-Sept. daily 8

a.m.-6 p.m., the rest of the year Mon.-Sat. 8:30 a.m.-5:30 p.m.

In summer, information booths also operate in Stanley Park and downtown on the corner of Granville and Georgia Streets.

On Granville Island, **Granville Island Information Centre,** 1398 Cartwright St., tel. (604) 666-5784, is open daily 9 a.m.-6 p.m. in summer, closed Monday the rest of the year.

South
If you approach Vancouver from the south, **Peace Arch Visitor Info Centre** is just north of the border at 15150 Russell Ave., tel. (604) 536-6844. If you miss it, try **Delta Visitor Info Centre,** 6201 60th Ave. (take the Delta exit and follow the signs), tel. (604) 946-4232, or **Richmond Visitor Info Centre,** to the east just past the George Massey Tunnel crossing the Fraser River, tel. (604) 271-8280 or (877) 247-0777. All three centers are open daily in summer, weekdays only the rest of the year. **Vancouver International Airport** has information booths on the arrivals levels of the international and domestic terminals; both are open every day 6:30 a.m.-11:30 p.m.

North
North Vancouver Visitor Info Centre, 131 E. 2nd St., tel. (604) 987-4488, website www.cofcnorthvan.org, is open Mon.-Fri. 9 a.m.-5 p.m. A more handy source of information north of the harbor is the small information center in the historic building beside Lonsdale Quay, which is open in summer daily 9 a.m.-6 p.m.

East
If you're approaching the city from the east, **Coquitlam Visitor Info Centre,** 1180 Pinetree Way, tel. (604) 464-2716, is a convenient stop along the

HEADING FARTHER AFIELD?

When you've finished experiencing the delights of Vancouver, there's a whole province and then the rest of the country to explore. This is the spot where we must recommend the *British Columbia Handbook,* the *Alaska/Yukon Handbook,* the *Canadian Rockies Handbook,* and the *Alberta and the Northwest Territories Handbook* for onward travel.

- **Tourism BC,** tel. (250) 387-1642 or (800) HELLOBC (435-5622), website www.hellobc.com, and the following regional offices can also assist in planning your trip through the rest of the province:

- **Tourism Victoria,** 812 Wharf St., Victoria, BC V8W 1T3, tel. (250) 953-2033 or (800) 663-3883, website www.travel.victoria.bc.ca

- **Tourism Vancouver Island,** 302/45 Bastion Square, Victoria, BC V8W 1J1, tel. (250) 382-3551, website www.islands.bc.ca

- **Thompson/Okanagan Tourism Association,** 1332 Water St., Kelowna, BC V1Y 9P4, tel. (250) 860-5999 or (800) 567-2275, website www.travel.bc.ca/region/ok

- **Tourism Rockies,** P.O. Box 10, Kimberley, BC V1A 2Y5, tel. (250) 427-4838, website www.bc.rockies.com

- **Cariboo Country Tourism Association** (Central British Columbia), P.O. Box 4900, Williams Lake, BC V2G 2V8, tel. (250) 392-2226 or (800) 663-5885, website www.cariboucountry.org

- **Northern British Columbia Tourism Association,** P.O. Box 1030, Smithers, BC V0J 2N0, tel. (250) 847-5227 or (800) 663-8843, website www.travel.bc.ca/region/north

For travel to neighboring provinces and Alaska, contact:

- **Tourism Yukon,** tel. (403) 667-5340 or (800) 789-8566, website www.touryukon.com

- **Alaska Division of Tourism,** tel. (907) 465-2010, website www.commerce.state.ak.us/tourism

- **Alberta Tourism,** tel. (403) 427-4321 or (800) 661-8888, website www.travelalberta.com

- **Northwest Territories Economic Development and Tourism,** tel. (403) 873-7200 or (800) 661-0788, website www.nwttravel.nt.ca

TransCanada Hwy. on the west side of the Fraser River. Off the TransCanada Hwy. is **Surrey Visitor Info Centre,** 14439 104th Ave., tel. (604) 581-7130, website www. surreycoc.com, which is closed weekends outside of the busy summer season. Farther out along the TransCanada Hwy. are: **Langley Visitor Info Centre,** 5761 Glover Rd., tel. (604) 530-6656; **Fort Langley Visitor Info Centre,** 23325 Mavis Ave., tel. (604) 513-8787; **Abbotsford Visitor Info Centre,** 2462 McCallum Rd., tel. (604) 859-9651; and **Chilliwack Visitor Info Centre,** 44150 Luckakuck Way, tel. (604) 858-8121 or (800) 567-9535. If you're traveling into the city on the north side of the Fraser River, along the Lougheed Hwy. from Harrison Hot Springs, stop at **Mission Visitor Info Centre,** 34033 Lougheed Hwy., tel. (604) 826-6914, or, closer to the city, **Maple Ridge Visitor Info Centre,** 22238 Lougheed Hwy., tel. (604) 463-3366.

BOOKS AND BOOKSTORES

Vancouver Public Library

In November 1995, after two years of construction and $100 million, Vancouver Public Library, 350 W. Georgia St., tel. (604) 331-3600, opened its doors to the public. The magnificent new nine-story facility is a far cry from the city's first library, which opened with a grant of £250 back in 1887. Its facade contains a glass-walled promenade rising six stories above a row of stylish indoor shops and cafés. Once inside, you'll soon discover that the city also found enough money to stock the shelves; the library holds over one million books. To help you find that one book you're searching for, use the self-guided tour brochure available at the information desk. The library is open year-round Mon.-Wed. 10 a.m.-9 p.m., Thurs.-Sat. 10 a.m.-6 p.m., and also Sunday 1-5 p.m. from October to April.

Over 20 other affiliated libraries are spread across the city. Call (604) 331-3600 for addresses and opening hours. One branch library of particular interest is the **Carnegie Reading Room,** on the corner of E. Hastings and Main Streets. It is named for its benefactor, U.S. philanthropist Andrew Carnegie, whose $50,000 donation went a long way toward its 1903 completion as Vancouver's first permanent library.

General Bookstores

Per capita, residents of Vancouver buy more books than the residents of any other North American city. And they buy them from a huge number of bookstores scattered throughout the city. **Duthie Books** is a local success story, with nine outlets in the city, including right in the heart of downtown on busy Granville St. Mall at 650 W.

Georgia St., tel. (604) 687-0083. With over 90,000 titles, newspapers from around the world, and sections devoted entirely to both Vancouver and British Columbia authors, Duthie's should have what you're looking for. The hours should suit you as well: Mon.-Thurs. 8 a.m.-10 p.m., Fri.-Sat. 8 a.m.-midnight, Sunday 10 a.m.-10 p.m. Other Duthie's bookstores are at 345 Robson St. (Library Square), tel. (604) 602-0610; 710 Granville St., tel. (604) 689-1802; 919 Robson St., tel. (604) 684-4496; and 4255 Arbutus St., tel. (604) 738-1833. The Canadian bookstore giant **Chapters** has two Vancouver shops, each stocking over 100,000 titles; both have in-

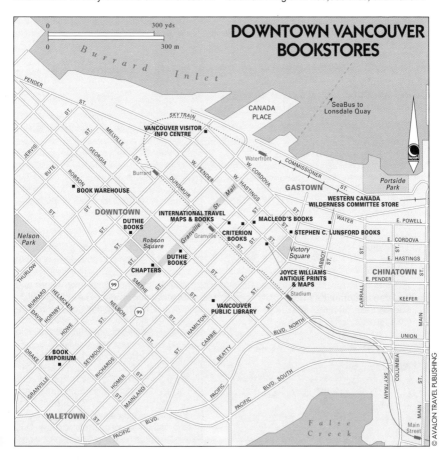

DOWNTOWN VANCOUVER BOOKSTORES

© AVALON TRAVEL PUBLISHING

house coffee shops. Downtown, Chapters is at 788 Robson St., tel. (604) 682-4066, and in Central Vancouver it's at 2505 Granville St. (at Broadway), tel. (604) 731-7822. To save a few bucks on current titles or pick up new books at bargain prices, search out the **Book Warehouse** at either 1150 Robson St., tel. (604) 685-5711, or 632 W. Broadway, Central Vancouver, tel. (604) 872-5711. On Granville Island, **Blackberry Books,** 1663 Duranleau St., tel. (604) 685-6188, stocks touristy-type coffee-table books and a wide range of western Canadiana.

UBC Bookstore

Until Chapters began opening its megastores across the city, the bookstore on the campus of the UBC, 6200 University Blvd. (at Westbrook Mall), tel. (604) 822-2665, held Vancouver's largest stock of books. Still, with almost 100,000 titles, it is an impressive place to browse. Books on just about every subject imaginable are stocked, and the staff can lay their hands on requested titles very quickly. Closed Sunday.

Travel Bookstores

International Travel Maps and Books, downtown at 552 Seymour St., tel. (604) 687-3320, website www.itmb.com, is the city's most central specialty travel bookstore. It's open seven days a week. Another, smaller branch of International Travel Maps and Books is at 345 W. Broadway, tel. (604) 879-3621. With over 10,000 titles, Canada's largest travel bookstore is **Wanderlust,** 1929 W. 4th Ave., Kitsilano, tel. (604) 739-2182. Also in Kits is the **Travel Bug,** 2667 W. Broadway, Kitsilano, tel. (604) 737-1122, website www.swifty.com/tbug. For environmentally aware literature head for the **Western Canada Wilderness Committee Store,** 227 Abbott St., Gastown, tel. (604) 687-2567.

Secondhand and Antiquarian Bookstores

Vancouver has some fantastic secondhand bookstores, including a few specializing entirely in nonfiction. The largest concentration lies along

W. Pender St. between Richards and Hamilton Streets. **Macleod's Books,** 455 W. Pender St., tel. (604) 681-7654, stocks a wide range of antiquarian titles, including many of the earliest works on western Canada. Across the road, **Criterion Books,** 434 W. Pender St., tel. (604) 685-2224, stocks newer titles, but the western Canada section is just as good. One block east is **Joyce Williams Antique Prints and Maps,** 346 W. Pender St., tel. (604) 688-7434. On the corner of W. Hastings and Hamilton Streets is **Stephen C. Lunsford Books,** tel. (604) 681-6830, with plenty of old Canadian nonfiction titles. The **Book Emporium,** 1247 Granville St., tel. (604) 682-3019, offers an excellent section of fiction (downstairs) and nonfiction (upstairs), all of which is organized by author or subject.

NEWSPAPERS AND PERIODICALS

Vancouver's two newspapers are the *Province,* website www.vancouverprovince.com, published daily except Saturday, and the *Vancouver Sun,* website www.vancouversun.com, published daily except Sunday. Both are published by the same company, Pacific Press, with the *Province* more tabloid-driven than the *Sun.* Both are available at newsstands and vending machines throughout the city for under a buck. Canada's two national dailies, the *Globe and Mail* and the *National Post,* are both based in Toronto but are readily available in Vancouver.

Many free publications are distributed throughout the city. The weekly *Georgia Strait* features articles on local issues, as well as a full entertainment rundown for the city. The *Westender,* also a weekly, spotlights downtown issues and has good restaurant reviews. The fortnightly *Terminal City* and, for the hip set, *Loop* both have offbeat articles and music and entertainment diaries. *Coast* is a lifestyle magazine focusing on outdoor recreation in the region, while the quarterly *Common Ground* is dedicated to health and personal development.

VICTORIA BASICS
GETTING THERE

AIR

Victoria International Airport
Vancouver Island's main airport is on the Saanich Peninsula 20 km north of Victoria's city center. The terminal building houses a cocktail lounge, café, and various rental car agencies. P.B.M. Transport, tel. (250) 475-2010, operates the **Airporter** bus between the airport and major downtown hotels every 30 minutes; $15 per person each way. A taxi costs approximately $45 to downtown.

For general information pertaining to both Vancouver and Victoria, such as entry requirements, currency, and communications, see the Vancouver Basics chapter, above.

Airlines
Air Canada, tel. (250) 360-9074 or (888) 247-2262, website www.aircanada.com; **Canadian Airlines,** tel. (250) 382-6111 or (800) 665-1177, website www.cdnair.com; and various regional connectors fly to Victoria from most western Canada cities and Seattle. **Horizon Air,** tel. (800) 547-9308, flies daily into Victoria International Airport from Seattle.

Also from Seattle, **Kenmore Air,** tel. (206) 486-1257 or (800) 543-9595, offers scheduled floatplane flights between the north end of Lake Washington and Victoria's Inner Harbour.

Smaller airlines, including those with floatplanes and helicopter services, provide a direct link between Victoria and Vancouver, departing from downtown Vancouver and landing on or beside the Inner Harbour. These include **Harbour Air,** tel. (250) 384-2215 or (800) 665-0212, website www.harbour-air.com (the least expensive option; $90 one-way); **West Coast Air,** tel. (250)

388-4521 or (800) 347-2222, website www.west-coastair.com; and **Helijet Airways**, tel. (250) 382-6222 or (800) 665-4354, website www.helijet.com.

BUS

From Vancouver

The main Victoria **bus depot** is behind the Empress Hotel at 710 Douglas Street. **Pacific Coach Lines**, tel. (604) 662-8074 or (250) 385-4411, website www.pacificcoach.com, operates bus service between Vancouver's Pacific Central Station and downtown Victoria, via the Tsawwassen–Swartz Bay ferry. In summer the coaches run hourly 6 a.m.-9 p.m.; $25 one-way, $51 roundtrip, which includes the ferry fare. The trip takes three and a half hours. This same company also runs three daily buses from Vancouver International Airport directly to Victoria; $30.50 one-way, $59 roundtrip. If you take the ferry over independently, you can catch the **Victoria Regional Transit System** bus no. 70, tel. (250) 382-6161, from the Swartz Bay ferry terminal to downtown for $2.50.

FERRY

From Tsawwassen (Vancouver)

Ferries run regularly across the Strait of Georgia from Tsawwassen, 30 km south of Vancouver, to the **Swartz Bay Ferry Terminal,** 32 km north of Victoria. Through summer, ferries run hourly 7 a.m.-10 p.m., the rest of the year slightly less frequently. The crossing takes 90 minutes. You can expect a wait in summer; limited vehicle reservations are accepted. Peak fares are adult $9, child 5-11 $4.50, vehicle $32, motorcycle $16, bicycle $2.50, canoe or kayak $4. For information, call **BC Ferries** at (250) 386-3431 or (888) 223-3779 (within B.C.), website www.bc-ferries.bc.ca.

From Seattle

Clipper Navigation offers a fleet of foot-passengers-only ferries connecting Seattle's Pier 69 with Victoria's Inner Harbour. Its turbojet catamaran, the *Victoria Clipper IV,* is North America's fastest passenger ferry, traveling at speeds of up to 45 knots (over 80 kph). This speedy vessel makes the crossing in two hours and costs adult US$66 one-way, US$109 roundtrip. The company's other vessels make the trip in two and a half hours and cost adults US$58 one-way, US$94 roundtrip. The service runs year-round. In summer, up to five sailings a day are offered, with some stopping off at Friday Harbor in the San Juan Islands (US$58 one-way, through to Victoria). All vessels feature spacious seating arrangements, writing tables, complimentary tea and coffee, and light snacks. Discounts apply outside of the busy summer months and to tickets purchased 14 or more days in advance. Seniors also get a break, and children travel for half price.

For those traveling from Seattle with a vehicle, Clipper Navigation operates the *Princess Marguerite III* between Seattle's Pier 48 and Victoria's Ogden Point Terminal. It runs mid-May to mid-October, departing Seattle daily at 1 p.m. and Victoria at 7:30 a.m. and taking four and a half hours each way. Facilities include a buffet restaurant (US$8 for a buffet breakfast or lunch), café, bar, solarium, and a gift shop with duty-free shopping. The one-way fare is US$49 for a vehicle and US$29 per passenger; a day room can be rented from US$29.

Clipper Navigation also offers a plethora of reasonably priced accommodations and tour packages in Victoria (from US$134 including transportation from Seattle; high season). For schedules and tour information, call (800) 888-2535, or drop by one of its offices: Pier 69, Seattle, tel. (206) 448-5000, or at the Inner Harbour terminal on Belleville St., tel. (250) 382-8100. The company's website is www.victoriaclipper.com.

From Anacortes

Washington State Ferries, tel. (206) 464-6400 or (250) 381-1551, runs a regular ferry schedule between Anacortes and the San Juan Islands, with the 8 a.m. sailing continuing to Sidney, on the Saanich Peninsula 32 km north of Victoria. The one-way fare is adult US$10, car and driver US$41. Reservations must be made at least 24 hours in advance.

From Port Angeles

The **MV** *Coho* crosses Juan de Fuca Strait in just over 90 minutes, arriving in Victoria's Inner Harbour. It makes four crossings daily in each direction from mid-May to mid-October, two crossings daily the rest of the year. Advance reservations are not accepted—phone a day or so before your planned departure for estimated waiting times. The one-way fare is adult US$6.75, child US$3.45, vehicle US$28.50. Checks and credit cards are not accepted; neither are reservations. For details call Black Ball Transport Inc. at (250) 386-2202 in Victoria, or (206) 457-4491 in Port Angeles, website www.northolympic.com/coho.

GETTING AROUND

BUS AND TAXI

Victoria Regional Transit System

Most of the inner-city attractions can be reached on foot. However, the local bus network is excellent, and it's easy to jump on and off and get everywhere you want to go. Pick up an *Explore Victoria* brochure at the information center for details of all the major sights, parks, beaches, and shopping areas, and the buses needed to reach them. Bus fare for travel within Zone 1, which covers most of the city, is adult $1.75, senior or child $1.10. Zone 2 covers outlying areas such as the Swartz Bay ferry terminal; adult $2.50, senior or child $1.75. Transfers are good for travel in one direction within 90 minutes of purchase. A DayPass, valid for one day's unlimited bus travel, costs adult $5.50, senior or child $4. For general bus information call the automated Busline at (250) 382-6161 or surf the Internet to www.transitbc.com.

Taxi

Taxis operate on a meter system, charging $2.75 at the initial flag drop plus around $2 per kilometer. Call **Blue Bird Cabs** at (250) 382-4235 or (800) 665-7055; **Empress Taxi** at (250) 381-2222; or **Victoria Taxi** at (250) 383-7111.

CAR RENTAL

It's best to call around and compare prices for rental cars—some lesser-known agencies advertise cheaper daily rates than others, but their cars are often used, old, large, and less economical, and usually must be returned to Victoria. Renting by the week is better, and you often get a number of kilometers free. If you don't want to return the car to Victoria, you'll probably have to pay a drop charge; usually the farther up the island you go, the higher the fee. For a used car in the low season, rates start around $30 a day, plus 15 cents per kilometer, plus gas. As with accommodations and many attractions, prices are higher in peak tourist periods. Rental car agencies in Victoria include: **Ada Rent a Used Car,** tel. (250) 474-3455; **Avis,** tel. (250) 386-8468 or (800) 879-2847; **Budget,** tel. (250) 953-5300 or (800) 268-8900; **Enterprise,** tel. (250) 475-6900 or (800) 325-8007; **Hertz,** tel. (250) 656-2312 or (800) 263-0600; **Island Auto Rentals,** tel. (250) 384-4881; **National Tilden,** tel. (250) 386-1213 or (800) 227-7368; **Rent-a-wreck,** tel. (250) 384-5343; and **Thrifty,** tel. (250) 383-3659 or (800) 367-2277.

BIKES AND SUCH

Victoria doesn't have the great network of bicycle paths that Vancouver boasts, but bike-rental shops are nevertheless plentiful. Try: **Sports Rent,** 611 Discovery St., tel. (250) 385-7368; **James Bay Bicycle Works,** 1A-507 Simcoe St., tel. (250) 380-1664; or **Oak Bay Bicycle,** 1968 Oak Bay Ave., tel. (250) 598-4111. Expect to pay from around $8 an hour, $25 per day. As well as renting bikes, **Harbour Rentals,** directly opposite the information center at 811 Wharf St., tel. (250) 995-1661, rents strollers, scooters, and a variety of watercraft.

SERVICES AND INFORMATION

Emergency Services

In a medical emergency call 911 or contact **Royal Jubilee Hospital,** 1900 Fort St., tel. (250) 370-8000, or **Victoria General Hospital,** 1 Hospital Way, tel. (250) 727-4212. For non-urgent cases, a handy facility is **James Bay Medical Treatment Centre,** 230 Menzies St., tel. (250) 388-9934. The **Cresta Dental Centre** is at 3170 Tillicum Rd. (at Burnside St.), tel. (250) 384-7711. **Shopper's Drug Mart,** at 1222 Douglas St., tel. (250) 381-4321, is open daily 7 a.m.-7 p.m.

Other Services

The main **post office** is on the corner of Yates and Douglas Streets.

Public Internet access costs $3 for 15 minutes or $10 per hour at the **Victoria Cyber Café,** 1414 Douglas St., tel. (250) 995-0175.

To change your money to the colorful Canadian variety, head to any of the major banks or to **Currencies International,** 724 Douglas St., tel. (250) 384-6631, or **Custom House Currency Exchange,** 815 Wharf St., tel. (250) 389-6007.

Downtown Photo Centre, 1314 Douglas St., tel. (250) 383-8111, offers full photographic services, including 24-hour slide developing.

Maytag Homestyle Laundry is at 1309 Cook St., tel. (250) 386-1799.

Tourist Information

Tourism Victoria runs the bright, modern **Victoria Visitor Info Centre,** 812 Wharf St. on the Inner Harbour, tel. (250) 953-2033 or (800) 663-3883 (accommodations reservations), website www.tourismvictoria.com. The friendly staff can answer most of your questions. They also book accommodations, tours and charters, restaurants, entertainment, and transportation, all at no extra cost; sell local bus passes and map books with detailed area-by-area maps; and stock an enormous selection of tourist brochures. Also collect the free *Accommodations* publication and the free local news and entertainment papers—the best way to find out what's happening in Victoria while you're in town. The center is open year-round daily 9 a.m.-5 p.m. Coming off the ferry from Vancouver, stop in at **Sidney Visitor Info Centre,** three km south of the terminal, tel. (250) 656-0525; open daily 9 a.m.-5 p.m. For **weather forecasts** call (250) 656-3978, or for **marine weather** forecasts call (250) 656-7515.

Books and Bookstores

Greater Victoria Public Library is at 735 Broughton St., at the corner of Courtney St., tel. (250) 382-7241. It's open Mon.-Fri. 9 a.m.-6 p.m., Saturday 9 a.m.-1 p.m. **Crown Publications,** 521 Fort St., tel. (250) 386-4636, is a specialty bookstore with a great selection of western Canadiana and maps. Right downtown, **Munro's Bookstore,** 1108 Government St., tel. (250) 382-2464 or (888) 243-2464, is in a magnificent neoclassical building that originally opened as the Royal Bank in 1909. Munro's may be the grandest bookstore in town, but it's not the largest. That distinction goes to **Chapters,** at 1212 Douglas St., tel. (250) 380-9009, open Mon.-Sat. 8 a.m.-11 p.m., Sunday 9 a.m.-11 p.m. For new books at discounted prices, head to **Book Ends,** 907 Yates St., tel. (250) 380-0740. **Snowdon's Bookstore,** 619 Johnson St., tel. (250) 383-8131, holds a good selection of secondhand titles.

BOOKLIST

HISTORY

Coull, Cheryl. *A Traveller's Guide to Aboriginal B.C.* Vancouver: Whitecap Books, 1996. Although this book covers native sites throughout the province, the Lower Mainland chapter is very comprehensive.

Duff, Wilson. *The Indian History of British Columbia: The Impact of the White Man.* Victoria: University of British Columbia Press, 1997. In this book Duff deals with the issues faced by natives in the last 150 years, but also gives a good historic overview of their general history.

Jenness, Diamond. *The Indians of Canada.* Toronto: University of Toronto Press, 1977. Originally published in 1932, this is the classic study of natives in Canada, although his conclusion, that they were facing certain extinction by "the end of this century" is obviously outdated.

Johnson, Pauline. *Legends of Vancouver.* This just-published book contains the writings of Pauline Johnson, a well-known writer and poet in the early part of the 1900s. She spent much of her time with native peoples, and this is her version of myths related to her by Joe Capilano, chief of the Squamish.

Kluckner, Michael. *Heritage Walks around Vancouver.* Vancouver: Whitecap Books, 1992. Perfect for history buffs, this guide details historic buildings in eight neighborhoods.

Kluckner, Michael. *Vancouver the Way It Was.* Vancouver: Whitecap Books, 1993. An easy-to-read history of Vancouver since the arrival of the first Europeans.

Lavallee, Omer. *Van Horne's Road.* Montreal: Railfare Enterprises, 1974. William C. Van Horne was instrumental in the construction of Canada's first transcontinental railway. This is the story of his dream, and the boomtowns that sprung up along the route. Lavallee devotes the final chapter to Vancouver and how the arrival of the railway affected the young city and created a Canadian gateway to the Orient.

McDonald, Robert A.J. *Making Vancouver 1863-1913.* Vancouver: University of British Columbia Press, 1996. Describes the formative years of Vancouver and the people who helped shape the city during this early period.

McMillan, Alan D. *Native Peoples and Cultures of Canada.* Vancouver: Douglas & McIntyre, 1995. A comprehensive look at the archaeology, anthropology, and ethnography of the native peoples of Canada. The last chapters delve into the problems facing these people today. The author is a professor at the local Simon Fraser University, so the chapters on the Pacific Northwest are particularly strong.

Nicol, Eric. *Vancouver.* Toronto: Doubleday Canada, 1970. An often-humorous look at Vancouver and its colorful past through the eyes of Eric Nicol, one of Vancouver's favorite columnists of the 1960s. It's been reprinted a few times, and although it has been out of print for many years, Vancouver's second-hand bookstores usually have multiple copies in stock.

Reksten, Terry. *Rattenbury.* Victoria: Sono Nis Press, 1998. The biography of Francis Rattenbury, British Columbia's preeminent architect at the turn of the last century. The history of his Vancouver buildings is given, and the final chapter looks at his infamous murder at the hands of his wife's young lover.

Rossiter, Sean. *The Hotel Georgia.* Vancouver: Douglas & McIntyre, 1998. A complete history of Vancouver's oldest and grandest accommodation in a coffee table-style book.

Suttles, Wayne. *Handbook of North American Indians,* Volume 7, *Northwest Coast.* Washington, D.C.: Smithsonian Institution, 1990. This volume is probably the most comprehensive piece ever written dedicated entirely to the natives of the Pacific Northwest.

Vancouver—A City Album. Vancouver: Douglas & McIntyre, 1991. A pictorial history of Vancouver using historical photographs from archives across Canada.

RECREATION GUIDES

Bodegom, Volker. *Bicycling Vancouver.* Edmonton, Alberta: Lone Pine Publishing, 1992. Trail descriptions, road logs, and maps of cycling routes throughout the city.

Hudson, Rick. *Gold, Gemstones, and Mineral Sites of British Columbia.* Victoria: Orca Books, 1999. This still-evolving series currently has two volumes in print. Volume 1 details sites on Vancouver Island, while Volume 2 covers sites around Vancouver and within a day's drive of the city. The history of each location, along with a map, what the site holds today, and interesting related facts make this a must-read for keen rockhounds.

Lebrecht, Sue, and Judi Lees. *52 Weekend Activities around Vancouver.* Vancouver: Douglas & McIntyre, 1995. There's something for everyone in this popular book, whether it be nude beaches or skiing at Whistler.

Macaree, Mary, and David Macaree. *109 Walks in British Columbia's Lower Mainland.* Vancouver: Douglas & McIntyre, 1997. The fourth edition of this guide details more than 100 easy walks throughout Vancouver, the Fraser River Valley, and as far north as Whistler. Two pages are devoted to each walk, accompanied by detailed text, a hand-drawn map, and a black-and-white photo.

Macaree, Mary, and David Macaree. *103 Hikes in Southwestern British Columbia.* Vancouver: Douglas & McIntyre, 1994. In the same format as above, this guide details longer and

more difficult trails (generally half-day or longer) through the region, but there is crossover on many trails. Also includes hikes in Manning Provincial Park and as far north as Pemberton.

Pratt-Johnson, Betty. *101 Dives from the Mainland of Washington and British Columbia.* Surrey, B.C.: Heritage House Publishing, 1997. This book and its companion volume, *99 Dives from the San Juan Islands in Washington to the Gulf Islands and Vancouver Island in British Columbia,* are the best sources of detailed information on diving in British Columbia.

Steele, Mike. *Vancouver's Famous Stanley Park—The Year-round Playground.* Vancouver: Heritage House Publishing, 1993. A complete guide to Stanley Park, including history, sights, walks, and maps.

ARTS AND CRAFTS

Allen, D. *Totem Poles of the Northwest.* Surrey, BC: Hancock House Publishers Ltd., 1977. Describes the importance of totem poles to native culture and totem pole sites and their history.

Kew, Della, and P.E. Goddard. *Indian Art and Culture of the Northwest Coast.* Surrey, BC: Hancock House Publishers Ltd., 1997.

Twigg, Alan. *Vancouver and its Writers.* Vancouver: Harbour Publishing, 1986. Vancouver has produced many fine writers, while other writers have moved to the city from elsewhere. This book gives short biographies on them all.

OTHER GUIDEBOOKS

Accommodations

Canadian Automobile Association. *Tour Book: Western Canada and Alaska.* Another free booklet available to members.

Pantel, Gerda. *The Canadian Bed and Breakfast Guide.* Toronto: Penguin Books Canada,

1999. Lists all bed and breakfasts prepared to pay a fee, so the reviews aren't very objective. Also lists prices.

Tourism British Columbia. *Accommodations.* Updated annually, this free booklet is available at information centers throughout British Columbia or by calling (250) 387-1642 or (800) HELLOBC (435-5622).

Western Canadian Bed and Breakfast Innkeepers Association. Contact this association for a copy of its annual accommodations guide, tel. (604) 255-9199, website www.wcbbia.com. It contains descriptions and prices of over 100 properties.

Food

Garber, Anne. *Vancouver Cheap Eats.* Burnaby: Serious Publishing, 1998. The author has thoroughly researched over 350 "cheap eats" throughout Vancouver. They are listed alphabetically, but cross referencing is easy with multiple indexes listing them by area, by specialty, and by other features, such as "Great Fish and Chips" and "Open Early." The descriptions concentrate on the food rather than the setting and ambience.

General

Bennett, Guy. *Guy's Guide to the Flipside.* Vancouver: Arsenal Pulp Press, 1992. A humorous look at the "wrong" side of the city, with firsthand descriptions of the worst bars, the strangest hairdressing saloons, and the most expensive funeral homes.

Blore, Shawn. *Vancouver: Secrets of the City.* Vancouver: Arsenal Pulp Press, 1998. Compiled from "secrets" revealed in the *Vancouver* magazine, this book delves into the darkest corners of the city. Many of the secrets will be of little interest to casual visitors, but the book does make for interesting reading.

Hempstead, Andrew, and Jane King. *British Columbia Handbook.* Chico: Moon Publications, 2000. Comprehensive coverage of all of British Columbia in the same format as this book.

Wilson, Kasey. *Vancouver Best Places.* Seattle: Sasquatch Books, 1997. A review of Vancouver's best recreation pursuits, entertainment, shopping, accommodations, and restaurants. The restaurant section is particularly good.

MISCELLANEOUS

Cannings, Richard. *British Columbia: A Natural History.* Vancouver, Douglas & McIntyre, 1996. The natural history of the province divided into 10 chapters, from the earliest origins of the land to problems faced in the new millennium. It includes lots of color photos, diagrams, and maps.

Haig Brown, Roderick. *Return to the River.* Vancouver: Douglas & McIntyre, 1997. Although fictional, this story of the life of one salmon and its struggle through life is based on fact— a classic read for both anglers and naturalists. It was originally published in 1946, but it has recently been reprinted and is available at most city bookstores.

Leighton, Douglas (photographer). *British Columbia.* Canmore: Altitude Publishing, 1998. A coffee table book photographed by one of western Canada's better known commercial cameramen.

Osborne, Graham (photographer). *British Columbia: A Wild and Fragile Beauty.* Douglas & McIntyre, 1993. In my opinion this coffee table book depicts the natural beauty of British Columbia better than any other edition currently in print. Each photograph is accompanied by a short section of moving text.

Wynn, Graeme. *Vancouver and its Region.* Vancouver: Univeristy of British Columbia Press, 1992. An in-depth look at the city, its geography, and the history of its urbanization through aerial photography, maps, graphs, and descriptive passages.

ACCOMMODATIONS INDEX

VANCOUVER

Alhambra Hotel: 18
Anmore Camplands: 77
Anne Manor B&B: 74
Barclay Hotel: 69
Best Western Chelsea Inn: 72
Best Western Coquitlam Inn: 72
Best Western Tsawwassen Inn: 72
Best Western Vancouver Downtown: 64-65
Biltmore Hotel: 71
Blue Horizon Hotel: 69
Bosman's Motor Hotel: 64
Buchan Hotel: 70
Burnaby Cariboo RV Park: 77
Burrard Motor Inn: 64
C&N Backpackers Hostel: 75
Capilano RV Park: 76
Century Plaza Hotel: 65
Coast Plaza Suite Hotel at Stanley Park: 70
Coast Vancouver Airport Hotel: 72
Crowne Plaza Hotel Georgia: 68
Cultus Lake: 77
Days Inn Metro Vancouver: 71
Days Inn Vancouver Downtown: 64
Deep Cove B&B: 74
Delta Pacific Resort & Conference Centre: 71
Delta Town and Country Inn: 72
Delta Vancouver Airport Hotel: 71
Dogwood Campgrounds of B.C.: 77
Dominion Hotel: 64
English Bay Inn: 73
ferry terminal accommodations: 72
Four Seasons Hotel: 68
Glencoe Motel: 38
Global Village Backpackers: 75
Globetrotter's Inn: 75
Golden Ears: 77
Granville Island Hotel: 71
Greenbrier Hotel: 69
Harrison Hot Springs Hotel: 38

Hilton Vancouver Airport: 71
Holiday Inn Chilliwack: 72
Holiday Inn Express: 72
Holiday Inn Express Vancouver Airport: 71
Holiday Inn Express Vancouver North Shore: 70
Holiday Inn Hotel and Suites: 65
Holiday Inn Metrotown: 72
Holiday Inn Vancouver Centre: 71
Horseshoe Bay Motel: 70-71
Hostelling International Vancouver Downtown: 74-75
Hostelling International Vancouver Jericho Beach: 75
Hotel Europe: 18
Hotel Vancouver: 65
Hyatt Regency Vancouver: 65-68
Kingston Hotel: 64
Listel Vancouver: 69
Lonsdale Quay Hotel: 70
Mountainside Manor: 74
Pacific Palisades Hotel: 69
Pan Pacific Hotel Vancouver: 68
Parkcanada RV Inns: 76-77
Parkhill Hotel: 68
Park Royal Hotel: 70
Patricia Hotel: 64
Paul's Guest House: 73
Peace Arch RV Park: 77
Penny Farthing Inn: 73
Pillow 'n Porridge Guest Suites: 73
Porteau Cove Provincial Park: 77
Quality Hotel–The Inn at False Creek: 65
Quality Inn Airport Hotel: 72
Quality Inn Metrotown: 72
Radisson President Hotel and Suites: 71
Rainbow Motor Inn: 72
Ramada Limited Downtown Vancouver: 65
Renaissance Vancouver Hotel: 68
Riviera Hotel: 69
Rosellen Suites: 70
Shady Island Seafood: 29
Sheraton Wall Centre Hotel: 68
Simon Fraser University: 76

Sutton Place Hotel: 68
Sylvia Hotel: 69
Travelodge Vancouver Centre: 64
2400 Motel: 71
University of British Columbia Housing and Conference Centre: 76
Vancouver International Airport accommodations: 71-72
Waterfront Centre Hotel: 65
West End Guest House: 73
Westin Bayshore: 69
Westin Grand: 68-69
YMCA: 75-76
YWCA Hotel: 75

VICTORIA

Admiral Motel: 115
Aerie Resort: 116-117
Ambleside Bed and Breakfast: 118
Anderson House Bed and Breakfast: 117
Bedford Regency: 115
Canterbury Flag Inn: 116
Cedarwood Motel: 117
Cherry Bank Hotel: 114
Coast Victoria Harbourside Hotel: 116
Craigmyle B&B Inn: 118
Crystal Court Hotel: 114
Dashwood Manor: 118
Days Inn on the Harbour: 115
Days Inn Victoria Waterway: 116
Dominion Hotel: 115
Dunsmuir Lodge: 117
Empress Hotel: 99, 116
Fort Victoria RV Park: 119
Fountain Inn: 116
Gatsby Mansion B&B: 117, 118
Goldstream Provincial Park: 120
Harbour Towers Hotel: 116
Haterleigh Bed and Breakfast: 117-118
Heritage House: 118
Holland House Inn: 115
Hotel Douglas: 114-115

Island View Beach RV Park: 120
James Bay Inn: 115
KOA Victoria West: 120
Laurel Point Inn: 115
Magnolia Hotel & Suites: 116
Malahat Ocenaview Motel: 116
McDonald Provincial Park: 120
Oak Bay Guest House: 118

Ocean Pointe Resort: 116
Olde England Inn: 104, 116
Quality Inn Waddling Dog: 117
Renouf House: 118
Strathcona Hotel: 115
Surf Motel: 115
Swans Suite Hotel: 115
Thetis Lake Campground: 119-120

Traveller's Inn Downtown: 115
Traveller's Inn on Douglas: 115
University of Victoria dormitories: 119
Western 66 Motel: 117
Westwind Plaza Hotel: 116
YMCA/YWCA of Victoria: 119

RESTAURANT INDEX

VANCOUVER

Aqua Riva: 81
Bacchus Ristorante (Wedgewood Hotel): 84
Backstage Lounge: 52, 91
Bagel St. Cafe: 87
Bar 98: 32
Bar None: 51
Blarney Stone: 51
Blenz: 87
Bojangles: 89
Boss Bakery and Restaurant: 86
Bread Garden: 87-88
Bridges: 91
Brother's Restaurant: 85
Buddhist Vegetarian Restaurant: 86-87
Bud's Halibut and Chips: 89
Cactus Club Cafe: 88
Café de Paris: 89-90
Cafe La Cantina: 88
Caper's: 87
Caper's Courtyard Café: 91
Carlos and Bud's: 81
Checkers: 52
Cheers: 94
Chef and the Carpenter, The: 88
Chicken on the Way: 81
CinCin: 88
Cordova Cafe: 85
Cows: 21, 87
Crystals Café: 88
Daniel le Chocolate Beige: 21
Delilah's: 89
Doll and Penny's: 80
East Hastings Street: 86
Edge, The: 80
Elbow Room: 80
Falafel King: 88
Fish House at Stanley Park: 90
Five Sails: 81
Fleuri Restaurant (Sutton Place Hotel): 84
Fresgo Inn: 80
Fu Wah: 86
Gain Wah Restaurant: 86
Grade A Café: 79

Grand Union: 51
Grouse Nest Restaurant: 32
Grove Inn: 88
Hamburger Mary's: 80
Hanada: 90
Hon's Wun Tun House: 86
Il Giardino: 84
Inlets Bistro: 88
Irish Heather: 51
Joe Fortes Seafood and Chop House: 21, 51-52, 87
Joe's Grill: 91
Johnny's Pizza Factory: 79
Kent's Kitchen: 85-86
Kettle of Fish, A: 81
Kisho: 84-85
Korner Restaurant: 80
La Luna Cafe: 85
Las Margaritas: 92
Le Crocodile: 84
Le Grec: 92
Livingroom: 92
Lonsdale Café: 94
Lonsdale Market: 93-94
Lui's Villa Café and Pies: 80
Malone's: 91-92
Marbella: 88
Mescalero: 89
Misaki: 85
Monterrey Lounge and Grill: 88
Mr. Pickwicks: 81
Mulvaney's: 91
Naam: 92
Nakornthai: 93
900 West (Hotel Vancouver): 84
Nyala African Hotspot: 93
Old Spaghetti Factory: 85
Olympia Seafood Market and Grill: 87
Only Cafe: 86
Ovaltine Café: 86
Pastel's: 85
Pomodori: 84
Ponchos: 89
Prospect Point Café: 90
Queens Cross Neighbourhood Pub: 52
Raincity Grill: 89
Raintree: 85

Rasputin's: 93
Reno's: 93
Revolving Restaurant: 81
Richard and Co.: 79
Riley Waterfront Café: 91
Robson Public Market: 21
Rooster's Quarters: 89
Rusty Gull Neighbourhood Pub: 52
Salmon House on the Hill: 94
Salonika: 88
Sami's: 93
Scoozis: 79
Seasons in the Park: 92
Sophie's Cosmic Café: 91
Spuntino Bakery and Caffe: 80
Stamp's Landing Neighbourhood Pub: 52
Starbucks: 21, 87
Steamrollers: 80
Steamworks Brewing Co.: 51
Stepho's: 84
Stock Market: 91
Surat Sweet: 92
Tanpopo: 90
Tapastree Restaurant: 89
Taste of India, A: 88
Teahouse Restaurant: 90
Templeton, The: 79
Tojo's Restaurant: 93
Topanga Cafe: 92
Two Parrots Taverna: 81
Urban Well: 92
Vij's: 93
Villa del Lupo: 84
Water St. Cafe: 85
White Spot: 79
Woodlands Natural Food Restaurant: 93
Yale Hotel: 80
Zagros: 80-81

VICTORIA

Aerie Resort: 123
Barb's Place: 122
Bavarian Bakery: 121
Bengal Lounge: 122

Blenz: 121-122
Cafe Mexico: 123
Capital Iron: 121
Chandlers: 122
Cherry Bank Hotel Rib House: 123
Company's Coming: 122
Cross' Quality Meats: 121
Don Mee Restaurant: 124
Electric Juice Café: 121
Elephant and Castle: 122
Empress Hotel: 122
Fowl & Fish Café: 122
Garden Cafe: 122
Garlic Rose Café: 124

Green Cuisine: 123
Herald Street Caffe: 123-124
Hunan Village Cuisine: 124
James Bay Inn: 123
John's Place: 121
Lotus Pond: 124
Marina Restaurant: 102
Med Grill: 124
Millos: 124
Murchies: 121
Nasty Jacks: 122
Olde England Inn: 104
Old Vic Fish & Chips: 122
Pablo's Dining Lounge: 124
Pagliacci's: 123

Paradiso: 121
Periklis Greek Restaurant: 124
QV Cafe and Bakery: 124
Sam's Deli: 122
Sooke Harbour House: 123
Sour Pickle Cafe: 122
Spinnakers Brew Pub: 123
Starbucks: 122
Strathcona Hotel: 111
Swans Hotel: 111, 122-123
Vin Santo: 124
Wah Lai Yuen: 124
Wharfside Eatery: 122
Willies Bakery: 121

INDEX

A

Abbotsford: 38
Abbotsford International Airshow:
   60
Air Canada Championship: 42, 61
airlines/air travel: see
   transportation
Alaska Marine Highway: 132-133
Alaska travel: 141
Alcan Dragon Boat Festival: 58-
   59
Alhambra Hotel: 18
Anne Hathaway's Thatched
   Cottage: 104
aquariums: see marinelife
area codes: 139
Art Gallery of Greater Victoria:
   103
auto travel: see transportation

B

backpacker lodges: 74-76, 119;
   see also hiking
banks: hours 139; see also
   currency exchange
Barclay Heritage Square: 20
Bard on the Beach: 59
bars: see specific place,
   nightlife/nightclubs
basketball: 49
Bastion Square: 101
Bathtub Race: 60
B.C. Ferries: 133
B.C. Golf Museum: 27-28
B.C. Lions: 49
B.C. Place Stadium: 23-24
B.C. Rail: see transportation
beaches: 43-44, 109
Beacon Hill Park: 102
bed and breakfasts: see
   accommodations index
beer: see microbrew
Belcarra Regional Park: 35
Belfry Theatre: 111
Benson & Hedges Symphony of
   Fire: 60
biking: see cycling
birds: 4-5; George C. Reifel Bird
   Sanctuary 30
Blackcomb: 47

Bloedel Floral Conservatory: 28
Blood Alley: 18
Blue Grouse Interpretive Trail: 32
boating: 45; Alcan Dragon Boat
   Festival 58-59; Wooden Boat
   Festival 60; see also specific
   activity
books/bookstores: 141-143, 147;
   booklist 148-150
Bowen Island: 33-34
Brentwood Bay: 105
British Empire Games (1954): 10
Brockton Point: 22
Burnaby: 35
Burnaby Mountain: 41-42
Burnaby Mountain Park: 35
business hours: 139
bus tours/travel: 49-50, 130-131,
   145; disabled passengers 134;
   see also transportation, tours
Butchart Gardens: 105-108
Butchart, R.P.: 108
Butterfly Gardens: 108
Byrnes Block: 18

C

cafés: see specific place, Internet
   services
Campbell River: 106
camping: 76-77, 119-120; see
   also accommodations index,
   hiking
Canada Day: 59
Canada Place: 13
Canadian Craft Museum: 15
Canadian Football League: see
   football
Canadian port of entry: by ferry
   132
canoeing: 43-45
Capilano Salmon Hatchery and
   Regional Park: 31
Capilano Suspension Bridge: 31
Carr, Emily: 13
Carr House: 102
Cathedral Place: 17
Centennial Square: 102
CFB Esquimalt Naval & Military
   Museum: 104
children's sights: 22, 36, 58

Chilliwack: 38
Chinatown (Vancouver): 19-20
Chinese New Year: 62
Christ Church Cathedral: 17; 103
Christmas Carol Ship Parade: 61
churches: see specific place
cinema: 54, 61
Clayburn Village: 38
Clayoquot Sound: 106
Cleveland Dam: 31
climate: 5
Cloverdale Rodeo and Exhibition:
   58
Clover Point: 102
coal: 7-8
Coal Harbour: see Stanley Park
Coast Salish: 6
comedy: see nightlife/nightclubs,
   festivals, performing arts
Coquitlam: 35-36
Courtney: 106
Craigdarroch Castle: 103-104
Craigflower Manor and
   Schoolhouse: 104
cruises: 50-51, 132
Crystal Garden: 101
Crystal Pool: 109
Cultus Lake Provincial Park: 38
currency exchange: 137, 147
customs: 136-137
cyber cafés: 139, 147
cycling: 42, 109, 146; see also
   transportation
Cypress Bowl: 48
Cypress Provincial Park: 32-33

D

dance: see performing arts
Deadman's Island: 22
Deas Island: 29
Deep Cove: 32
Deighton, "Gassy Jack:" 8, 18
Delta: 29
disabled travelers: 134, 138
Dominion Hotel: 18
Douglas Border Crossing: 31
Dr. Sun Yat-Sen Classical
   Chinese Garden: 20
Du Maurier International Jazz
   Festival: 59

E
Elgin Heritage Park: 30
Elk Lake: 109
emergency services: 138, 147
Emily Carr Institute of Art and
    Design: 25
employment abroad: 136
Empress Hotel: 99
English Bay Beach: 20
Esquimalt Lagoon: 105
Europeans: 7
events: 57-62
Expo86: 11

F
False Creek: 11, 23-25, 40-41;
    ferries 135
fauna: 4-5; see also marinelife
Ferguson Point: 23
ferries: 131-133, 135, 145-146
Festival of Lights: 61
festivals: Vancouver 57-62;
    Victoria 112-113
Fisgard Lighthouse: 105
fish/fishing: 45-46; see also
    marinelife
flightseeing: 32, 51
flora: 4-5
football: 49; B.C. Place Stadium:
    23-24; see also sports
Forest Alliance of B.C. Information
    Centre: 17
forestry: 17
Fort Langley National Historic
    Park: 37
Fort Rodd Hill National Historic
    Site: 105
Fort Victoria: 98
Fox, Terry: 50
Fraser River: 29-31
Fraser River Valley: 37-39
fringe theater: 61, 113; see also
    performing arts
Fringe, The—Vancouver's
    Theater Festival: 61

G
Gaolers Mews: 18
"Gassy Jack:" see Deighton,
    "Gassy Jack"
Gastown: 8, 17-19
geography: see specific place
George C. Reifel Bird Sanctuary:
    30

ginseng: 19
Girl in Wet Suit: 22
Golden Ears Provincial Park: 39
Goldmine Trail: 105
Goldstream Provincial Park: 105,
    120
golf: 42-43; Air Canada
    Championship 61; B.C. Golf
    Museum 27-28
"Golf Ball, The:" see Science
    World
Gordon MacMillan Southam
    Observatory: 26
Government House: 103
Granville: 8
Granville Island: 24-25
Greenpeace: 11
Grouse Mountain: 31-32, 48
Gulf of Georgia National Historic
    Site: 29

H
handicrafts: see arts/architecture,
    shopping
Harrison Bay: 39
Harrison Hot Springs: 38
Harrison Lake: 38
Hathaway, Anne (Thatched
    Cottage): 104
health: 138
helicopter tours: 32, 51
Helmcken House: 100
Heritage Village: 35
hiking: 32, 39, 40-42, 105, 107;
    see also parks, camping
history: see specific place
holidays, public: 57
Hongkong Bank: 17
horse racing: 49
Horseshoe Bay: 33
hostelling: 74-75, 119
Hotel Europe: 18
Hotel Vancouver: 17
Hyack Festival: 58

IJ
ICA FolkFest: 112-113
ice hockey: 48-49
immigration: 11;see also customs
Indy racing: 60-61
information centers: 140-141
Inner Harbour: 99
international border crossing: by
    private craft 136; see also

ferries, customs
    Internet services: 139, 147
Irving House: 37
Johnson, Pauline: 23

K
kayaking: 34, 43-45, 106, 109-110
kids: see children's sights
Kilby Historic Store and Farm: 38-
    39
Kitsilano Showboat: 59

L
land: see specific place
Landing, The: 17
Langley: 37
laundry: 147
Laurel Point: 101
libraries: 141-143, 147
Lighthouse Park: 33
Little Mountain: 28
Lookout!, The: 16
Lost Lagoon: 23
Lower Falls Trail: 39
Luxton Fall Fair: 113
Luxton Pro Rodeo: 112
Lynn Canyon Park: 32

M
Malkin Bowl: 21
Maple Tree Square: 18
maps: 140, 143
Marathon of Hope: 50
Maritime Museum of British
    Columbia: 101-102
Marsh Trail: 105
McDonald Provincial Park: 120
McPherson Playhouse: 111
measurement system: 139
media: 143
medical services: 138, 147
metric system: 139
microbrew: 111
Mill Bay: 105
Miniature World: 101
mining: coal 7-8, 17
Molson Indy Vancouver: 60-61
Mondo Pride: 59
money: 137-138, 147
Mount Seymour Provincial Park: 2
Museum of Anthropology: 27
Museum of Archaeology and
    Ethnology: 35
museums: Canadian Craft

Museum 15; CFB Esquimalt Naval & Military Museum 104; Maritime Museum of British Columbia 101-102; Museum of Anthropology 27; New Westminster Museum 37; Pacific Mineral Museum 17; Royal British Columbia Museum 99-100; Sport Fishing Museum 25; Vancouver Art Gallery 13-15; Vancouver Centennial Police Museum 19; Vancouver Maritime Museum 26; Vancouver Museum 25; *see also* art/architecture
music: *see* nightlife/nightclubs, festivals, performing arts
Musqueam: 7

NO

Nanaimo: 106
National Geographic Theatre: 100
native crafts: *see* art/architecture, shopping
Nature House: 23
Netherlands Centennial Carillon: 100
newspapers: 143
New Westminster: 36-37
Niagara Falls: 105
nightlife/nightclubs: Vancouver 51; Victoria 111-112; *see also* performing arts
Nine o'-Clock Gun: 22
Nitobe Memorial Garden: 27
North Shore: 10, 16-17, 42
Oak Bay: 103-104
Only Cafe: 86

PQ

Pacific Mineral Museum: 17
Pacific Opera Victoria: 111
Pacific Rim National Park: 106
Pacific Space Centre: 25
Pacific Spirit Regional Park: 26-27, 41
Pacific Undersea Gardens: 101
parliament buildings: 100-101
people: 11-12; *see also* museums, art/architecture
performing arts: 21, 53-54, 61, 100, 111-113; *see also* festivals, nightlife/nightclubs
periodicals: 143

photography: 139-140, 147
Pinecone Burke Provincial Park: 35-36
plants: *see* flora, gardens
Playland: 36
Point Ellice House and Garden: 104
Point Roberts: 30
Polar Bear Swim: 61-62
population: 12
Port Alberni: 106
Porteau Cove Provincial Park: 77
Port Hardy: 106
postal services: 139, 147
publications, media: 143
Queen Elizabeth Park: 28

R

rail travel: *see* transportation
railway: 8-9; miniature 36
Richmond: 29
Richmond Nature Park: 29
Robson Street: 21
Rockland: 103-104
rodeos: Cloverdale Rodeo and Exhibition 58; Luxton Pro Rodeo 112
Roedde House Museum: 20
Royal British Columbia Museum: 99-100
Royal Hudson: 50
Royal London Wax Museum: 101
Royal Theatre: 111
Royal Victoria Yacht Club: 102-103
running: 58
RVs: *see* camping

S

Saanich Peninsula: 105-108
sand sculpture: 61
Science World: 24, 36
Score: 60
scuba diving: 46, 110
Seawall Promenade: 22-23
Semiahoo Park: 31
Seymour Ski Country: 48
shopping: Vancouver 55-57; Victoria 112
Sidney: 108
Sidney Info Centre: 147
Simon Fraser University: 35, 76
Siwash Rock: 22
skiing: 46-48, 106

snowboarding: 47
Snug Cove: 34
soccer: 49
Southern Gulf Islands: 106
Sport Fishing Museum: 25
sports: B.C. Golf Museum 27-28; B.C. Place Stadium 23-24; Score 60; Sport Fishing Museum 25; *see also specific sport*
Squamish: 7
Stanley Park: 16, 20-23
steam clock: 17-18
Steveston: 29
Strathcona Provincial Park: 106
studying abroad: 136
submarine, Russian: 37
Sumas Mountain Provincial Park: 38
Surrey: 30-31
Swartz Bay: 105
Swiftsure International Yacht Race: 112
swimming: Polar Bear Swim 61-62; *see also* beaches
Symphony Splash: 113

T

taxes: *see* money
taxis: 135, 146
tea: 19
Telegraph Cove: 106
telephone services: 139
TerriVic Jazz Party: 112
theater: *see* performing arts
Thetis Lake: 109
Third Beach: 22-23
Thunderbird Park: 100
time: zone 139; business hours 139
Tofino: 106
totem poles: 6, 22; Thunderbird Park 100
tourist information centers: 140-141
tours: 32, 49-51, 98, 102-103, 110-111; *see also* transportation, hiking
trails: *see specific trail,* hiking
train travel: *see* transportation
Translink: 133-134
transportation: to and from Vancouver 127-133; transportation *(continued):* around

Vancouver 133-136; disabled travelers 134, 138; to and from Victoria 144-146; around Victoria 146; *see also* tours

U

University of British Columbia (UBC): 26-28; bookstore 143; Botanical Garden 27; Housing and Conference Centre 76
University of Victoria: 103

V

Vancouver: 1-94; accommodations 63-77; food 78-94; recreation 40-62; sights 13-39; travel basics 127-143; *see also* transportation
Vancouver Aquarium: 21-22, 36
Vancouver Art Gallery: 13-15
Vancouver Canucks: 49
Vancouver Centennial Police Museum: 19
Vancouver Chamber Music Festival: 59
Vancouver Folk Music Festival: 59
Vancouver, George: 7
Vancouver International Airport: 127; information booth hours 139; *see also* transportation
Vancouver International Children's Festival: 36, 58
Vancouver International Comedy Festival: 59
Vancouver International Film Festival: 61
Vancouver International Marathon: 58
Vancouver International Writer's Festival: 61
Vancouver Maritime Museum: 26
Vancouver Museum: 25
Vancouver Playhouse International Wine Festival: 57
Vancouver Sun Run: 58
Van Dusen Botanical Garden: 28
Vanier Park: 25
Victoria: 95-124; accommodations 114-120; food 121-124; recreation 109-113; sights 99-108; travel basics 144-147; *see also* transportation
Victoria Fringe Festival: 113
Victoria Harbour Ferry: 110-111
Victoria International Airport: 144
Victoria Summer Theater: 111, 113
Victoria Visitor Info Centre: 147
visas: 136-137

WXYZ

walking: *see* hiking
weather: 5; forecasts 147
West Canyon Trail: 39
West Coast Trail: 107
West End: 20
whalewatching: 110
Whistler: 47
White Rock: 31
whitewater rafting: 41
Willows Beach: 109
wine: Vancouver Playhouse International Wine Festival 57
Wooden Boat Festival: 60
working abroad: 136
World Championship Bathtub Race: 60
World Championship Sand Sculpture Competition: 61
World's Narrowest Office Building: 20
World War I: 10
yachting: 45
Yat-Sen, Dr. Sun Classical Chinese Garden: 20

ABOUT THE AUTHOR

Andrew Hempstead has spent many years exploring, writing about, and photographing western Canada and has a strong affinity with Vancouver through his work as co-author of *British Columbia Handbook*. He is also the author of *Alberta and the Northwest Territories Handbook* and *Canadian Rockies Handbook* and is co-author of *Australia Handbook* (Moon Publications). He has been writing since 1989, when, after leaving a promising career in the field of advertising, he took off for Alaska, linking up with veteran travel writer Deke Castleman to help research and update the fourth edition of *Alaska-Yukon Handbook*. Andrew has also traveled to New Zealand on assignment to write and photograph for Moon Publications and The Guide Book Company, and traveled purely for pleasure through most of the United States, Europe, the South Pacific, and India.

When not working on his books, Andrew is happiest hiking, fishing, golfing, camping, and enjoying the simple pleasures in life, such as skimming stones down on the river. He calls Canmore, Alberta, home.

LOSE YOURSELF IN THE EXPERIENCE, NOT THE CROWD

For more than 25 years, Moon Travel Handbooks have been the guidebooks of choice for adventurous travelers. Our award-winning Handbook series provides focused, comprehensive coverage of distinct destinations all over the world. Each Handbook is like an entire bookcase of cultural insight and introductory information in one portable volume. Our goal at Moon is to give travelers all the background and practical information they'll need for an extraordinary travel experience.

The following pages include a complete list of Handbooks, covering North America and Hawaii, Mexico, Latin America and the Caribbean, and Asia and the Pacific.To purchase Moon Travel Handbooks, check your local bookstore or check our Web site at **www.moon.com** for current prices and editions.

"An in-depth dunk into the land, the people and their history, arts, and politics."
—*Student Travels*

"I consider these books to be superior to Lonely Planet. When Moon produces a book it is more humorous, incisive, and off-beat."
—*Toronto Sun*

"Outdoor enthusiasts gravitate to the well-written Moon Travel Handbooks. In addition to politically correct historic and cultural features, the series focuses on flora, fauna and outdoor recreation. Maps and meticulous directions also are a trademark of Moon guides."
—*Houston Chronicle*

"Moon [Travel Handbooks] . . . bring a healthy respect to the places they investigate. Best of all, they provide a host of odd nuggets that give a place texture and prod the wary traveler from the beaten path. The finest are written with such care and insight they deserve listing as literature."
—*American Geographical Society*

"Moon Travel Handbooks offer in-depth historical essays and useful maps, enhanced by a sense of humor and a neat, compact format."
—*Swing*

"Perfect for the more adventurous, these are long on history, sightseeing and nitty-gritty information and very price-specific."
—*Columbus Dispatch*

"Moon guides manage to be comprehensive and countercultural at the same time . . . Handbooks are packed with maps, photographs, drawings, and sidebars that constitute a college-level introduction to each country's history, culture, people, and crafts."
—*National Geographic Traveler*

"Few travel guides do a better job helping travelers create their own itineraries than the Moon Travel Handbook series. The authors have a knack for homing in on the essentials."
—*Colorado Springs Gazette Telegraph*

MEXICO

"These books will delight the armchair traveler, aid the undecided person in selecting a destination, and guide the seasoned road warrior looking for lesser-known hideaways."
—*Mexican Meanderings* Newsletter

"From tourist traps to off-the-beaten track hideaways, these guides offer consistent, accurate details without pretension."
—*Foreign Service Journal*

Archaeological Mexico	**$19.95**
Andrew Coe	420 pages, 27 maps
Baja Handbook	**$16.95**
Joe Cummings	540 pages, 46 maps
Cabo Handbook	**$14.95**
Joe Cummings	270 pages, 17 maps
Cancún Handbook	**$14.95**
Chicki Mallan	240 pages, 25 maps
Colonial Mexico	**$18.95**
Chicki Mallan	400 pages, 38 maps
Mexico Handbook	**$21.95**
Joe Cummings and Chicki Mallan	1,200 pages, 201 maps
Northern Mexico Handbook	**$17.95**
Joe Cummings	610 pages, 69 maps
Pacific Mexico Handbook	**$17.95**
Bruce Whipperman	580 pages, 68 maps
Puerto Vallarta Handbook	**$14.95**
Bruce Whipperman	330 pages, 36 maps
Yucatán Handbook	**$16.95**
Chicki Mallan	400 pages, 52 maps

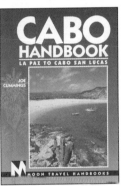

"Beyond question, the most comprehensive Mexican resources available for those who prefer deep travel to shallow tourism. But don't worry, the fiesta-fun stuff's all here too."
—*New York Daily News*

LATIN AMERICA AND THE CARIBBEAN

"Solidly packed with practical information and full of significant cultural asides that will enlighten you on the whys and wherefores of things you might easily see but not easily grasp."

—*Boston Globe*

Belize Handbook	**$15.95**
Chicki Mallan and Patti Lange	390 pages, 45 maps
Caribbean Vacations	**$18.95**
Karl Luntta	910 pages, 64 maps
Costa Rica Handbook	**$19.95**
Christopher P. Baker	780 pages, 73 maps
Cuba Handbook	**$19.95**
Christopher P. Baker	740 pages, 70 maps
Dominican Republic Handbook	**$15.95**
Gaylord Dold	420 pages, 24 maps
Ecuador Handbook	**$16.95**
Julian Smith	450 pages, 43 maps
Honduras Handbook	**$15.95**
Chris Humphrey	330 pages, 40 maps
Jamaica Handbook	**$15.95**
Karl Luntta	330 pages, 17 maps
Virgin Islands Handbook	**$13.95**
Karl Luntta	220 pages, 19 maps

NORTH AMERICA AND HAWAII

"These domestic guides convey the same sense of exoticism that their foreign counterparts do, making home-country travel seem like far-flung adventure."

—*Sierra Magazine*

Alaska-Yukon Handbook	**$17.95**
Deke Castleman and Don Pitcher	530 pages, 92 maps
Alberta and the Northwest Territories Handbook	**$18.95**
Andrew Hempstead	520 pages, 79 maps
Arizona Handbook	**$18.95**
Bill Weir	600 pages, 36 maps
Atlantic Canada Handbook	**$18.95**
Mark Morris	490 pages, 60 maps
Big Island of Hawaii Handbook	**$15.95**
J.D. Bisignani	390 pages, 25 maps
Boston Handbook	**$13.95**
Jeff Perk	200 pages, 20 maps
British Columbia Handbook	**$16.95**
Jane King and Andrew Hempstead	430 pages, 69 maps

Canadian Rockies Handbook	**$14.95**
Andrew Hempstead	220 pages, 22 maps
Colorado Handbook	**$17.95**
Stephen Metzger	480 pages, 46 maps
Georgia Handbook	**$17.95**
Kap Stann	380 pages, 44 maps
Grand Canyon Handbook	**$14.95**
Bill Weir	220 pages, 10 maps
Hawaii Handbook	**$19.95**
J.D. Bisignani	1,030 pages, 88 maps
Honolulu-Waikiki Handbook	**$14.95**
J.D. Bisignani	360 pages, 20 maps
Idaho Handbook	**$18.95**
Don Root	610 pages, 42 maps
Kauai Handbook	**$15.95**
J.D. Bisignani	320 pages, 23 maps
Los Angeles Handbook	**$16.95**
Kim Weir	370 pages, 15 maps
Maine Handbook	**$18.95**
Kathleen M. Brandes	660 pages, 27 maps
Massachusetts Handbook	**$18.95**
Jeff Perk	600 pages, 23 maps
Maui Handbook	**$15.95**
J.D. Bisignani	450 pages, 37 maps
Michigan Handbook	**$15.95**
Tina Lassen	360 pages, 32 maps
Montana Handbook	**$17.95**
Judy Jewell and W.C. McRae	490 pages, 52 maps
Nevada Handbook	**$18.95**
Deke Castleman	530 pages, 40 maps
New Hampshire Handbook	**$18.95**
Steve Lantos	500 pages, 18 maps
New Mexico Handbook	**$15.95**
Stephen Metzger	360 pages, 47 maps
New York Handbook	**$19.95**
Christiane Bird	780 pages, 95 maps
New York City Handbook	**$13.95**
Christiane Bird	300 pages, 20 maps
North Carolina Handbook	**$14.95**
Rob Hirtz and Jenny Daughtry Hirtz	320 pages, 27 maps
Northern California Handbook	**$19.95**
Kim Weir	800 pages, 50 maps
Ohio Handbook	**$15.95**
David K. Wright	340 pages, 18 maps
Oregon Handbook	**$17.95**
Stuart Warren and Ted Long Ishikawa	590 pages, 34 maps

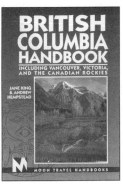

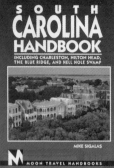

Pennsylvania Handbook	**$18.95**
Joanne Miller	448 pages, 40 maps
Road Trip USA	**$24.00**
Jamie Jensen	940 pages, 175 maps
Road Trip USA Getaways: Chicago	**$9.95**
	60 pages, 1 map
Road Trip USA Getaways: Seattle	**$9.95**
	60 pages, 1 map
Santa Fe-Taos Handbook	**$13.95**
Stephen Metzger	160 pages, 13 maps
South Carolina Handbook	**$16.95**
Mike Sigalas	400 pages, 20 maps
Southern California Handbook	**$19.95**
Kim Weir	720 pages, 26 maps
Tennessee Handbook	**$17.95**
Jeff Bradley	530 pages, 42 maps
Texas Handbook	**$18.95**
Joe Cummings	690 pages, 70 maps
Utah Handbook	**$17.95**
Bill Weir and W.C. McRae	490 pages, 40 maps
Virginia Handbook	**$15.95**
Julian Smith	410 pages, 37 maps
Washington Handbook	**$19.95**
Don Pitcher	840 pages, 111 maps
Wisconsin Handbook	**$18.95**
Thomas Huhti	590 pages, 69 maps
Wyoming Handbook	**$17.95**
Don Pitcher	610 pages, 80 maps

ASIA AND THE PACIFIC

"Scores of maps, detailed practical info down to business hours of small-town libraries. You can't beat the Asian titles for sheer heft. (The) series is sort of an American Lonely Planet, with better writing but fewer titles. (The) individual voice of researchers comes through."

—*Travel & Leisure*

Australia Handbook	**$21.95**
Marael Johnson, Andrew Hempstead,	
and Nadina Purdon	940 pages, 141 maps
Bali Handbook	**$19.95**
Bill Dalton	750 pages, 54 maps
Fiji Islands Handbook	**$14.95**
David Stanley	350 pages, 42 maps
Hong Kong Handbook	**$16.95**
Kerry Moran	378 pages, 49 maps

Indonesia Handbook		**$25.00**
Bill Dalton		1,380 pages, 249 maps
Micronesia Handbook		**$16.95**
Neil M. Levy		340 pages, 70 maps
Nepal Handbook		**$18.95**
Kerry Moran		490 pages, 51 maps
New Zealand Handbook		**$19.95**
Jane King		620 pages, 81 maps
Outback Australia Handbook		**$18.95**
Marael Johnson		450 pages, 57 maps
Philippines Handbook		**$17.95**
Peter Harper and Laurie Fullerton		670 pages, 116 maps
Singapore Handbook		**$15.95**
Carl Parkes		350 pages, 29 maps
South Korea Handbook		**$19.95**
Robert Nilsen		820 pages, 141 maps
South Pacific Handbook		**$24.00**
David Stanley		920 pages, 147 maps
Southeast Asia Handbook		**$21.95**
Carl Parkes		1,080 pages, 204 maps
Tahiti Handbook		**$15.95**
David Stanley		450 pages, 51 maps
Thailand Handbook		**$19.95**
Carl Parkes		860 pages, 142 maps
Vietnam, Cambodia & Laos Handbook		**$18.95**
Michael Buckley		760 pages, 116 maps

OTHER GREAT TITLES FROM MOON

"For hardy wanderers, few guides come more highly
recommended than the Handbooks. They include good
maps, steer clear of fluff and flackery, and offer plenty of
money-saving tips. They also give you the kind of
information that visitors to strange lands—on any budget—
need to survive."

—US News & World Report

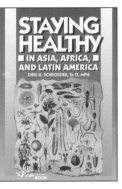

Moon Handbook	**$10.00**
Carl Koppeschaar	150 pages, 8 maps
The Practical Nomad: How to Travel Around the World	**$17.95**
Edward Hasbrouck	580 pages
Staying Healthy in Asia, Africa, and Latin America	**$11.95**
Dirk Schroeder	230 pages, 4 maps

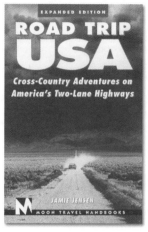

U.S.~METRIC CONVERSION

1 inch = 2.54 centimeters (cm)
1 foot = .304 meters (m)
1 yard = 0.914 meters
1 mile = 1.6093 kilometers (km)
1 km = .6214 miles
1 fathom = 1.8288 m
1 chain = 20.1168 m
1 furlong = 201.168 m
1 acre = .4047 hectares
1 sq km = 100 hectares
1 sq mile = 2.59 square km
1 ounce = 28.35 grams
1 pound = .4536 kilograms
1 short ton = .90718 metric ton
1 short ton = 2000 pounds
1 long ton = 1.016 metric tons
1 long ton = 2240 pounds
1 metric ton = 1000 kilograms
1 quart = .94635 liters
1 US gallon = 3.7854 liters
1 Imperial gallon = 4.5459 liters
1 nautical mile = 1.852 km

To compute celsius temperatures, subtract 32 from Fahrenheit and divide by 1.8. To go the other way, multiply celsius by 1.8 and add 32.

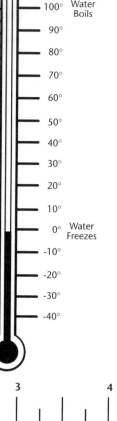

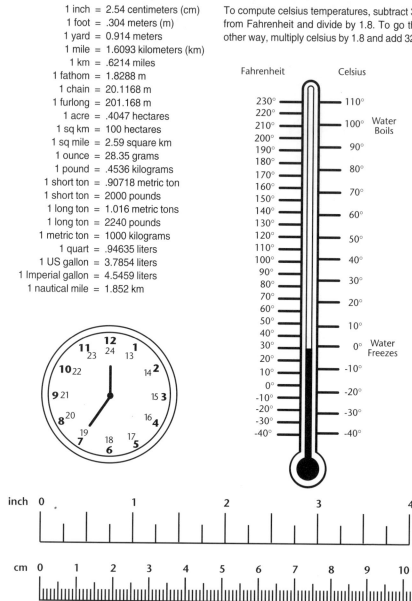

IF YOU CAN'T AFFORD TO TRAVEL, JOIN THE CLUB

American Youth Hostels
733 15th Street, NW, Suite 840
Washington, DC 20005 USA

Robert Murphy
123 Rodeo Ave.
Denver, Co 43711

Expires end 11/99
Robert Murphy

10/74
Date of birth

Adult
Category

4,500 Hostels, 70 Countries, One Card, One Call ...

Traveling in the United States doesn't have to mean hotels that cost $200 a night. With a Hostelling International Membership Card, you can stay in New York for just $22, Miami Beach for $14, Seattle for $16, or any one of the other 140+ HI hostels in the U.S. for less than the price of this book! Your HI Card will also get you all kinds of special discounts on everything from museum fees and restaurants, to special excursions and a variety of transportation. So if you're looking for a less   expensive way to travel, join the club! Call 202-783-6161. Or check out our Website at http://www.hiayh.org.

HOSTELLING INTERNATIONAL

The new seal of approval of the International Youth Hostel Federation.

HOSTELLING
INTERNATIONAL

Next time, make your *own* hotel arrangements.

Yahoo! Travel

Do You YAHOO!